Out
and
About
PORTLAND
with
KIDS

The Ultimate
Family Guide for
Fun and Learning

SECOND EDITION

BY NELLE NIX

ACKNOWLEDGEMENTS

With special thanks to Elizabeth Hartzell DeSimone, author of the first edition of Out and About Portland With Kids.

CONTRIBUTORS
Sara Kirschenbaum
Michael Clapp

IBSN: 0-9715644-0-X

Layout and Design: John Rusnak

TABLE OF CONTENTS

HOW TO USE THIS BOOK:

The listings in *Out and About Portland with Kids* were current at press time, but I urge you to confirm locations, hours, and prices of selected destinations.

The Quick Index, beginning on page 193, offers outing suggestions that meet specific needs.

Four icons appear regularly throughout:

Offers classes and/or workshops for children

Offers birthday-party packages

Offers field trips for schools or large groups

Features facilities that are accessible to persons in wheelchairs

INTRODUCTION

Portland's reputation as a city of parks precedes it.

So when my family settled in the City of Roses in the mid 1990s, one of the first things we did was track down a brochure listing all of the region's parks. We wanted to know which parks had the best swings, where we could spot a great blue heron, and where to find the most glorious fall colors. Aside from the occasional break for an afternoon nap, we were dogged in our pursuit, excited to explore neighborhoods near and far.

As our family has grown and grown-up (at least a bit), we have continued our pursuit, although we have changed what we look for a bit. We've long since expanded our quest to include family-friendly experiences.

Until I began updating this book, I thought we had been pretty thorough. But, in truth, we are creatures of habit. Like so many other families we know, we've tended to beat a path to our favorite trailheads, parks, museums and restaurants.

Researching this book, though, gave us all a new excuse to ask everyone we ran into to divulge their own favorite locales. The happy result? It's all on the pages that follow.

I think you'll find, as we did, that there's something for everyone in Portland — whether you're looking for a cultural afternoon or a seasonal fair, a kid-friendly restaurant or a new team to root for.

Whatever the case, I hope that *Out and About Portland With Kids* leads you to discover many new favorites for your own family.

Happy exploring,

Nelle Nix

January 2002

Chapter 1
KID CULTURE

The signs are universal and pre-dictable: Feet wiggle with anticipation inches above the floor, bottoms bob in the plush seats, and necks crane anxiously for a clear view around the hairdo in front. Then the curtain rises, and there's a squeal of delight, a sigh of satisfaction.

You've given your child a gift. Though he may not thank you out-right, he will hum a tune that cap-tures his senses, he will make a draw-ing inspired by one that he saw, he will tote home a library book to show you the story he remembers, he will point out the Big Dipper on a clear night, and he will ask to go again.

And then you know you've done a good thing; you've opened up a new door. Exciting, intimidating, enlight-ening—culture is all these things. Whether you take your child to a live theater performance or to see a show at a museum, you're encourag-ing him to walk through a door that will enrich and broaden his world.

MUSEUMS AND EXHIBITS: ESPECIALLY FOR KIDS

ESPECIALLY FOR KIDS

A.C. Gilbert's Discovery Village

116 Marion St NE, Salem 97301
503-371-3631
www.acgilbert.org
Hours: Mon-Sat, 10 am-5 pm; Sun, noon-5pm (The Village is closed on some holidays.)
Admission: $4/person, $3/senior, free/child 3 & under; $3/after 3:30 pm daily except Sun

This museum was named for Salem native A.C. Gilbert, who founded the Gilbert Company and manufactured educational toys, including the Erector Set and American Flyer trains. It occupies three historic Victorian houses on Salem's downtown riverfront. Opened in 1989 and expanded in 1992, the museum showcases a revolving selection of stimulating, interactive exhibits in the sciences, arts and humanities as well as the National Toy Hall of Fame, which features such illustrious toys as the Slinky, Tonka trucks and Silly Putty.

New exhibits include "Earth's Fury," an earth science room where visitors build structures and then test their integrity in a simulated earthquake. Other popular recent exhibits have included a bubble room, optical illusion room and the Astronaut Fitness Challenge.

In 1998, the museum added the Discover Center, a 20,000-square-foot outdoor science center that includes a spacious playground with hands-on experiments and other activities.

Carnegie Center Children's Museum

606 John Adams St,
Oregon City 97045
503-557-9199
Hours: Call for hours
Admission: $2.50/child or adult, free/adult with child, $2/child in groups of 10 or more if scheduled two weeks in advance

This Oregon City building, sited on a flat, square block beside a small playground, was the public library for 82 years before its rebirth as a community center. Closed for renovation for most of 2001, the Carnegie Center Children's Museum reopened in mid-November with new exhibits and an expanded ability to offer children's classes in arts and crafts. Upstairs is an art gallery; downstairs, the basement has been outfitted for exploratory play.

The kid sister to the Children's Museum 2nd Generation (see below), the Carnegie Center is equipped with pint-size versions of a grocery store, diner, hospital, post office and credit union. Young visitors vie for a turn in the wheelchair and at the typewriter. After an afternoon of play, kids gather in the upstairs coffee shop for juice and cookies.

CM2/Children's Museum 2nd Generation

4015 SW Canyon Rd, Portland 97221
503-223-6500
www.portlandcm2.org
Hours: Tues-Thurs & Sat, 9 am-5 pm; Fri, 9 am-8 pm; Sun, 11 am-5 pm; closed Mon except for some school holidays
Admission: $5/adult or child 1 & over

Situated in the heart of Washington Park, just across from the Oregon Zoo, the CM2 opened during the summer of 2001, in a spot with three times more usable space than its former Second

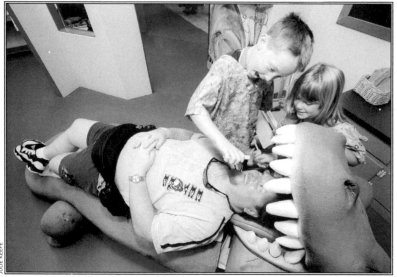

JULIE KEEFE

Lane and Victoria Duras check out dad's choppers in the Wally Gator dental chair in the Kid's Clinic.

Ave location. The renovation of this building, which used to house OMSI, cost $9.9 million. It was completed through the efforts of the Children's Museum, Rotary International and Portland Parks and Recreation.

The museum is especially popular with the younger set. Among the favorite new exhibits:

• "Water Works." Using cranks, pull cords and valves, kids of all ages can send water cascading through Rube Goldberg-style contraptions that combine everything from roof gutters to industrial-size windshield wipers and toilet floats.

• "Me and My Shadow." Light and shadow are in the spotlight here as visitors use projectors to cast their own creative designs and images on a wall-size screen.

• "KidCity Market." A child-size version of a grocery store, this hot spot has everything from miniature carts to fab-

ulous fake food, and it's right next door to the Café, where kids are encouraged to play with their food.

Also fun, especially for the littlest ones, are "Baby's Garden," designed to give the museum's youngest visitors a multisensory experience in a magical forest; "Once Upon a Time," where little actors can bring their favorite fairy tales to life using scenery, props and costumes; and "Kids' Clinic," where junior doctors can "operate" on each other, care for newborn babies and practice dentistry on Wally Gator.

Oregon Museum of Science and Industry (OMSI)
1945 SE Water Ave, Portland 97214
503-797-4000
503-797-4600 (advance tickets)
www.omsi.edu
Hours: Winter: Tues-Sun, 9:30 am-5:30 pm. Summer: Tues-Sun, 9:30 am-7 pm. Discovery Space closes at 5 pm

MUSEUMS AND EXHIBITS: ESPECIALLY FOR KIDS

Admission: $7/adult 14-62, $3.50-$10/senior 63 & over or child 3-13

The Oregon Museum of Science and Industry resides in a gleaming steel-and-glass structure on the east bank of the Willamette River.

Always popular are Omnimax Theater, where such films as *Dolphins* and *Destiny in Space* make use of the five-story domed screen and a pulsating sound system; the Murdock Planetarium, with its regular slate of shows; and the USS *Blueback*, a naval submarine in service for 30 years and now permanently docked in the river.

part in, along with hands-on high-tech and computer activities in the Vernier Technology Lab.

Exciting visiting exhibits make their way to OMSI as well. "Richard Scarry's Busytown" is always popular with the younger set when it tours OMSI, and "A T. Rex Named Sue" thrilled dinosaur fans in fall 2001.

OMSI engages kids on a number of levels with interactive exhibits (left). Above, exploring periscopes on the permanently docked USS Blueback.

OMSI's own engaging, interactive activities reach patrons on many levels. It's almost enough to devote a visit to one of the permanent displays. The Life Science Exhibit Hall explores human growth, fetal development and the structure and function of the human body. The Earth Science Exhibit Hall focuses on geology, biology and weather. The High Tech Hall showcases computers, communication and electronics, all in interactive exhibits that visitors can take

A place like OMSI will make you glad you live in Portland, because you'll want to visit this facility over and over. Tourists are likely to feel overwhelmed by the possibilities and frustrated by lack of time and energy. The size and scope of OMSI are overwhelming (imagine how small a toddler must feel in the cathedral-like lobby), so it's important to plan your visits accordingly.

Don't attempt to do too much. Little children are perfectly content to play with the pulleys, magnets, sand and goo in the Discovery Space (for those ages newborn to 7 years only). Older kids never tire of experimenting with the engineering stations in the

Physical Science Exhibit Hall or riding in the wheelchairs in the "Breaking Down Barriers" exhibit.

If possible, plan your arrival for off-hours. Crowds are not always a problem, but to be sure you miss the rush, arrive by 9:30 am or late in the afternoon. Holiday weekends, particularly in inclement weather, and exhibit openings are bound to be busy.

Pack snacks. OMSI exhibits are challenging and ambitious; even adults tend to flag after a few hours of deep concentration. Carry some munchies in a backpack and break for a picnic outside, where the kids can roll on the lawn and run along the riverside pathways. An attractive cafeteria with views out over the water serves light meals and snacks.

FAMILY MEMBERSHIPS

If your family is the kind that likes to visit and revisit a local attraction—such as a museum or the zoo—purchasing a family membership can make a lot of sense. The benefits often include more than just admission for your own brood. Newsletters, gift shop discounts and guest passes often are part of a membership package. Most museums offer a variety of family memberships. A sampling of some the area's museums is below, along with the cost of a basic family membership. Call individual facilities for details about memberships that are beyond the basic.

- **A.C. Gilbert's Discovery Village**, 116 Marion St NE, Salem 97301; 503-371-3631; $50
- **American Advertising Museum**, 211 NW Fifth Ave & Davis, Portland 97204; 503-226-0000; $75

- **CM2/Children's Museum 2nd Generation**, 4015 SW Canyon Rd, Portland 97221; 503-223-6500; $65
- **End of the Oregon Trail Interpretive Center**, 1726 Washington St, Oregon City 97045; 503-657-9336; $50
- **Oregon History Center**, 1200 SW Park Ave, Portland 97205; 503-306-5198; $60
- **Oregon Museum of Science and Industry (OMSI)**, 1945 SE Water Ave, Portland 97214; 503-797-4000; 503-797-4600; $55
- **Oregon Zoo**, 4001 SW Canyon Rd, Portland 97221; 503-226-1561; $59
- **Pearson Air Museum**, 1115 E Fifth St, Vancouver (Washington) 98661; 360-694-7026; $35
- **Portland Art Museum**, 1219 SW Park Ave, Portland 97205; 503-226-2811; $75
- **Audubon Society of Portland**, 5151 NW Cornell Rd, Portland; 503-292-6855; $38

MUSEUMS AND EXHIBITS:
EXPLORING THE PAST

A 60-minute presentation at the Oregon Trail Interpretative Center tells of the history, spirit and heritage of immigrants who were part of the wagon train.

Exploring the Past

American Advertising Museum
211 NW Fifth Ave & Davis
Portland 97204
503-226-0000
www.admuseum.org
Hours: Wed-Sun, noon-5 pm
Admission: $5/adult, $4/senior,
student with valid ID or child 4-12

Though many parents endeavor to shield their children from advertising, it permeates society and has a vital, enlightening history of its own. All this becomes frightfully clear at the American Advertising Museum, a vital downtown exhibit space in its own right. Since opening in June 1986, the museum has amassed the industry's most comprehensive collection of advertising and business artifacts. Shows are remarkably engaging.

Displays highlight, through print and broadcast advertising, nearly 300 years of social history and trends. The museum is best for children over age 6 who will get a kick out of admiring the 6-foot-tall Bob's Big Boy, the 15-foot tall Jantzen diver hanging from the ceiling and the museum's neon sign collection.

Exhibits in the front gallery change every three months. Recent shows: "Twenty Ads that Shook the World," based on the book of the same title, which looks at 20 ad campaigns from the 20th century and how they affected our cultural mind-sets; "Clio Winners," an exhibit of recent award-winning ads; and the 80th annual traveling exhibit from the New York Art Directors Club.

End of the Oregon Trail
Interpretive Center
1726 Washington St
Oregon City 97045
503-657-9336

MUSEUMS AND EXHIBITS: EXPLORING THE PAST

www.endoftheoregontrail.org/
Hours: Mon-Sat, 9 am-5 pm;
Sun, 10 am-5 pm.
Admission: $6.50/adult, $5.50/senior,
$4/child 5-12, free/child 4 & under

From I-205, you can't miss it: three Paul Bunyan-size covered wagons in conference on Abernethy Green. This is the End of the Oregon Trail Interpretive Center—not quite museum, not quite theater. The live, 60-minute presentation inside helps enlighten visitors as to the history, heritage and spirit of the immigrants who arrived here via wagon train in the mid-19th century.

Enter first the barnlike Provisioner's Depot and take a seat among crude barrels, flour sacks and earthenware jugs to hear a living history interpreter describe the shopping trips and other preparations that preceded the 2,000-mile trek. Move next to the Cascades Theatre for a mixed-media dramatization of the journey that blends 100-year-old photographic images with 20th-century film footage and surround sound, lighting and special effects. Then visit the gallery, with its collection of artifacts, including a Barlow Road toll book, clothing, tools and household items used by early settlers. And last, stop in at the Willamette Trades and Crafts Building, which features ever-changing, hands-on pioneer living activities. Here kids can practice loading supplies for the trail into a life-size wagon bed, or they can learn how to grind wheat into flour, make old-fashioned splints, tinker with old-fashioned toys or learn different sewing stitches.

Bring your lunch and take advantage of the covered picnic area. If you're going with a group of 12 or more, ask about group rates and be sure to make reservations.

Fort Vancouver
1501 E Evergreen Blvd
Vancouver (Washington) 98661
800-832-3599, 360-696-7655
www.nps.gov/fova/
Hours: Winter: daily, 9 am-4 pm.
Summer: daily, 9 am-5 pm
Special reenactments: Year-round
Admission: $3/adult, $5/family,
free/senior with Golden Age Pass or
child 16 & under

The hub of regional activity during its heyday in the early 19th century, Fort Vancouver still draws between 75,000 and 80,000 visitors each year. And with ongoing reconstruction at this once politically pivotal site, the attraction is getting stronger all the time. Most recently, reconstruction projects have focused on historic roads around the fort and the village area.

In a brash move to claim dominion over Oregon Country, a territory rich in furs, England established headquarters for its Hudson's Bay Trading Company at Fort Vancouver in 1825 and enjoyed 20 years of prosperity. In 1846, following the mass migration of American pioneers to the West, Oregon Country was divided and Fort Vancouver was on U.S. soil. By 1860 the trading company had moved out, and within six years fires and decay had destroyed what was once a bustling headquarters.

Much of the fort has since been reconstructed by the National Park Service. At the entrance is a period garden planted with the same vegetables and grains consumed at the fort. A half-dozen buildings are enclosed in a stockade, including the chief factor's residence, a blacksmith's shop, bakery, trade shop, fur store, wash house, kitchen, carpenter shop and jail.

MUSEUMS AND EXHIBITS: EXPLORING THE PAST

Climb the three-story bastion to touch a cannon and spy on "enemies," handle beaver hats and pelts, watch blacksmithing and baking demonstrations. On-site archaeologists are busy identifying and cataloguing the thousands of objects (glass trade beads, ceramic shards, iron pieces, etc.) that have been uncovered in excavations here.

The park staff continues to add events to the calendar so that virtually every month features a living history event; check the fort's Web site or call for details.

Also within the Vancouver National Historic Reserve, check out the Gen. O.O. Howard House Visitor Center. Here, an exhibit titled "One Place Across Time" tells the story of Native Americans' use of the Columbia River, the British fur trade at Fort Vancouver, the U.S. Army's northwest headquarters at Vancouver Barracks, the Army Air Corps' use of nearby Pearson Airfield and the activity at the shipyards in Vancouver during World War II.

If you're looking to delve even deeper into the fort's history, consider a trip to tour the home of Dr. John McLoughlin in Oregon City (see Restored Houses). Fort Vancouver would not have risen to regional prominence were it not for McLoughlin's organizational prowess and business acumen. After retiring as the fort's chief factor when the new boundary was drawn, McLoughlin settled in Oregon City.

Museum of the Oregon Territory
211 Tumwater Dr, Oregon City 97045
503-655-5574
www.endoftheoregontrail.org/cchs.html
Hours: Mon-Fri, 10 am-4 pm; Sat-Sun & holidays, 1-5 pm

Admission: $4/adult, $3/senior, $2/child, $10/family (up to 5 members)

Opened in 1990, this museum (also known as the Clackamas County Museum of History) is a striking contemporary structure on the bluffs above Willamette Falls. It provides a thorough overview of the inhabitants of Clackamas County, from prehistory to the present day. Arrowheads and stone tools are among the artifacts on display from early settlements. A covered wagon sits packed and ready for adventure. The shelves of a replica pharmacy are stacked with hundreds of colorful, tiny bottles. And display cases reveal the tools used by practitioners of various trades. Children are asked not to touch these and other artifacts, many of which are not under glass.

Admission to the museum includes a visit to the Stevens-Crawford Museum (see Restored Houses).

Old Aurora Colony Museum
Second Ave & Liberty St
Aurora 97002
503-678-5754
www.oldaurora.com
Hours: Early March-mid-October: Tues-Sat, 10 am-4 pm; Sun, noon-4 pm. Mid-October-early March: Fri-Sat, 10 am-4 pm, Sun, noon- 4 pm (or by appointment)
Guided tours: Sat, 11 am & 2 pm; Sun, 2 pm
Admission: $3.50/adult, $3/senior, $1.50/child 5 & up

In 1856 Dr. William Keil established a communal society, named for his daughter Aurora, on several hundred acres around a gristmill and sawmill in

Oregon. For 27 years this colony attempted to live out a Christian experiment in brotherhood similar to those practiced by the Harmony, Amana and Shaker communities in the eastern United States.

The only such settlement in the Pacific Northwest, the Aurora Colony left behind an old ox barn, two homes, a communal wash house, a farm-machinery building, a log cabin and an outhouse. In spring and again in September, schoolchildren are invited to experiment with pioneer tasks, including cutting wood and spinning yarn.

The museum also offers summer programs for kids, including a quilting camp.

Oregon History Center
1200 SW Park Ave, Portland 97205
503-306-5198, 503-222-1741
www.ohs.org
Hours: Tues-Sat, 10 am-5 pm (Thurs, until 8 pm); Sun, noon-5 pm
Admission: $6/adult, $3/student, $1.50/child 6-12, free/child 5 & under, free/seniors on Thurs

Operated in the heart of downtown Portland by the Oregon Historical Society, the Oregon History Center is increasingly creating exhibits and special programming that cater to families. Closed for renovations in 2002, the museum will reopen in early 2003 with the "Oregon Country" exhibit, which will occupy 7,000 square feet and will be dedicated to Oregon artifacts and information about the Oregon Country.

Oregon Maritime Center and Museum
113 SW Naito Pkwy, Portland 97204
503-224-7724
Hours: Fri-Sun, 11 am-4 pm

Admission: $4/adult, $3/senior, $2/child 8-17, $10/family

Located on the waterfront in a historic building, the Oregon Maritime Center and Museum features dozens of model ships, including those of sailing vessels and early sternwheelers that plied the Columbia and Willamette rivers. One room is devoted to artifacts from Portland's shipbuilding industry.

Children enjoy inspecting the ships in bottles and hefting the Navy diving helmet and leaden boots. Admission includes a tour of the *Portland*, a restored stern-wheel steam tugboat built in 1947 to help ships navigate the Willamette River.

Pearson Air Museum
1115 E Fifth St
Vancouver (Washington) 98661
360-694-7026
www.pearsonairmuseum.org
Hours: Tues-Sun, 10 am-5 pm
Admission: $5/adult, $4/senior, $3/student 13-18, $2/child 6-12, free/child 5 & under.
Summer tours: $1/student, $3/adult

Located at the nation's oldest operating airfield (it dates to 1905), the Pearson Air Museum is dedicated to preserving the field and its rich aviation heritage. Visitors can view as many as a dozen fully restored planes that predate World War II and visit the aircraft restoration center. Watch footage of the Soviet transpolar flight, which touched down at Pearson in 1937. And learn of the accomplished career of Lt. Alexander Pearson, for whom the airfield was named in 1925.

A multimillion-dollar project has

MUSEUMS AND EXHIBITS:
EXPLORING THE PAST / RESTORED HOUSES

resulted in two restored buildings, one that was part of a barracks and another that was a munitions building. These buildings now hold offices and museum archives. Interactive exhibits teach the principles of flight, such as gravity and lift.

One Sunday each month (usually the third Sunday of the month) is designated as "family fun day." These days offer seasonally appropriate activities that are both educational and fun.

Washington County Museum
Portland Community College
Rock Creek Campus
17677 NW Springville Rd
Portland 97229
503-645-5353
Hours: Mon-Sat, 10 am-4:30 pm
Special events: May & September
Admission: $2/adult, $1/child 6-17; free every Mon

This small museum and research library features rotating exhibits that illuminate various periods of Washington County history, from the early Atfalati Indians to the influx of today's high-technology companies. Some examples: "Our County Collects," a changing selection of private local collections; and "Victorian Pastimes," a room decorated in the style of the late Victorian era. You can get a quick overview of the county's history from a single-wall exhibit titled "The History of Washington County in a Nutshell." There's also a display of women's clothing with samples from the 1890s forward.

Western Antique Powerland
(See Active Play: Outdoor Fun, Trains and Trolleys, "All Aboard.")

Restored Houses

Some children are fascinated by glimpses of yesteryear. For these children—and you probably know if your child is one of them—a trip to the restored home of a prominent local person can be fun. After all, restored houses provide private snapshots of family life at distinct periods in Oregon history.

Many museum volunteers are quite good at tailoring their talks to suit the ages and interests of young guests, especially when they're given a little advance notice. So if you have questions or want to arrange a special tour, call first.

Pittock Mansion, a stately restored home in northwest Portland, hosts a special holiday showcase each year in December.

Hoover-Minthorn House Museum
115 S River St, Newberg 97132
503-538-6629
Hours: March-November: Wed-Sun, 1-4 pm. December & February: Sat-Sun, 1-4 pm. Closed January. Tours available by appointment.
Admission: $2/adult, $1.50/senior or student, 50 cents/child 5-11

McLoughlin House
713 Center St, Oregon City 97045
503-656-5146
Hours: Tues-Sat, 10 am-4 pm; Sun, 1-4 pm. Closed January, Mondays and holidays

Admission: $4/adult, $3/senior,
$2/student 6-17, free/child 5 & under
with parent

Pittock Mansion
3229 NW Pittock Dr, Portland 97210
503-823-3624
Hours: Daily, noon-4 pm
Admission: $5/adult, $4.50/senior,
$2.50/child 6-18

Rose Farm
Holmes Ln (at Rilance Ln)
Oregon City 97045
503-656-5146
Hours: May-September, Sun, 1-4 pm
Admission: Nominal

Stevens-Crawford Museum
603 Sixth St, Oregon City 97045
503-655-2866
Hours: Wed-Fri, noon-4 pm; Sat-Sun,
1-4 pm
Admission: $4/adult, $3/senior,
$2/child 6-18, $10/family of 5 or more
(includes admission to Clackamas
County Museum of History)

Go Wild!

Hart's Reptile World
11264 S Macksburg Rd, Canby 97013
503-266-7236
www.hartsreptileworld.com/
Hours: Daily, 11 am-5 pm
Admission: $5/person 7 & over,
$4/child 3-6, free/child 2 & under

At the end of a rutted road on the
outskirts of Canby sits a large barn. This
is Hart's Reptile World, a menagerie of
some 200 snakes, iguanas, geckos,
lizards, turtles, tortoises, alligators and

crocodiles. Lovingly cared for by Mary
Hart, a renowned West Coast reptile
handler, these creatures (and their surroundings) may not be pretty, but
they're pretty intriguing.

Far from a conventional museum,
Hart's Reptile World is a slice of jungle,
where the creatures look more comfortable than the people. Many inhabitants
are available for "petting," including
Binky, the 17.5-foot tame python, and
SeeMore, the iguana. The newest addition here is a Nile crocodile named Daisy.

Cupboards along the walls harbor
incubating snake eggs and other treasures; ask for a peek, but beware an
escaped mouse or wandering iguana.

Feeding time at Hart's Reptile World
is not for the squeamish. Smaller
snakes are fed on Saturday at 3 pm,
and larger snakes are fed on Sunday at
3 pm. The alligators are fed Wednesday and Saturday at 3 pm.

Oregon Zoo
4001 SW Canyon Rd, Portland 97221
503-226-1561
www.oregonzoo.org
Hours: October 1-March 31, daily, 9
am-4 pm; April 1-September 30, daily,
9 am-6 pm. Grounds are open for an
hour after entry gates close; zoo is
closed on Christmas Day
Admission: $7.50/adult, $6/senior,
$4.50/child 3-11, free/child 2 & under;
free/second Tues of month, 1 pm-clos-
ing; $2-$2.75/train (April-September)

Set amid the forest and rolling lawns
of Washington Park, the Oregon Zoo has
managed to maintain its own park like
identity, with attractive landscaping, bubbling brooks, a vast amphitheater centerpiece and intimate alcoves with
benches for resting. Indeed, like the

MUSEUMS AND EXHIBITS: GO WILD!

PHOTO COURTESY OF THE OREGON ZOO

The Oregon Zoo boasts the world's most successful elephant breeding program.

nation's best "natural-style" parks, the zoo invites visitors to wander, to discover; even regulars stumble upon unfamiliar paths and new pieces of statuary. Also a botanical garden, the zoo has identification plaques on many of its trees.

Tigers, monkeys, bears and elephants—they're all here, and apparently quite happy in their capacious enclosures. The zoo boasts the world's most successful elephant-breeding program and has staked its reputation on its innovative toys. Admitting that the animals' enclosures fall far short of the challenging environments of the wild, the zoo has outfitted animal habitats with big plastic balls, Styrofoam shapes, "blood balls" (balloons filled with frozen meat juices) and great, hanging tree trunks. It is believed that equipment of this kind, in addition to multilevel climbing structures and sprinklings of cinnamon, herbs and other exotic scents, can help to keep the animals physically fit and mentally alert.

Zoos nowadays struggle to achieve a balance between imitating the animals' native habitats and appeasing the public, which wants to see the beasts up close. Peek into the shade of a great boulder or up onto a cantilevered tree limb—that's where you're likely to find a sleeping cat or lazy bear.

Keepers (in blue denim shirts with name tags) and docents (in red polo shirts with name tags) wander the grounds, answering visitors' questions. In summer, keepers schedule special talks at select exhibits throughout the zoo. Check the handout map for subjects and times, and for the feeding schedule (the penguins receive a public feeding daily, year-round).

It's the unexpected that is most intriguing here. The quarter-mile Cascade Nature Trail, tucked into a back hillside, showcases native plants and ani-mals: beavers, river otters, fish and waterfowl. An indoor cafeteria overlooks the lush vegetation and colorful tropical birds of an enclosed aviary. In the Kongo Ranger Station, children clamor for a seat behind the wheel of a full-size jungle jeep. The train ride, with its three dif-ferent locomotives, veers deeper into Washington Park along a wooded, 4-mile ravine route.

Founded in 1887 at the rear of a downtown pharmacy, the zoo is Ore-gon's leading paid attraction. And with new exhibits being added all the time, it seems sure to stay that way.

In 2000, the zoo opened Steller Cove, which simulates the Northwest coastal habitat. Named for the large sea lions that inhabit this exhibit, it also features sea otters, tide-pool animals, fish, inver-tebrates and plants. The exhibit is pop-ular, and its inhabitants have thrived: just six months after the exhibit opened, a

southern sea otter pup was born. Dubbed Oz, the pup has the distinction of being the first sea otter in the world to be conceived, born and raised by its mother at a zoo or aquarium.

In fall 2001, the zoo opened the Amazon Flooded Forest. Named for the watery world created by six months of torrential rains, this exhibit is one of the first of its kind at any zoo. It features the full spectrum of species—mam-mals, fish, birds, reptiles, amphibians and invertebrates—living in this ecosys-tem on the banks of the great South American river. Keep an eye out here for animals that are both colorful and mysterious: howler monkeys and a two-toed sloth, toucans and tanagers, an emerald tree boa and a massive ana-conda, and many more.

With all there is to see, it's best to select a few exhibits and not try to see everything in one fell swoop. You might want to purchase a zoo key ($2) at the souvenir shop near the exit gates, then hunt down the talking boxes for tidbits and trivia. Or plan a backwards visit, so your energy gives out at a dif-ferent cage.

Break up the afternoon with a pic-nic lunch or snack (food from home is allowed, and you can rent a wagon to transport the cooler). Most people grav-itate to the amphitheater at lunch time, where the kids can somersault and wrestle on the lawn. Another option is to set up on a bench along the Cas-cades Trail, a serene, forested corner back behind the big cats.

Visit in the early morning and in winter to see different animals at their best—and to avoid traffic snarls in the parking lot. If you can't resist the zoo on a sunny summer day, you'll be in good company, and chances are, if you don't take the MAX to get here, you'll

PHOTO COURTESY OF THE OREGON ZOO

Howler monkeys are part of the new Amazon Flooded Forest habitat at the Oregon Zoo.

MUSEUMS AND EXHIBITS:
GO WILD! / EXPLORE NATURE

have to park in the overflow lot (near the Sylvan exit of Hwy 26). Have the driver drop an adult and children at the entrance gate first, then meet the group inside. The return trip to the overflow lot via shuttle bus is an almost-welcome detour because the door-to-door service cuts down on the walk. There's no denying it: A trip to the zoo means a lot of walking. Take a stroller for the toddler (or rent one for $2.50).

(For extra fun, check out the Kid's Zone on the zoo's Web site. There you'll find amazing animal facts, a behind-the-scenes tour and pictures to print out and color.)

Explore Nature

John Inskeep Environmental Learning Center
19600 S Molalla Ave
Oregon City 97045
503-657-6958 ext. 2351
http://depts.clackamas.cc.or.us/elc/
Hours: Daily, dawn-dusk
Haggart Observatory
Hours: Winter: Wed & Fri- Sat (weather permitting), 7:30-11:30 pm.
Summer: Wed & Fri- Sat, 9-11:30 pm
Admission for observatory:
$2.50/person

  (except observatory)

Part museum, part park, this site on the Clackamas Community College campus wasn't always so inviting. In the early 1970s what is now home to a native wetlands nursery, small exhibit hall and observatory was an abandoned industrial complex. Restored by volunteers, the eight-acre John Inskeep Environmental Learning Center stands as a model for cooperative projects of this kind.

Plan a daytime visit to enjoy the gravel trails that meander beside Newell Creek. Inspect the buildings, made almost entirely of salvaged and recycled materials.

Then return at night to view the stars. A 40-foot tower, Haggart Memorial Astronomical Observatory, houses a 26-inch reflecting telescope. Staffed by volunteer astronomers, stargazing parties are open to the public year-round.

Planetarium Sky Theater
Mount Hood Community College
26000 SE Stark St, Gresham 97030
503-491-7297
www.starstuff.com/stars.htm
Public shows: One weekend per month, January-August; Sat, 1 pm & 2:30 pm; Sun, 2 pm
Admission: $1/person

With its newly remodeled 30-foot hemispherical dome, comfortable seating for 70, special effects and enhanced audio system, the Mount Hood Community College Planetarium puts on a star-studded show. Planetarium director Douglas McCarty, an astronomy instructor for more than 25 years, tailors the monthly public shows to his audience. Children are always welcome (McCarty welcomes questions), and the programs use the current night sky as a springboard to discuss recent discoveries in astronomy and space science. Visitors are seated on a first-come, first-served basis, so arrive early to be sure of a seat.

World Forestry Center
4033 SW Canyon Rd, Portland 97221
503-228-1367
www.worldforestry.org
Hours: Winter, daily, 10 am-5 pm; summer (Memorial Day-Labor Day), daily, 9 am-5 pm

WORLD FORESTRY CENTER

Visitors to the World Forestry Center can view a Pygmy family from Africa's Ituri Forest.

Admission: $4.50/adult, $3.50/senior or child 6-18

The World Forestry Center is a non-profit organization whose mission is to "educate and inform people about the world's forests and trees and their relationship to all life, in order to promote a balanced and sustainable future."

Located in Washington Park, it features permanent exhibits, including "Tropical Rainforest: A Disappearing Treasure" and "Old Growth Forest: Treasure in Transition," and traveling exhibits ranging from unique and rare photographs to tribal masks from the Amazon rain forests. Future plans call for the development of a kid-friendly, hands-on, interactive forest lab, as well as displays on how forests have shaped civilizations and how civilizations have shaped forests.

Sports Anyone?

Oregon Sports Hall of Fame and Museum
321 SW Salmon, Portland 97208
503-227-7466
www.oregonsportshall.org
Hours: Mon-Sat, 10 am-6 pm; Sun, noon-5 pm
Admission: $4/adult, $3/student 7-21 or senior 55 & over, free/child 6 & under; $10/family; call ahead for group rates

This 7,000-square-foot facility is full of interactive exhibits centered on great Oregon athletes, including runner Steve Prefontaine, basketball star Clyde Drexler, baseball's Dale Murphy, golf's Peter Jacobsen and many more.

Youngsters love climbing up on a rodeo saddle, testing their mettle in a racing wheelchair, powering out of starting blocks, lifting a full-size shot

MUSEUMS AND EXHIBITS:
SPORTS ANYONE? / ART

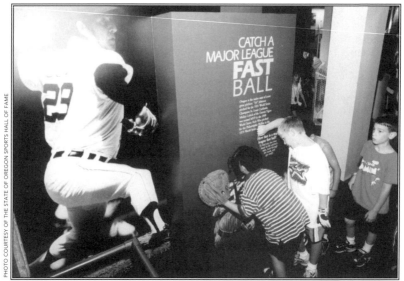

PHOTO COURTESY OF THE STATE OF OREGON SPORTS HALL OF FAME

Kids enjoy the interactive exhibits at the Oregon Sports Hall of Fame and Museum.

put and discus, catching a fastball and trying out full hockey goalie gear.

Special visiting exhibits highlight such sports events as the Berlin Olympics of 1936 and the Winter Olympics.

Each year the museum honors a new slate of six inductees and awards multiple scholarships to exceptional Oregon student athletes who attend Oregon colleges.

Art

Portland Art Museum
1219 SW Park Ave, Portland 97205
503-226-2811
www.portlandartmuseum.org
Hours: Tues-Sat, 10 am-5 pm (Wed & first Thurs, until 8 pm); Sun, noon-5 pm
Admission: $10/adult, $9/senior, student 18 & over, $6/child 5-18, free/child 4 & under

The region's oldest and largest visual- and media-arts center, the Portland Art Museum was established in 1892 by seven successful Portland businessmen. Transplanted Northeasterners, they believed in the power of art to create enlightened citizens. In the century since, the museum has amassed a substantial collection of more than 30,000 objects that span 35 centuries of Asian, European and American art.

Allied with the Northwest Film Center, the city's most visible arts institution continues to play an important role in directing the region's cultural life. To that end, the Portland Art Museum has increasingly pursued collections that underscore the variety of artistic origins and expressions. For instance, its renowned collection of Native American art features examples from nearly every cultural region of North America.

Especially for kids, Museum Family Sundays are scheduled four or five times a year in conjunction with different exhibitions. And legions of kids—with their parents—come to these free-for-all open houses. Each event (usually free with museum admission) is designed to augment the theme of a current installation—Japanese art, Rodin sculpture or Impressionism, for example. Local cultural groups, artists and educators lead interactive activities, performances and demonstrations that help make the exhibits more tangible and accessible to children. Most activities are in the North Wing, and they're likely to include, for example, learning calligraphy, watching a tea ceremony, building a sculpture from pipe cleaners and coat hangers, or making a mosaic picture using squares of colored construction paper.

Museum Family Sundays (generally 1 pm to 5 pm) are worth planning for. Call ahead for a schedule of upcoming events (organizers try to have a year-round calendar ready in July), then be the first in line when doors open at 1 pm. Usually the hours between 2 pm and 3:30 pm are the most crowded. If you haven't visited all the activity stations by

then, feel free to step outside for a snack and a walk, then return later in the afternoon when the place isn't so mobbed.

Families have become a real priority for the museum, and its efforts to provide family programming have won it national notice. An interactive resource center within the gallery is quite popular with families, who find it easy to learn more about an exhibit by using computers and engaging in hands-on interaction with the collection. Watch, too, for docent-led family tours, offered on special dates during each exhibition (for information, call the education department at 503-276-4225).

In addition, the museum opened a family education center in its new wing in summer 2000. With "First Look," the museum aims to introduce children ages 3 to 5 (accompanied by their parents) to art. And hands-on art classes are offered for everyone age 5 and up.

Fire/Police

Jeff Morris Fire Museum
55 SW Ash, Portland 97204
503-823-3615

This walk-by museum (with viewing from the sidewalk only) is adjacent to the Portland Fire Bureau building on SW Ash. It's dedicated to the memory of Jeff Morris, a loyal firefighter who pioneered the bureau's safety-education program and died of cancer in 1974 at age 46. Signage describes the historic equipment inside, much of which tells its own story of the past—from hand-drawn hand-pumpers and ladder trucks (1860s to 1870s) to a horse-drawn steam-pumper from 1911.

Museum Family Sundays at the Portland Art Museum feature hands-on activity stations.

THE ALARM BELL

The 4,000-pound alarm bell that used to be housed in the Jeff Morris Fire Museum has a new home.

Look for it today in a covered bell house just behind Campbell Fountain at Firefighters Memorial Park, located at SW 18th and Burnside.

Commissioned in 1873 following a tragic fire to which volunteer firefighters responded belatedly, the huge bell (it could be heard in Oregon City) arrived from New York in time to usher in a new, paid fire department.

Portland Police Museum
Justice Center
1111 SW Second Ave, 16th floor,
Portland 97204
503-823-0019
Hours: Mon-Thurs, 10 am-3 pm

Tucked away on an upper story of the Justice Center are the three small rooms and dozens of display cases of the Portland Police Museum, an operation run by volunteer members of the Portland Police Historical Society. Children clamor to sit atop the vintage Harley-Davidson motorcycle and in its sidecar. Everything else is under glass: bulletproof vests, firearms and other confiscated weapons, drug paraphernalia, uniforms, badges, arrest logs and historic photographs.

Music

Chamber Music Northwest
522 SW Fifth Ave, Ste 725
Portland 97204
503-294-6400 (box office), 503-223-3202
www.cmnw.org
Dates: Late June-late July
Tickets: $5/family concert, $16-$29 other concerts; free events during summer

For nearly 30 years, Chamber Music Northwest has been building a national reputation on the strength of its programming and informal, intimate settings. The 25-concert summer series with performances at both Catlin Gabel School (8825 Barnes Rd) and Reed College's Kaul Auditorium (3203 SE Woodstock Blvd) is serious business—and popular with metro-area music-lovers.

Children younger than age 7 are not admitted to evening performances. Instead they are offered a special matinee (with refreshments afterward) that's designed to serve as a nonthreatening introduction to classical music.

Family concerts, lasting just 45 minutes, are held during both spring and summer. Recent musical selections have included "Tyrannosaurus Sue" and "Tough Turkey in the Big City." These

Chamber Music Northwest offers special family concerts.

events allow children to ask questions and to see the instruments up close.

Chamber Music Northwest is also involved in educational outreach programs throughout the year.

Columbia Symphony Orchestra
P.O. Box 6559, Portland 97228
503-234-4077
www.columbiasymphony.org
Season: October-April
Tickets: $14/adult, $11/senior, $7/student; season subscription available

Founded in 1983 at Lewis and Clark College, the Columbia Symphony Orchestra is a semiprofessional metropolitan group. The orchestra takes pride in performing works that are considered undiscovered classics and offers audiences the chance to hear and meet some of the finest classical musicians in the Portland area.

During its eight-month season, the orchestra performs six concerts in the First United Methodist Church at SW 18th and Jefferson. In addition to its regular concert series, each January the orchestra rings in the new year with a standing-room-only gala presentation of Johann Strauss' comic operetta *Die Fledermaus* in the Grand Ballroom of the Governor Hotel.

Oregon Symphony
923 SW Washington, Portland 97205
503-228-1353 (ticket office)
503-228-4294 (administration)
www.orsymphony.org
Season: September-June
Tickets: $5-$70; season subscription available

The Oregon Symphony is commit-

ted to reaching diverse audiences with a 10-month season of varied music, including newly commissioned works, works dropped from active repertoires and works of contemporary composers and U.S. composers. Under the leadership of music director and conductor James DePreist, the orchestra, which performs at the Arlene Schnitzer Concert Hall (SW Broadway & Main), has grown increasingly active in the areas of education and outreach.

Its popular Kids Concerts series is consistently rated among the city's highest-caliber children's musical events. Recent series selections have included *Where in the World of Music Is Carmen Sandiego?*, *The Snowman* and *Peter and the Wolf*.

These fast-paced performances are kept to about an hour in length and are designed to introduce children age 4 and up to the instruments and sounds of the orchestra. Each of the three Sunday-matinee concerts is performed twice, and seating is reserved.

Read the symphony's season concert schedule for other family offerings, such as the ever-popular annual holiday concert, and periodic Special Events Concerts, including appearances by guests such as Linda Ronstadt and the Temptations.

Metropolitan Youth Symphony
825 NE 20th, Portland
P.O. Box 5254, Portland 97208
503-239-4566
www.metroyouthsymphony.org
Season: September-June
Tickets: $6-$29; season subscription available

The Metropolitan Youth Symphony (MYS) draws more than 450 student musicians (elementary-school-age and

MUSIC

up) from throughout northwest Oregon and even southern Washington to perform in its eight orchestras and bands. Under the direction of musical director Lajos Balogh since 1974, the MYS holds rehearsals every Saturday during the school year. Emphasis is placed on enjoyment through learning and satisfaction through accomplishment.

The annual performance schedule features three major concerts at the Arlene Schnitzer Concert Hall (SW Broadway & Main), in December, March and June, as well as several free concerts at local schools.

Auditions are held each summer to welcome new students. If your child is interested, call early to find out more.

Portland Opera

1515 SW Morrison, Portland 97205
503-241-1802 (box office)
www.portlandopera.org
Season: September-May
Tickets: $24-$100; season subscription available

Having adopted an "anything but stuffy" style in order to reestablish public enthusiasm for opera, Portland Opera consistently plays to sell-out audiences at Keller Auditorium (SW Third Ave & Clay). Ranked as one of the nation's top 20 professional opera companies (out of 106), Portland Opera is a distinguished member of the metro area's arts community.

Its five-show season tends to blend traditional with innovative performances.

Recent performances have included *La Traviata* and *The Pearl Fishers*.

Ambitious education and outreach programs help expose school groups throughout the region to talented young opera and musical-theater pro-

fessionals. Dress-rehearsal performances are reserved for students and educators, and the demand for these discounted tickets attests to the success of Portland Opera's attempts to shed its highbrow image without compromising the integrity of its productions.

Portland Youth Philharmonic

1119 SW Park Ave, Portland 97205
www.portlandyouthphil.org
503-223-5939
Season: November-May
Tickets: $9-$25

The nation's oldest youth orchestra, the Portland Youth Philharmonic (PYP) was founded in 1924 and continues its long-standing commitment to excellence in musical education. Students ages 9 to 22 audition for seats in the PYP, the Preparatory Orchestra and the Young String Ensemble each season. About 200 are selected, and some choose to travel from as far as Eugene and Tillamook for rehearsals and performances.

The PYP is far from a kiddie company. Its ambitious repertoire mirrors that of major professional orchestras, and it performs four concerts a year at Arlene Schnitzer Concert Hall (SW Broadway & Main) and the Newmark Theatre (next door to the Schnitzer). In addition, it offers more-informal recitals for local school groups; some 10,000 children see these concerts each year.

Singing Christmas Tree

11040 SW Barbur Blvd, Ste 102
Portland 97219
503-557-TREE (8733), 503-244-1344
Season: Late November-early December
Tickets: $8-$50
 (signed performance also)

PHOTO COURTESY OF THE SINGING CHRISTMAS TREE

The Singing Christmas Tree pageant is an annual holiday tradition for many local families.

From its perch atop a 26-foot-tall, 34-foot-wide lighted and flocked Christmas "tree," a 300-member volunteer choir performs with a 60-piece orchestra and 50 children in one of the city's most popular and enduring holiday extravaganzas. Performed at Keller Auditorium (SW Third Ave & Clay) beginning Thanksgiving weekend, the pageant "does" Christmas by incorporating Santa and popular commercial Christmas music with the Christ child and more-traditional carols. With a nearly 40-year history, this production has it all. As participants say, "It's not just a concert; it's not just a performance; it's not just a show. It's an experience."

Waterfront Blues Festival

Tom McCall Waterfront Park, Naito Pkwy, near Hawthorne Bridge
503-282-0555
www.waterfrontbluesfest.com
Dates: Fourth of July weekend; hours vary
Fee: Nominal cash donation, plus a food donation

Surely it's sacrilegious to be caught smiling at a blues festival, but this four-day Fourth of July mega-jam has all the makings of a good time: three stages of world-class blues acts (Junior Wells, Charlie Musselwhite, Canned Heat and Elvin Bishop, among others); a wide swath of lawn with ample room for dancing and tumbling; a view of the Willamette River; a grand fireworks display on July 4; and food booths with enough variety to satisfy finicky as well as more sophisticated palates. To top it all off, you can feel good about coming. Donations benefit the Oregon Food Bank. In 2001, volunteers at the gate collected $302,000 and some 103,000 pounds of canned food.

Summer Concert Series

A picnic at an outdoor summer concert has got to be as American as baseball, hot dogs and apple pie. And if we're lucky, the sun shines just long enough in Portland for families to get their fill of all of the above.

In reality, the Rose City seems to have more than its fair share of concert series in the summer. Virtually every municipality with a patch of green lawn hosts one. Not that we're complaining. Events such as these have "family" written all over them. Yours won't be the only kids digging for ants and stepping on neighboring blankets.

Many of the concerts are free, but some are not. Call for details. The listing below is merely a sampling.

- **Concerts on the Commons:** July-August, Fri, 6:30 pm. Tualatin Commons, 8325 SW Nyberg, Tualatin; 503-691-3061.
- **Forest Music Series:** June-August, Sun, 2 pm. Tryon Creek State Park,

The Jefferson Dancers work in all dance styles: tap, ballet, jazz, modern, ethnic and musical theater numbers.

PHOTO COURTESY OF JEFFERSON HIGH SCHOOL

11321 SW Terwilliger Blvd; 503-636-4398.

- **High Noon Tunes:** July-August, Wed, noon-1 pm. Pioneer Courthouse Square, SW Broadway between Yamhill & Morrison; 503-223-1613.
- **Lunchbox Concerts:** June-August, Wed, noon-1 pm. Oregon Square Courtyard, NE Holladay between Seventh & Ninth; 503-233-5696.
- **Oregon Symphony in the Neighborhood:** August-early September, various dates and locations; 503-228-4294.
- **Performance Series:** July-August, Fri, times vary. Beaverton Town Square, 11665 SW Beaverton-Hillsdale Hwy, Beaverton; 503-526-2288.
- **Wells Fargo Summer Concert Series at the Oregon Zoo:** Mid-June-August, days vary, 7 pm. Oregon Zoo Amphitheater, 4001 SW Canyon Rd; 503-226-1561.

Dance

Jefferson Dancers
Jefferson High School
Performing Arts Department
5210 N Kerby Ave, Portland 97217
503-916-5180
www.pps.k12.or.us/depts/arts/dance/
Season: April-early May
Tickets: $7-$13

Established in 1974, the Jefferson Performing and Visual Arts Magnet Program was devised to improve inner-city school enrollment, along with student motivation and self-esteem. Drawing from a racially integrated student body of nearly 500 high-schoolers, the program offers training in dance, theater, music, television and visual arts.

One of the Performing Arts Center's unbridled success stories is the Jefferson Dancers. An ensemble composed of the department's most advanced dance students, the Jefferson Dancers tour the Northwest and western Canada each year, returning to Portland in late spring for a series of performances at the Center for Performing Arts (1111 SW Broadway).

Unlike most professional companies, this dance troupe maintains an ambitious repertoire of works in all dance styles—tap, ballet, jazz, modern, ethnic and musical-theater numbers. The resulting potpourri productions are all the more exciting to children.

Oregon Ballet Theatre

818 SE Sixth, Portland 97214
503-2-BALLET (222-5538), 503-227-0977
www.obt.org
Season: October-June
Tickets: $5-$80; season subscription available

Established in 1989, Oregon Ballet Theatre (OBT) is the metro area's flagship dance company. With an annual season of four productions at the Keller Auditorium (SW Third Ave & Clay) and Newmark Theatre (1111 SW Broadway), this 23-member troupe is developing a uniquely American repertoire and style.

Artistic director James Canfield offered local families a magical holiday present in 1993 when his company unveiled an opulent new *Nutcracker.* Set in czarist Russia and augmented by regal costumes and Fabergé-inspired scenery, this jewel of a production plays to full houses in December each year. Act I, with its pantomime party scene, is particularly beloved by young children. Act II showcases more traditional pas de deux.

Nutcracker is an opulent show, a vast improvement over the tired, dowdy productions many dance companies mount year after year. Think twice about taking young children, however, because this version—with all its pomp and circumstance—is two and a half hours long. Kids younger than age 6 will likely lose interest after intermission. Be forewarned, as well, that parents dress up and dress up their kids for *The Nutcracker.* Lace, velvet, bow ties and blue blazers are de rigueur.

In late August, OBT takes to the streets with a special two-week outdoor rehearsal program (daily, 10 am-4 pm). Housed on a tented stage behind the

Oregon Ballet Theatre's annual production of The Nutcracker *is a highlight of Portland's dance season.*

Arlene Schnitzer Concert Hall (SW Broadway & Main), *OBT Exposed!* premiered in 1995 to enthusiastic crowds and has since returned for an annual run. In full view of the public, company dancers go about their business, attending classes and rehearsals in preparation for the season opener.

Pacific Festival Ballet
4620 SW Beaverton-Hillsdale Hwy, Portland 97221
503-245-5269
www.pacificfestivalballet.org
Tickets: $19/adult, $17/senior or child for *The Nutcracker*; group discounts available

Founded by professional ballet dancer John Gardner in 1980, this community-based nonprofit organization performs *The Nutcracker* each year to growing and enthusiastic audiences. While professionals fill the principal roles, some 100 students from throughout the metropolitan area dance in supporting roles to much acclaim in late November and early December. Staged at Portland Community College's Sylvania Campus Forum Theatre (12000 SW 49th St), this version is a good introduction to *The Nutcracker* for younger audiences. In fact, the company typically takes its show on the road, performing in several schools during the holiday season. The company also performs a spring concert in June and is considering adding another production during the year as well (call for ticket prices on these).

Northwest Afrikan American Ballet
P.O. Box 11143, Portland 97211
503-287-8852
www.nwaab.org
(Call for information on season and tickets)

Northwest Afrikan American Ballet, the first traditional African dance company in the northwest United States, performs full concert productions nationally and internationally to more than 60,000 audience members per year. Founded in 1982 by lead drummer and dancer Bruce Smith, the company features original choreography inspired by traditional dances indigenous to Senegal, Gambia, Mali and Guinea, West Africa. Each performance allows the audience to feel that they have just witnessed a true African village ritual with its ceremonial grandeur.

In addition, with its interactive educational outreach programs, the company aims to teach the culture of West Africa, develop sensitivity to diversity in the community and foster appreciation and respect for similarities and differences.

Theater

Broadway Rose Theatre Company
P.O. Box 231004, Tigard 97281
503-620-5262
www.bwayrose.com
Season: Summer
Tickets: $18/adult, $15/student or senior, $9/child 12 & under, $6/children's show

The metro area's only professional summer-stock theater troupe, the Broadway Rose Theatre Company got its start in 1991, when a group of four experienced actors, directors and designers began mounting professional—and affordable—productions at Tigard High School's 600-seat Deb Fennell Auditorium (9000 SW Durham Rd, Tigard). Its ambitious eight-week season consists of three main-stage shows and two children's musicals. Recent productions have included *Phantom, The Odd Couple, The Taffetas, Snow White* and *Robin Hood.*

The theater also runs summer camps for budding actors, one for ages 8 to 11 and the other for ages 12 to 16.

Chickadee Children's Theater

Cedar Hills Recreation Center
11640 SW Park Wy, Portland 97225
503-644-3855
Season: Fall & spring
Tickets: $1-$2

Under the aegis of the Tualatin Hills Park and Recreation District in Beaverton, Karolyn Pettingell Ainsworth's company was launched in 1993 to a receptive local audience. A teacher of puppetry and acting at the Cedar Hills Recreation Center for many years, and a former manager of a children's entertainment facility in Sacramento, Ainsworth writes and directs two plays at the center each year. Performances are in December and June.

With a cadre of talented actors (both children and adults), a set designer and other technical assistants, Chickadee Children's Theater plays to full houses. Recent productions include *Do You Know These Muffins, Man?* and *The Friendlier Brothers Grimm.*

With the group's 10th anniversary slated for 2003, a huge celebration is in the works.

Children's Theater Series

Beaverton Community Center, 12350 SW Fifth Ave, Beaverton 97005
503-526-2288
www.ci.beaverton.or.us/departments/arts/
Season: October-December, one Sun each month
Tickets: $5/adult, $4/senior, $3/child

With invaluable assistance from a committed citizens' board of directors, the Beaverton Arts Commission, an agency of the city of Beaverton, has for nearly 10 years raised the funds necessary to mount an increasingly diverse series of live theatrical events for chil-

FOR A LIVELY LUNCH . . .

Friends of the Performing Arts Center's Brown Bag Lunch Series features open rehearsals and selected highlights from resident companies' upcoming performances. A good way to preview a show or concert and the attention span of your youngster, the free hourlong events convene at PCPA venues at noon on various weekdays, October through June.

Recent events have included selections from Portland Opera productions, scenes from Tygres Heart Shakespeare Company plays, workshops based on Oregon Children's Theatre productions *Stuart Little* and *Tuck Everlasting,* and selections from Tears of Joy Puppet Theater productions. For a schedule, call 503-274-6555 or check www.pcpa.com/friends/friends.html.

THEATER

dren. In addition to nurturing future audiences of the arts, the series seeks to promote multicultural understanding and empathy in youths ages 4 to12.

Performed at Elsie Stuhr Center in Beaverton, these productions have included *The Toad Prince* from Tears of Joy Puppet Theatre, *A Midsummer Night's Dream* from Oregon Children's Theater Company and *Swingin' On a Star* from Northwest Children's Theatre. Face painting and refreshments precede each show.

Do Jump! Movement Theater
Echo Theatre, 1515 SE 37th Ave, Portland 97214
503-231-1232
www.dojump.org
Season: October-June
Tickets: $10-$14

Imago Theater frogs

Under the direction of Robin Lane, a performance artist of the best kind, Do Jump!, founded in 1977, has outlasted all comparably sized local arts organizations. Yet what it does continues to do is to defy description. "Cirque du Soleil meets Oregon Ballet Theatre" may have to suffice.

With a repertoire that consists of nearly 50 segments, the seven-member company is in the enviable position of being able to shuffle and reshuffle its programs to fill a nine-month season with elements of dance, acrobatics, physical comedy, aerial movement and live original music.

The December holiday show features special appearances by Poptarts, student performers from the Do Jump! after-school program. Each Sunday show culminates in an all-ages, all-out juggle-in.

Built as a silent-movie house in 1910, the Echo Theatre has been out-

fitted with high-tech lighting and aerial equipment to serve as a community arts center and home for Do Jump!

Imago Theatre
17 SE Eighth Ave, Portland 97214
503-231-9581
www.imgagotheatre.com
Season: August-May
Tickets: $10-$23

Recognized as one of the nation's most innovative mask ensembles, Imago continues to grow and evolve. Having established its reputation with the family favorite *Frogz*, the company has since staged complex, even dark, adult dramas that center on classic themes from literature by Dante and Sophocles, for example. Its performance space, completed in 1993, has spawned a second theater upstairs. Now more than 20 years old, Imago is developing a new family show called *Squid.*

Still, it's hard to imagine anything upstaging good old *Frogz*, in which amphibians with a sense of humor intermingle with ethereal globes and an overfed baby. The show tours internationally and plays to an appreciative home crowd once a year.

Ladybug Theater
503-232-2346
www.ladybugtheater.com
Season: September-May; special Halloween, Christmas & spring break productions
Tickets: $2.50-$6.50
(At press time, Ladybug Theater was in a state of flux; call for information about location and times for productions.)

Originally housed at the Oregon Zoo in a ladybug-shaped building (hence its name), this Portland theater institution has been performing for the region's youngest audiences for more than 40 years.

There's nothing timeworn about this company, though. Ladybug's core of a half-dozen or so adult improvisational actors continues to refashion classic fairy tales and nursery rhymes into zany, original productions. Grimm's scary witches and abusive stepmothers land on the cutting-room floor, to be replaced by silly dimwits and their slapstick antics.

Committed to providing preschoolers with their first theater experiences, Ladybug has adopted an informal, ad-lib style that invites audience input. Sometimes the cast is hard put to squelch the little cut-ups, but the show must go on!

For children age 2 ½ and up, the troupe offers quickie Wednesday- and Thursday-morning productions. (Preschool groups are welcome either day.) Older children flock to the weekends' more elaborate shows, where they sit in a heap on the floor, as close to the action as possible.

After the finale, the cast members form a receiving line by the front door to greet the audience and answer questions. Kids get a kick out of inspecting the costumes and makeup up close.

Lakewood Theatre Company
Lakewood Center for the Arts, 368 S State St, Lake Oswego 97034
503-635-3901
www.lakewood-center.org
Children's season: Fall, winter (December) & spring
Tickets: $5-$9

Its primary emphasis may be on adult theater, with half a dozen productions scheduled annually, but the Lakewood Theatre Company is also dedicated to theater-arts education. In hosting an array of drama workshops for children and three children's theater productions each year, LTC continues to serve its suburban community with engaging arts experiences.

Each season's trio of kids' shows, mostly adaptations of fairy tales, feature young actors, many of whom are students in Lakewood classes. In partnership with Lake Oswego high schools, LTC also sponsors a holiday breakfast-theater event for children in December.

Lakewood Theatre Company also offers classes for children (in grades 3 through 12) in spring, fall and winter, as well as a popular summer drama camp.

Miracle Theatre Group
425 SE Sixth Ave, Portland 97214
503-236-7253
www.milagro.org
Season: September-May

Students from Ainsworth Elementary School participate in a Miracle Theatre workshop.

Tickets: $15; subscription available

Miracle Theatre Group oversees three performance companies: Miracle Mainstage, Teatro Milagro and the Milagro Bailadores.

While Miracle Mainstage presents artistically challenging productions in Portland, Teatro Milagro and the Milagro Bailadores are theatrical and dance touring companies respectively that present bilingual and Spanish-language performances throughout the West.

Miracle Mainstage presents both adult and family-oriented productions performed in El Centro Milagro's intimate, 120-seat theater in inner southeast Portland. Teatro Milagro takes current global issues and crafts them into cutting-edge dramatic plays infused with Latino culture, Spanish language and original music. And the Milagro Bailadores performs dances from several Latin American cultures and also produces three original dance and theater works: *Milagro Bailadores on Tour, El Dia de los Muertos Festival*

(Festival of the Day of the Dead) in the fall and *¡Viva Baile!* (Long Live Dance) in spring. Milagro Bailadores presentations are original, interactive programs that are performed in El Centro Milagro as well as toured to schools, festivals and community events.

Missoula Children's Theatre
200 N Adams
Missoula, Montana 59802
406-728-1911
www.mctinc.org
Season: Year-round
Tickets: Prices vary

Each year this Montana-based band of traveling actor/directors crisscrosses the globe overseeing full-length productions starring legions of singing schoolchildren in nearly 900 communities. Hired by a school, recreation department, church or scout troop to put on a show, an MCT duo arrives on Monday to audition and cast 50 to 60 students. Tuesday through Friday afternoons are devoted to rehearsals and to costume and set preparation. Saturday is the performance. And on Sunday the

MIRACLE THEATRE GROUP

MCT team packs up and drives to the next town to do it all over again.

With almost 30 years spent directing shows in this fast-forward, soup-to-nuts fashion, MCT has developed quite a system. Seventeen productions—each one an original musical adaptation of a popular fairy tale—are in circulation annually among 26 teams of professional actors. Chosen for their backgrounds in the arts and education, these folks are very good at what they do.

MCT makes many visits to the Portland metro area during the school year and summer. Call your local school or recreation department to learn of a planned residency, or contact MCT directly to arrange for one. Cost of a weeklong program (actors are boarded by sponsor families): $2,300.

Perhaps the most visible metro-area visit by MCT each summer is the one at the Lake Oswego Festival of Arts. Sponsored by Lake Oswego's Parks and Recreation Department, this production takes place in late June. Tickets to the show sell quickly. For more information about time, location and cost, call 503-636-9673.

Northwest Childrens Theater and School

Northwest Neighborhood Cultural Center, 1819 NW Everett St.
Portland 97209
503-222-4480, 503-222-2190
www.nwcts.org
Season: October-May
Tickets: $8-$15; season subscription available

This nationally recognized company operates out of the Northwest Neighborhood Cultural Center with a three-tiered organization centered on entertainment, in the form of stage productions; education, in the form of acting classes and workshops; and enrichment, in the form of educational outreach and scholarship programs.

NWCT has a reputation for showcasing top-quality classic plays and original adaptations of children's liter-

Rehearsing at the Oregon Children's Theatre. The company frequently features plays based on favorite children's books.

THEATER

Portland Revels is best known for its Christmas Revels production. The shows include a large volunteer chorus of children and adults.

ature (a recent season featured *A Wrinkle in Time* and *The Magic Mrs. Piggle Wiggle*, among others) using both professional actors and children.

For season subscribers, NWCT offers a mix-and-match package of tickets to four or more productions on the main stage.

(Just for fun, keep an eye out for word on the school's annual fund-raising event, a costume rummage sale, that takes place in late October.)

Oregon Children's Theatre Company
600 SW 10th Ave, Ste 501
Portland 97205
503-228-9571
www.octc.org
Season: Late November-early May
Tickets: $10-$19; season subscription available

A nonprofit professional theater company and a resident of the Portland Center for the Performing Arts, OCT presents two full-scale productions at the Keller Auditorium (SW Third Ave &

Clay) along with one holiday show each year. It also plays to more than 80,000 children, parents and educators throughout Oregon and Washington each year.

The selected scripts tend to be based on favorite children's books, such as *Stuart Little* and *Tuck Everlasting*, so audiences benefit not only by experiencing live theater, but also by being exposed to great literature.

Broadway in Portland
Portland Opera, 1515 SW Morrison, Portland 97205
503-241-1407
www.portlandopera.org
Season: Year-round
Tickets: $22-$65; season subscription available

A unique partnership between Portland Opera and Clear Channel Entertainment, this multishow series is a local favorite, with more than 5,000 season subscribers. Booking top-quality touring productions, Portland's Broadway Theater Season showcases many of the musicals that make headlines in New York City. Some are suitable for children. Among recent visitors to Keller Auditorium (SW Third Ave & Clay): *Beauty and the Beast, Cats* and *Cinderella.*

Portland Revels

503-224-7411
www.portlandrevels.org
Season: Year-round
Tickets: Prices vary by event

The Portland affiliate of this national organization provides unique opportunities for communal celebration, usually centered around the changing of the seasons. The Revels' events blend traditional music, dance, drama, comedy and ritual, and will appeal to just about everyone in the family, although they are not recommended for children under 4. The shows are presented by a large volunteer chorus of children and adults drawn from the community along with a number of highly talented professional actors, musicians, artists, directors and "bearers of tradition" from many cultures.

While Portland Revels marks the passing of the seasons with celebrations throughout the year (including a May Day celebration and an autumn harvest party), they are most widely known for the Christmas Revels. Each Christmas Revels production is different, though all are historic in character. Most center on the medieval period and feature songs, dances, comedy and the playing of instruments that are characteristic of the period. The Christmas Revels (held in early December at the Scottish Rite Theater, SW Morrison & 15th) always brings a welcome message of hopefulness, even in the face of the shortest, darkest day of the year. Admission in 2001 was $21/adult, $15/senior or student, $10/child 12 and under.

Audience participation is a hallmark of Revels productions, so if you go to one of these shows, be prepared to sing along on some songs and to join the cast in an audience-wide dance.

New for the Portland Revels is what's being billed as Fool School. Taught by the Revels' own resident fool, Burl Ross, a professional actor who has appeared in many of the local productions, these multiday sessions teach such skills as juggling, mime and how to pull off a physical joke. A spring session is geared for children; in the fall, adults have their own turn.

Shakespeare in the Parks

Portland-area parks
503-321-0710
www.portlandactors.org
Season: July-August, weekends
Tickets: Free

For more than 30 years, a band of volunteer actors, writers and artists who call themselves Portland Actors Ensemble has been organizing a minstrel-like summer Shakespeare series in metro-area parks. Sometimes traditionally Elizabethan, other times set in the golden age of Hollywood, the Wild West or sometime in the near future, for example, these free plays are largely faithful to the Bard's text.

Each season brings a new title (*The Tempest, Romeo and Juliet* and *Comedy of Errors* made the rounds in past years), which is then performed on consecutive weekend afternoons before being repeated the following week in a different neighborhood park, library or college campus. Because the stage is designed to conform to its natural surroundings with minimal props and sets, each new location adds an unexpected twist to the proceedings. Audiences are encouraged to picnic on the grounds while watching the show.

THEATER

For a schedule of performance locations and times, check *The Oregonian's* A&E section on Fridays and *Willamette Week* beginning in late July, or visit the ensemble's Web site (see above). Final shows coincide with Labor Day weekend.

Student/Senior Matinee Series
Interstate Firehouse Cultural Center, 5340 N Interstate Ave, Portland 97217
503-823-4322
Season: Varies year to year
Tickets: $5/student or senior

Housed in a historic 1910 firehouse in north Portland, the nonprofit Interstate Firehouse Cultural Center sponsors performing-, literary- and visual-arts events and programs that emphasize the cultural heritage and diverse ethnic traditions of area residents. The Student Matinee Series consists of theater productions designed primarily for school groups (the public is invited, provided enough seats are available in the theater). Productions are done on weekdays.

The series has recently seen grade-school students treated to performances by Northwest Asian-American

OUTREACH FOR DISABLED

Three local theater companies—Tygres Heart, Northwest Childrens Theater and Oregon Children's Theatre Company—make an effort to reach disabled persons with special sign-interpreted and audio-described performances. Call the box offices for dates and other details.

Theatre, shadow puppets, marionettes and multicultural storytellers.

Tears of Joy Puppet Theatre
P.O. Box 1029
Vancouver (Washington) 98666
503-248-0557, 360-695-0477
Season: November-April
Tickets: $9-$14; season subscription available

Tears of Joy develops inspirational productions that entertain and enlighten audiences about distant peoples and far-off lands.

The puppets, custom-built for each show, are otherworldly—big as sequoias or small as shrews. Visit with the puppeteers after the show to touch their creations and learn how they're manipulated. No doubt you'll be surprised at how versatile the performers are; most take on multiple parts. Almost better than the puppets is the innovative use of simple materials and indigenous music in evoking a mood.

Typically, the company performs at Portland Center for the Performing Arts' Winningstad Theatre (1111 SW Broadway) and in Vancouver at the Royal Durst Theater (32nd and Main). Productions on the drawing board for coming years include *Perseus, Hero of Ancient Greece* and *Beanstalk!*

The theater offers puppet classes for children each June in Portland.

Theatre in the Grove
2028 Pacific Ave, Forest Grove 97116
503-359-5349
www.theatreinthegrove.org/
Season: October-June
Tickets: $8-$15

SUPPORT YOUR LOCAL (HIGH SCHOOL) ACTORS

The best children's-theater deal in town isn't something most people ever consider. Local acting students from after-school and summer programs throughout the city typically culminate their course work with a performance or two for family and friends.

Actually, anyone's welcome. Beyond providing free, informal entertainment, these shows are a good way to assess local theater-arts programs, should you be in the market for performance classes for your kids. Just call local theater schools (many are listed here) and ask for details regarding their term-ending productions.

Also keep an eye out for flyers from your local high school and consider going to student productions. Many schools put on captivating musicals, seasonal productions and student-directed children's plays, which are quite popular.

Following are a few of the high schools that local theater professionals tout when asked where they've seen quality productions. Call or check their Web sites to find out what's slated for the upcoming season. (For a list with links to all of the state's high schools, check the Eugene School District 4J's site: www.4j.lane.edu/schools/high.html.)

- **Aloha High School**, 18550 Kinnaman Rd, Aloha 97007; 503-259-4700; www.beavton.k12.or.us/aloha/home.html
- **Beaverton High School**, 13000 SW Second St, Beaverton 97005; 503-259-5000; www.beavton.k12.or.us/beaverton/home.html
- **Jefferson High School**, 5210 N Kerby, Portland 97217; 503-916-5180; www.pps.k12.or.us/depts/arts/dance/
- **West Linn High School**, 5464 West A St, West Linn 97068; 503-673-7800; www.wlwv.k12.or.us/wlhs/
- **Westview High School**, 4200 NW 185th Ave, Portland 97229; 503-259-5218; www.beavton.k12.or.us/westview/index2.html
- **Wilson High School**, 1151 SW Vermont, Portland 97219; 503-916-5280; www.wilsonhs.pps.k12.or.us/

An amateur community theater troupe formed in 1970 to produce musicals, Theatre in the Grove continues to thrive in a remodeled Forest Grove movie theater. Its season consists of six shows, two of which are musicals.

Casts for these productions are often family affairs—with parents and children on stage side by side—and you can bet the audience is, too. Recent productions have included *Little Shop of Horrors*, *A Christmas Carol*, *Feather of the Eagle*, *Brigadoon* and *Charlotte's Web*. In the works as of fall 2001 were classes in theater and dancing for the theater.

Tygres Heart Shakespeare Company
309 SW Sixth Ave, Ste 102
Portland 97204
503-288-8400
www.tygresheart.org
Season: October-June
Tickets: $11-$33.50;
season subscription available

Founded in 1989 by artistic director Jan Powell, Tygres Heart Shakespeare Company has developed a winning formula of innovative staging and natural, vivid delivery, which results in productions that are fresh and bold. Staged in the unique courtyard setting of the Winningstad Theatre (1111 SW Broadway), the plays are also intimate. Recent productions include *The Tempest* and *Richard II.*

Though full-length productions are probably more than most children can sit still for, the company's narrated, abridged Sunday Family Matinee series makes a fine introduction to the Bard. Each play in the three-show season receives this special treatment once during its run. Call for specific dates and times.

Portland Center for the Performing Arts
503-248-4335
www.pcpa.com

PCPA entertains more than a million patrons a year at four theaters in town:

Arlene Schnitzer Concert Hall
SW Broadway & Main

Italian Rococo Revival architecture and the world's largest electronic organ. Resident companies include the Oregon Symphony and Portland Youth Philharmonic.

New Theatre Building
1111 SW Broadway

State-of-the-art facilities in an award-winning, contemporary building. Two theaters: the Newmark Theatre, whose resident companies include Portland Center Stage, and the Dolores Winningstad Theatre, whose resident companies include Tygres Heart Shakespeare Company and Tears of Joy Puppet Theatre.

Keller Auditorium
SW Third Ave. & Clay
503-274-6560

Excellent acoustics and sight lines. Accommodates national touring shows. Resident companies include Portland Opera, Oregon Ballet Theatre and Oregon Children's Theatre.

BY THE BOOK

Though an afternoon at the theater is well spent if you and your child haven't read the book, the experience is all the richer when you have. So, before planning your family's theater outings, do a little research; contact some of the companies listed here and ask to receive their season brochures. Northwest Childrens Theater and Oregon Children's Theatre, in particular, create award-winning plays that are drawn from the pages of award-winning children's literature.

Movies

With VCRs—and now DVDs—in just about every household, going to the movies is not quite the treat that it was at one time. It's simpler, more economical and more convenient to rent a movie, take it home and settle in on the couch to watch it.

But when you do want to venture away from the house to try something a little different, check out the following theaters and drive-in.

Operated by the McMenamins chain of eateries (www.mcmenamins.com), the Bagdad Theatre, Edgefield Power Station Theatre, Kennedy School and Mission Theater show second-run pictures (as distinct from first-run blockbusters) in cinemas adjacent to full-service pubs. Order from the restaurant and eat while watching the movie. Families are restricted to off-peak hours. Call the movie line in advance to make sure that the current film is suitably rated for your family.

Bagdad Theater & Pub
3702 SE Hawthorne Blvd
Portland 97214
503-225-5555, ext 8831
Times: Sat-Sun, 2:30 pm (doors open at 2 pm)
Tickets: $2-$3/person, $1/child 11 & under

Edgefield Power Station Theater
2126 SW Halsey, Troutdale
503-225-5555, ext 8834
Times: Nightly, 6 pm
Tickets: $2-$3/person

Kennedy School Theater
5736 NE 33rd, Portland
503-225-5555, ext 8833
Time: Mon-Fri, 5:30 pm; Sat-Sun, 2:30 & 5:30 pm
Tickets: $1-$3/person

Mission Theater
1624 NW Glisan, Portland
503-225-5555, ext. 8832
Time: Sat-Sun, 2:30 pm
Tickets: $1-$3/person

Ninety-Nine West Drive-in
Hwy 99 West, just west of Springbrook Rd, Newberg (23 miles from Portland)
503-538-2738
www.99w.com
Season: Mid-April-late October (depending on weather)
Shows: Fri-Sun evenings, shows start at dark, arrive early for best parking spot
Admission: $6/adult, $3/child 6-11, free/child 5 & under ($8 minimum vehicle charge)

For a fun taste of the past, check out this drive-in, one of just a few in Ore-

PHOTO COURTESY OF NINETY-NINE WEST DRIVE-IN

The Ninety-Nine West Drive-in specializes in old-fashioned family fun.

gon still operating. The Ninety-Nine West Drive-in was built by the late J.T. Francis, the grandfather of the theater's current proprietor, and opened in August 1953. It's been open ever since.

Its popularity has waxed and waned, but now, with a capacity of 275 to 300 cars, the drive-in is quite popular. In fact, cars have been known to line up outside the theater—in hopes

CRYING ROOMS

If you're the parent of an infant and attempting to keep up with current films, you should know about the "crying rooms" at the KOIN Cinemas (SW Third Ave & Clay; 503-225-5555, ext 4608). This theater screens mostly independent art and foreign films. Each of its two crying rooms is equipped with four seats and a monophonic sound system. Situated at the rear of the theaters, behind a glass panel, the private annexes are virtually soundproof, so babies can carry on without disturbing anyone— except their parents. Tickets: $6.75/person, $4.50/senior or child, $4.50/before 6 pm, $5/student with valid ID.

of getting the best parking spot—as early as three hours before a show.

Films are usually suitable for families, but it's always best to call and check what's playing before you go. And don't miss a visit to the theater's original snack bar.

Storytelling

Bookstores

Before Barnes & Noble and Borders Books & Music were vying for prime real estate on every Main Street in America, Portland's own Powell's had a national reputation as the book emporium to beat all.

Many still swear by Powell's flagship store on W Burnside. New and used books are filed side by side at Powell's, and the store has a disordered, lived-in feeling suitable for bibliophiles. Portland still loves Powell's, but the national chains have a strong foothold in the city, as well.

Perhaps driven by that competition, booksellers are offering increasingly diverse and interesting free programs in hopes of enticing buyers inside. Most bookstores schedule weekly children's story hours. Many also feature monthly calendars of readings and signings with notable children's authors and illustrators, appearances of favorite storybook characters and even arts and crafts sessions.

Here is a sampling of bookstores around the area that offer storytimes:

- **A Children's Place**, 4807 NE Fremont, Portland 97213; 503-284-8294
- **Annie Bloom's Books**, 7834 SW Capitol Hwy, Portland 97219; 503-246-0053
- **Barnes & Noble**, 9078 SE Sunnyside Rd, Clackamas 97015; 503-794-9262
- **Barnes & Noble**, 1720 N Jantzen Beach, Portland 97217; 503-283-2800
- **Barnes & Noble**, 1317 Lloyd Center, Portland 97232; 503-335-0201
- **Barnes & Noble**, 18300 NW Evergreen Pkwy, Beaverton 97006; 503-645-3046
- **Barnes & Noble**, 10206 SW Washington Square Rd, Tigard 97223; 503-598-9455
- **Borders**, 708 SW Third Ave, Portland 97204; 503-220-5911

- **Borders**, 16920 SW 72nd Ave, Tigard 97224; 503-968-7576
- **Bridges**, 402 N State St, Lake Oswego 97034; 503-699-1322
- **In Other Words**, 3734 SE Hawthorne Blvd, Portland 97214; 503-232-6003

Public Libraries

Libraries around town also offer scheduled story hours throughout the school year. Toddlers and preschoolers are typically treated to separate sessions, and several libraries have instituted a periodic Book Babies series for parents and infants ages 6 to 18 months. For older kids, there are book groups at most library branches. Many of these groups are geared for parents and kids to participate in together. Multnomah County branches host an impressive array of craft sessions, pajama parties, puppet shows and other special events year-round. They pull out the stops, though, during summer vacation to inspire young readers to continue practicing.

Drop by your local library to pick up a program flyer, or call the appropriate department below for information about branches in your neighborhood.

- **Library Information Network of Clackamas County:** 503-723-4888
- **Multnomah County Library Administration:** 503-988-5402
- **Multnomah County Library KidsPage:** www.multnomah.lib.or.us/lib/kids/
- **Washington County Cooperative Library:** 503-846-3222

TICKET DISCOUNTS

Sampling Portland's arts and culture scene doesn't have to be an expensive proposition.

Consider becoming a season subscriber to an arts group that you and your child enjoy. Subscriber benefits often include discounted ticket prices, priority seating and ticket exchange privileges. If a subscription still seems a bit spendy, ask about special packages. Many groups offer deals that allow you to pick and choose tickets for several scheduled performances instead of requiring you to commit to a full season.

If you're the spontaneous type, there are deals to be had with Ticket Central's day-of-show, half-price tickets, available to walk-in customers for selected performances. Before you drop by the Ticket Central office, located in the Portland Oregon Visitors Association's office (Pioneer Courthouse Square, SW 10th between Morrison and Yamhill), check the availability of tickets by calling 503-275-8358 after 10 am on the day you are interested in attending an event. Ticket Central is open to walk-in customers Monday through Friday, 9:30 am–5 pm; Saturdays, 10 am–2 pm.

Chapter 2

PARKS

It doesn't take too much to win the heart of a child: a big shady tree, a swing, a patch of lawn, some sand.

In the Portland area, there seems to be a park around almost every corner. Surely there's one your family knows best of all—where Sister mastered the rings, Brother fell from the jungle gym, and Baby ate dirt. There's no replacing a comfortable neighborhood hangout. But when you want to branch out, you'll find parks that offer something different and perhaps unexpected: a child-designed, community-built wooden play structure; an extinct volcano; a trail under a waterfall; a bike path along a river; a koi pond; a duck pond; a waterplay stream; paddle boats. Such parks are destinations for a few hours, or a day of fun.

RESOURCES

The Portland area's two larger parks and recreation departments—Portland Parks & Recreation and Tualatin Hills Park & Recreation District—oversee community centers, swimming pools, recreation centers, senior centers, golf courses, and tennis courts, in addition to their playgrounds and nature parks. Residents are mailed quarterly program booklets with information about their parks department's hundreds of classes, seminars, lessons, and special events. District residents have priority at registration time; out-of-district residents pay a higher fee to enroll, but are otherwise welcome to participate in most programs.

Dedicated to acquiring regional trails, open spaces, and natural areas, Metro Regional Parks & Greenspaces oversees its own assortment of more than a dozen sites throughout the region. The biannual program guide, Metro GreenScene (www.metro-region.org/parks/greenscene/greenscene.html), details Metro-sponsored hikes, tours, cleanups, bike rides, river trips, and other special outdoor events.

USEFUL CONTACT INFORMATION:

- **Portland Parks & Recreation:** 503-823-2223; 503-823-PLAY (information hotline); 503-823-2525 (reservations); www.portlandparks.org
- **Tualatin Hills Park & Recreation District:** 503-645-6433; www.thprd.org/
- **Lake Oswego Parks & Recreation Department:** 503-636-9673; www.ci.oswego.or.us/parksrec/
- **City of Tualatin Parks & Recreation Department:** 503-692-2000; www.ci.tualatin.or.us/
- **Tigard Public Works Department:** 503-639-4171; www.ci.tigard.or.us/PARKS/PARKS.HTM
- **Gresham Parks & Recreation:** 503-618-2531; www.ci.gresham.or.us/departments/des/parksandrec/index.htm
- **Metro Regional Parks & Greenspaces:** 503-797-1850; www.metro-region.org/parks/parks.html
- **Oregon State Parks Information Center:** 800-551-6949; www.prd.state.or.us/
- **Reservations Northwest:** 800-452-5687 (state-park campgrounds in Oregon & Washington)

Kids hunt for creatures in Balch Creek.

Whether you're looking for a romp on a really cool slide or a hike among the wildflowers, metro-area parks easily provide an escape from the ho-hum humdrum of the daily routine.

Some of the parks listed below are known for their play structures, while others are renowned for the wildlife they harbor.

Wherever you go, it pays to do a little preparation before you pile the kids into the car. After all, just because it's sunny and hot at your house doesn't mean the weather's going to be exactly the same at your destination. So, dress in layers for flexibility, take good walking shoes just in case a wander through the woods seems like a good idea and fill a daypack or bag with water bottles, snacks, a first-aid kit and some Kleenex.

(Unless otherwise specified, the parks listed below are generally open to the public between dawn and dusk.)

Audubon Society Sanctuary
5151 NW Cornell Rd, Portland
503-292-6855
www.audubonportland.org

Nestled against Forest Park's southwestern flank, the Audubon Wildlife Sanctuary is deep, dark and tranquil. Home to the giant Pacific salamander (it barks like a dog and grows to be a foot long) and bats (look for wooden bat houses nailed high up in trees), in addition to a variety of bird species, the 150-acre park consists of dense forest and 4 miles of trails that are open dawn to dusk year-round. The maze of trails weaves and loops over bridges and boardwalks, past a pond, below a rough-hewn picnic hideout, alongside Balch Creek, and up and down steep hillsides. Two longer loops begin south of Cornell (be alert when crossing this busy road).

Stop by the trailhead at the Wildlife Care Center, where volunteers tend to injured birds and other forest creatures.

Peek in the windows to see them gently handle baby birds and drip nutrients into their beaks using syringes. Permanent residents, whose cages face the outdoor courtyard, include a hawk, a pygmy owl and a peregrine falcon.

Enter the Nature Center (Mon-Sat, 10 am-6 pm; Sun, noon-5 pm) for an up-close look at the backyard birds and squirrels who come to feast at a large platform feeder and at the display of birds, nests and eggs. Walk down Cornell Rd to Macleay Park, which sports green grass, picnic tables and additional rest rooms. (The Nature Center is wheelchair accessible, but trails are not.)

The Audubon Society of Portland hosts a regular selection of nature programs for families and children. Daycamp sessions—pick and choose classes of interest—are offered during winter, spring and summer vacations. Field trips and workshops are scheduled throughout the year. Call for a program guide or check the Web site, which is frequently updated. Especially good for families with young children is a group called Fledglings, which meets during the week on various days to explore nature together. Call the society for details.

In addition, watch for the guest speakers who make presentations at Nature Night, the second Tuesday of each month, 7 pm. Call ahead to assess suitability for children.

Beverly Cleary Sculpture Garden
Grant Park, NE 33rd Ave & Brazee
Portland

Oregon native and award-winning children's author Beverly Cleary mastered reading at a grammar school in northeast Portland, not far from the Klickitat Street she made famous in

A bronze statue of Ramona is at the Beverly Cleary Sculpture Garden for Children.

Henry Huggins and her many other books about childhood—and not far from Grant Park, site of this monument.

Dedicated in October 1996, the Beverly Cleary Sculpture Garden for Children features a central fountain surrounded by bronze statues of Ramona, Henry and his dog, Ribsy. Local sculptor Lee Hunt took pains to make the sculptures accessible to children (even toddlers can sit on Ribsy's back) and realistic, though whimsical: Henry is wearing a Band-Aid and Ramona has on rain boots. Rest rooms are adjacent to the nearby playground. To check out the garden before you go, visit this Multnomah County Library Web site, www.multnomah.lib.or.us/lib/kids/cleary.html.

Blue Lake Regional Park
Off Sandy Blvd & NE 223rd Ave
Portland
503-797-1850, 503-665-4995
Hours: 8 am-sunset; pets not allowed
Fee: $3/car, $6/bus

Operated by Metro Regional Parks and Greenspaces, Blue Lake Park is a 185-acre recreational paradise. The big draw is the 64-acre natural lake fed by underground springs. Rent a paddleboat, canoe or rowboat. Let the kids wade and splash in the swim park (no lifeguards) or water-play area.

But there's more to do than get wet at Blue Lake. Bring bikes to tour the interior or to explore the scenic 40-Mile Loop, which runs adjacent to the park. Fish for largemouth bass, bluegill, green sunfish and catfish from the docks. Hang from the jungle gym or slurp on a Popsicle. Then try horse-shoes or archery, or take a nature hike. (Most sports gear is provided on loan; bring your own fishing and archery equipment.)

Picnic tables and shelters abound, as do rest-room facilities. Bring a lunch or purchase hot dogs and other snack foods at the concession stand.

A popular location for corporate picnics, Blue Lake Park can get crowded on summer weekends. Plan instead a Wednesday visit, to coincide with the eight-week Especially for Kids program (mid-June through mid-August, Wednesdays, 2 pm). Each 45-minute performance spotlights premier local talent in a puppet show, play, concert or demonstration of educational value.

Nature Crafts, another summer kids' program, is a series of four hour-long art sessions that feature take-home projects using spruce cones, clay, dried nettles and origami paper (late June through early August, Tuesdays, 1 pm; $2/child).

Nature crafts at Blue Lake Regional Park.

Cedar Oak Park
4515 S Cedar Oak Dr, West Linn
503-557-4700 (West Linn Parks and Recreation)
Hours: Open to the public Sat-Sun & holidays, dawn-dusk; during summer vacation, daily, dawn-dusk; and on school days, 3:05 pm-dusk

At this park you'll find a wooden fantasy castle designed, with the input of schoolchildren, by noted playground architect Robert Leathers of New York (see also Columbia Park and Hallinan Park). The play structure was built in 1988 by parents, children and staff members on the grounds of Cedar Oak Elementary School. Twice a year volunteers from the community return to refurbish and repair the structure, which is surrounded by gravel.

You'll find playing fields, a tennis court and a few picnic tables here, but not much shade and no rest rooms. Park in the school parking lot, not on the street.

Classical Chinese Garden
121 NW Everett, Portland
503-228-8131
www.chinesegarden.org
Hours: Daily, 9 am-6 pm (last ticket sold at 5:15 pm)
Fees: $6/adult, $5/student or senior, free/child 5 & under

Located within Chinatown, this walled garden occupies an entire city block between NW Everett and NW Flanders and NW Second and NW Third. Here, you can walk along serpentine walkways, past ponds and across bridges through a meticulously arranged landscape of rock groupings, delicate trees and shrubs, lattice screens and pavilions. While it is a wonderful place to introduce a child to the Chinese culture, the garden is not a play-

Young bird watchers enjoy the wildlife at Crystal Springs Rhododendron Garden.

ground. To round out the experience, dine on dim sum at one of several nearby Chinese restaurants, such as House of Louie at NW Third and NW Davis.

Columbia Park

1600 SW Cherry Park Rd, Troutdale
503-665-5175 (Troutdale Parks and Facilities Department)

Columbia Park is famous for its community-built wooden play structure, yet another Robert Leathers design (see also Cedar Oak Park and Hallinan Park). Erected in 1994 behind Reynolds High School, Imagination Station is a circular, castlelike construction on a springy ground-cover cushion. The park itself, with its extensive playing fields, benefits from continued improvement. It now features walking trails, a picnic shelter and rest rooms.

Cook Park

South of Durham Rd at end of 92nd Ave
Tigard
503-639-4171 (city of Tigard)

At 79 acres, Cook Park, Tigard's prized play park, has long attracted metro-area families with its expansive playground, well-groomed fields and clusters of shaded picnic tables. Toddlers are content on the swings and slides, while older children get involved in games of volleyball, basketball and horseshoes. Adults tend to venture toward the Tualatin River, where there's a fishing dock, boat ramp and paved, mile-long trail that is wheelchair accessible. The park is currently being expanded to include a wetlands viewing gazebo, a butterfly meadow and trails to other community parks. Reservations for the large picnic shelter go fast in summer, so call early.

Crystal Springs Rhododendron Garden

SE 28th Ave, 1 block north of
Woodstock, Portland
503-771-8386
Season: March-early September,
daily, dawn-dusk
Fees: $3/adult, free/children 12 &
under; free Tues & Wed and if you
enter before 10 am or after 6 pm

Operated by the Rhododendron
Society on land owned by Portland
Parks and Recreation, this 6.5-acre
enclave is a paradise of birds. All man-
ner of ducks and other waterfowl flock
here, and local bird-watching groups
regularly visit to take a new census.
Bring binoculars, cracked corn and a
notebook to keep tally of the varieties
you see: mallards, wood ducks, domes-
tic ducks, widgeons, buffleheads, pie-
billed grebes and coots. The wooden
boxes nailed to tree trunks are for
wood ducks (with round door openings) and bats (without).

Surrounded by the Eastmoreland
Golf Course and fed by 13 different
springs, the peaceful gardens are
planted with hundreds of rhododendron species and azaleas, which generally reach their peak blooming
season in late April and early May.
Winding, paved trails loop around
lakes, over bridges, past waterfalls and
fountains, along a lagoon. There are no
tables or any shelter, but picnicking is
allowed on the lawn. Be aware that
while the garden is wheelchair accessible, the park's rest rooms are not.

And by the way, leave your stale
bread at home when you come. Ducks
prefer cracked corn, and so do park
supervisors. You can buy cracked
corn at the park's entrance booth, or
stop at a local bird shop or at the
nearby produce stand to buy some.

TAKE A HIKE!

When the nationally renowned Olmsted
brothers arrived from Boston in 1904 to
propose a park system for Portland as part
of the planning for the Lewis and Clark
Exposition, they recommended a 40-mile
loop trail that would encircle the city and
connect the region's scenic parks like
pearls on a necklace.

Since then Portland has grown. Like-
wise the 40-Mile Loop. Though it will
stretch 140 miles when complete and connect 30 metro-area parks along the
Columbia, Sandy and Willamette rivers, it
still goes by its historic moniker. Parts are
already in place, with Forest Park's Wildwood Trail (see this chapter) and the
Springwater Corridor (see Active Play:
Outdoor Fun, Biking) making the most significant contributions.

To order a colorful 40-Mile Loop map,
send a $3 check made out to "City of
Portland" and a stamped, self-addressed
envelope to: Portland Parks and Recreation,
Receptionist, 1120 SW Fifth Ave, Room 1302,
Portland, OR 97204. Find out more about
the 40-Mile Loop at the parks department's Web site, www.portlandparks.org.

Eastbank Esplanade is popular with walkers, bicyclists and skaters.

PHOTO COURTESY OF THE PORTLAND PARKS AND RECREATION

Eastbank Esplanade
Between Hawthorne Bridge and
Steel Bridge, Portland
503-823-PLAY (7529)

Just opened in 2001, the 1.5-mile-long Eastbank Esplanade is tucked between Interstate 5 and the Willamette River. With its fabulous views of downtown, the esplanade has become popular with walkers, bicyclists and skaters. Along the walk, 13 markers provide information about the river and the area's rich history. For those who tire along the way or who just want to savor the views, there are seating walls, benches and overlooks that invite visitors to stop and relax. Kids enjoy especially being right down at river level as they cross the 1,200-foot-long floating walkway, the longest such walkway in the United States.

From the east side, you can access the walk just north of the Hawthorne Bridge at the foot of Madison St, from the Morrison Bridge pedestrian ramp or from the overlook at the east end of the Steel Bridge, just across from the Rose Quarter transit station. From the west, cross the Hawthorne Bridge or use the new RiverWalk on the Steel Bridge. With the exception of the Morrison Bridge ramp, all entrances are wheelchair accessible. An additional exit is provided at the Burnside Bridge, which features a motorized lift.

On weekends, especially during Saturday Market season, it's fun to walk the esplanade, then cross over the river on the Burnside Bridge, hit the market for some pad thai or an elephant ear, and then continue walking along the river through Waterfront Park.

Forest Park

3339 NW Skyline to St. Helens Rd
Portland
503-823-PLAY (7529)

"Whose woods these are . . ." In Portland, these woods—5,000-acre Forest Park in the West Hills—belong to everybody, and we couldn't be luckier. The largest natural area in any U.S. city, this expansive tangle of firs, alders and maples is crisscrossed by some 50 miles of trails. Navigating the wilderness with children takes some forethought, though, because few of the paths make loops. Hoyt Arboretum (4000 SW Fairview; 503-228-8733) has free Forest Park trail maps and staff who can offer suggestions for family walks.

An obvious place to start is at the end of NW Thurman St (continue west from NW 25th Ave, across a small bridge to the dead end). Especially popular with cyclists, Leif Erickson Dr begins here. A public throughway that was closed in the 1950s, this broad trail is still paved in spots and relatively flat. Though it continues for about 7 miles, you will likely tire before then and turn for home.

Sample another bit of Forest Park from Cumberland Rd (ascend Westover from NW 25th Ave, then continue up Cumberland to the dead end). The dappled Cumberland Trail hugs the hillside along a ravine. Connect with the Wildwood Trail, then the Upper Macleay Trail, and emerge on Macleay Blvd for a short walk back to the car. Ambitious (and strong) hikers can remain on the Wildwood Trail for a steep climb to the Pittock Mansion (See Kid Culture, Restored Houses).

Hallinan Park

16800 Hawthorne Dr, Lake Oswego
503-635-0353

Hours: Open to the public Sat-Sun & holidays, dawn-dusk; during summer vacation, daily, dawn-dusk; on school days 4 pm-dusk

Erected by the Hallinan Elementary School community following an ambitious fund-raising campaign in 1988, the extensive play structures here were designed by New York playground architect Robert Leathers (see also Cedar Oak Park and Columbia Park). Tucked away in a quiet suburban neighborhood, the park is largely unknown outside its immediate environs. Facilities include picnic tables, playing fields, a running track and portable toilets.

Ibach Park

10455 SW Ibach St, Tualatin
503-691-3061

Surrounded by suburban sprawl, this award-winning play area (pronounced I-back) is a 19-acre oasis that translates history into an interactive educational play area for children of all abilities.

Young children rush to explore the dinosaur bones, splash in the water-play stream, scale the meteor and ride the trolley. Older children are no less inspired; they've never imagined a playground quite like this. Adults talk about it the way they would a work of art, and there are intriguing and varied sculptural references to many of the fixtures.

Learn of the Atfalati tribe, natives of the Tualatin River Valley, from interpretive signs posted along a paved pathway. Bring baseball equipment and tennis racquets. Spread a picnic

LOCAL AND REGIONAL

Kids are drawn to the pig sculpture at Jurgens Park.

blanket on the vast lawn or a tablecloth in the picnic shelter, and stay all day. There's little shade, so wear sunscreen and hats in summer.

A teen play area, requiring a bit more strength and dexterity, gives older youngsters a place to hang out while younger siblings play nearby. Parents can sit in between the themed area and the teen play area and keep an eye on both.

Jenkins Estate

8005 SW Grabhorn Rd, Aloha
503-642-3855
www.thprd.org/Facilities/Jenkins/
jenkins_estate.htm
Hours: Winter, daily, 8 am-5 pm;
Memorial Day weekend-September,
daily, 8 am-8 pm

Originally owned by heiress Belle Ainsworth Jenkins, the 68-acre Jenkins Estate was purchased by the Tualatin Hills Park and Recreation District in 1975. The main house—built to resemble an English hunting lodge—and stable and gatehouse have been restored and are available by reservation for private receptions and business functions.

With winding, hide-and-seek gravel paths, a rockery and a koi pool, the gardens were designed in the traditional English picturesque style. Rhododendrons and wildflowers are at their best in spring; the perennial gardens peak in summer.

Bring a picnic to spread out on a lawn, park bench or covered table. But be mindful that there are no public rest rooms, save one portable toilet in Camp Rivendale.

If the Jenkins Estate's lush landscaping isn't reward enough for your children, entice them with images of a pot of gold at trail's end. Walk south past the teahouse to Camp Rivendale, a clearing where outdoor sessions for youths with physical and learning disabilities are held each summer. There's a fine play structure here, an ample lawn and a picnic shelter. (The camp is in use on weekdays until 4 pm from mid-June to the end of August.) Best of all, well away from the peaceful estate, kids are free to shake their sillies out.

A fun time to visit the estate is the annual Spooktacular held each year on the last Saturday of October from 11 am to 5 pm. This not-so-spooky event is geared for children 10 and under and features carnival games, a spooky snack shack, pictures in the scarecrow garden and cookie decorating. Costumes are welcome. Admission is $7/child; adults are free.

Jurgens Park

10455 Hazelbrook Rd, Tualatin
503-691-3061

Opened in 1999, this 12-acre park is still sort of a hidden treasure. Neighborhood folks, though, are well aware of the wealth of fun that awaits kids here. Using a theme of agriculture and history, the park offers kids the opportunity to race up a wagon ramp to a covered bridge, search for "vegetables" embedded in the wall of the sand-play area and feed the pig sculpture that stands in the middle of the area above a water trough. Though a shelter is available, for now there are only portable toilets.

Mount Tabor Park

SE 60th Ave & Salmon, Portland
503-823-PLAY (7529)
www.portlandparks.org

To visit Mount Tabor is to experience a brush with danger . . . but not really. This peak is an extinct volcano, one of only two found in cities in the continental U.S. (Bend has one also.) Climb or bike the cone for a view (on a clear day) of downtown Portland and Mount Hood. Below are basketball and tennis courts, a recently updated playground, picnic shelters and rest rooms. An area near the reservoir is popular

GET A JUMP ON SUMMER

Metro Regional Parks and Greenspaces' group picnic facilities at Oxbow Park and Blue Lake Park are both hot commodities in summer. The reservation lines open January 1, and weekends book quickly. Reserve a weekday and receive a 20 percent discount. Picnic reservations include the use of a baseball diamond for two hours, plus sporting equipment for volleyball, horseshoes and basketball.

Park regulars may wish to consider purchasing an annual pass for $35. It's good for entry and parking at Oxbow Park, Blue Lake Park, Chinook Landing Marine Park and the James M. Gleason Boat Ramp (but not during special events). Pick up one at Oxbow Park, Blue Lake Park or the Metro Regional Center (600 NE Grand Ave), or by calling 503-797-1850.

A young visitor explores the specially designed children's area at the Oregon Garden.

with dog walkers. Cinders discovered in the park were used to surface its roads. Send the children off to hunt for volcanic rocks.

The Oregon Garden
Highway 213, on the south side of Silverton
503-874-8100;
877-ORGARDEN (877-674-2733)
www.oregongarden.org
Season/hours: Summer: daily, 9 am-6 pm; Winter: daily, 9 am-3 pm
Admission: $6/adult, $5/senior 60+, $5/student 14 -17, $3/child 8-13, free/child 7 and under

The plantings are still relatively fresh at the Oregon Garden, located in Silverton, 40 miles south of Portland. But designers have big plans for this new public display garden that encompasses 60 acres.

Eventually, the garden will expand to cover 240 acres, and plans call for it to become not only a botanically challenging, world-class facility but also a living laboratory of research and study that will evolve into a major tourism destination by the year 2010.

While adults will marvel at the diversity of plants found throughout the garden, kids will probably be most enthusiastic about a specially designed children's area that features funny Dr. Seussish plantings, an Alice-in-Wonderland-like archway tunnel that grows smaller the farther you walk into it, and by the sandbox where careful digging reveals dinosaur bones.

Concerts and educational programs are scheduled throughout the year. For up-to-date information on both concerts and educational programs for kids (such as Daffodil Fun, Creating with Native Plants and Winter Birds & Me), check the garden's frequently updated Web site. In the summer, there are several day camps for young gardening enthusiasts.

Oxbow Regional Park

3010 SE Oxbow Pkwy, Gresham
503-797-1850, 503-663-4708
www.metro-region.org/parks/
oxbowpage.html
Fee: $3/vehicle

Evidence indicates Native Americans inhabited the Oxbow Regional Park area 9,000 years ago, and it's easy to see what drew them here. Oxbow's 1,000 acres encompass an ancient old-growth forest and an oxbow in the Sandy, one of the state's most scenic rivers. Owned and managed by Metro Regional Parks and Greenspaces, Oxbow, the system's largest park, has been left relatively undeveloped.

Come to hike, bike or ride horseback on the 15 miles of trails throughout the park. (Please, leave your pets at home; they're not allowed, in or out of your vehicle, due to conflict with resident wildlife.)

Motorized boats are not allowed, but canoes, kayaks and rafts are welcome, as are anglers (consult park staff regarding regulations). In season, several small, rocky beaches provide access to the river for swimmers (brrr!).

Picnic tables and shelters dot the park, and there are two playgrounds. A newly expanded campground, open year-round, features 66 campsites that are available on a first-come, first-served basis. The campground now has two new rest-room/shower buildings that boast hot and cold running water, coin-operated showers, heated-air hand dryers, radiant floor heating and Oxbow's first flush toilets. The new rest-room facilities and two of the new campsites are accessible by wheelchair.

The park hosts regular nature programs for families throughout the year, but in summertime it's especially busy. Schoolchildren investigate park ecosystems and animal habitats in "Oxbow Adventures," a series of four hourlong sessions (June through mid-July; check for day and time). Campfire programs spotlight history lessons, storytellers and birds of prey (July through late August; times vary). Call for a schedule of these and other special events at 503-797-1850 or check online at the Web site address above.

Oxbow Park is also the site of the annual Salmon Festival, which coincides with the return of spawning Chinook salmon to the Sandy River in mid-October. Tiptoe beside the river for a chance viewing. Learn about the life cycle of these anadromous fish from park guides. Stay for a salmon-bake lunch, live entertainment and children's craft activities. Fee for Salmon Festival: $6/vehicle.

River discovery at Oxbow Regional Park.

LOCAL AND REGIONAL

Tualatin Hills Nature Park
15655 SW Millikan Blvd, Beaverton
503-644-5595

Opened in November 1997, this 219-acre nature park, once owned by St. Mary's Home for Boys, was developed courtesy of a 1994 bond measure that earmarked $2 million for this purpose. It's a smaller version of Tryon Creek State Park, and its wetlands, forest and wildlife sanctuary encompass the region where Cedar Mill Creek and Beaverton Creek merge.

Designed for contemplation and walking, Tualatin Hills Nature Park features 5 miles of trails (one of them handicapped accessible), a visitors' center and covered shelter. Bicycles are allowed on two different paved trails, each 0.75 mile in length. Picnic tables are located near the interpretive center.

In addition to offering "school day off programs" that focus on such topics as how wildlife survives in the city, the park also offers a program during the school year that is designed to let preschoolers (ages 3 to 5) get a close-up look at nature. Call for details.

Washington Park
Head of SW Park Pl, Portland

In 1871, when Portland's population stood at 8,000 and the city was surrounded by forest, hills and the river, the city purchased more woods—41 acres—from a private citizen for the then-steep price of $32,624. The 1901 Park Commission's report reads: "The purchase was at first regarded by most citizens with disapprobation or contempt." Fortunately, nothing came of this general dissatisfaction, and Washington Park is now among Portland's best-loved and most-used parks.

Many special sites are located within or adjacent to Washington Park's 130 acres, including Hoyt Arboretum, the International Rose Test Garden, the Oregon Zoo, CM2 (the new Children's Museum), the World Forestry Center and the Japanese Garden. (See Kid Culture, for details on the Oregon Zoo, CM2 and the World Forestry Center.)

*Hoyt Arboretum
4000 SW Fairview Blvd, Portland
503-228-8733

  Established in 1928, 175-acre Hoyt Arboretum boasts one of the nation's largest collections of conifers, including Brewer's weeping spruce, Himalayan spruce, dawn redwood, Chinese lacebark pine and a maturing grove of coast and giant redwoods. This city-owned garden of trees is adjacent to Washington Park, and many of its 10 miles of trails dip into its neighbor and link with Forest Park byways beyond.

When you arrive in Hoyt Arboretum for a walk, stop first at the visitors' center to get oriented (open daily, 9 am-4 pm). The rest rooms are here, and a large picnic shelter is directly across the street. Seasonal trail maps for spring's wildflower displays and autumn's fall foliage fiesta are free. A trail map is available for $1. While you're here, pick up a free Forest Park trail map to add to your collection.

The Vietnam Veterans Memorial Trail and Bristlecone Pine Trail are wheelchair accessible; most other trails are rugged and steep at times. Scenic outlooks over Portland and toward mountain peaks are worth the climb, even when you're toting a child. Wildflowers in spring, and colorful foliage and wild mushrooms in fall, are other seasonal treats.

*International Rose Test Garden
400 SW Kingston Ave,
Washington Park, Portland
503-823-3636
Hours: Daily, 7 am-9 pm

From its terraced hillside above the city, the International Rose Test Garden is more to Portland than a botany lab-oratory. But to serious rose hybridizers, this idyllic spot represents a confluence of conditions too good to be true.

Since 1917 the five-acre rose garden, one of only 25 such sites in the country, has been methodically conducting research into the performance levels of new rose varieties. Best Rose winners are

On a clear day, the view from the International Rose Test Garden is among the city's finest.

PHOTO COURTESY OF THE PORTLAND OREGON VISITORS ASSOCIATION

LOCAL AND REGIONAL

exhibited chronologically in the Gold Medal Garden. Roses still in the guinea-pig stage are designated by numeral only.

Tourists visit all the time, but Portlanders prefer to come on lazy Sunday afternoons after church or for wedding portraits against the scenic skyline backdrop. (Blooms are at their best from early June through early November.) Whether locals or not, visitors to the International Rose Test Garden bring their cameras.

Children may quickly lose interest in row upon row of flowers (8,000 plants, 532 varieties). Encourage them to study just a few closely and soon they'll initiate a hunt for a family favorite—be sure to factor in aroma, as well as color, shape and texture. Enjoy a giggle at the roses' funny "celebrity" names, then ask your children to select the varieties by which they would choose to be immortalized.

The adjoining two-acre amphitheater, which hosts summer concerts, is a great place to run and romp. Rest rooms and picnic shelters are located near the tennis courts and parking lots up above on Kingston Ave, as are a seasonal concession stand, a recently opened gift shop featuring all things roses and the zoo train depot. The Rose Garden Children's Park is an easy walk farther down Kingston.

*Rose Garden Children's Park
SW Kingston Blvd, adjacent to International Rose Test Garden, Washington Park, Portland

Originally envisioned by the Rotary Club of Portland as the nation's first park designed to fulfill the specific needs of children with disabilities, this park, open since 1995, may be too good to be true.

So surreptitious are the special handicapped aids—handrails, armrests on benches, Braille instructions—that one scarcely notices them. But then, it's hard to concentrate on much of anything amid the hustle-bustle of children here.

Themed "pods" feature a castle, spaceship, clock tower and tree house. In addition, the park offers a sand-play area, tube slides, a variety of swings and shaded lawns for picnicking. Nearby, the old zoo's elephant house is now a picnic shelter with rest-room facilities. Be warned: On sunny weekends this place is a beehive of activity and parking is scarce.

*Japanese Garden
611 SW Kingston, Washington Park, Portland
503-223-4070
www.japanesegarden.com
Hours: April 1-September 31: Mon, noon-7 pm; Tues-Sun, 10 am-7 pm. October 1-March 31: Mon, noon-4 pm; Tues-Sun, 10 am-4 pm. (Last admission is accepted one-half hour prior to closing.)
Fees: $6/adult, $4/senior 62 & over, $3.50/child 6-17 and college students with ID, free/child 5 & under
(Prices and hours are subject to change)

In 1990, at the 25th anniversary of the Japanese Garden, no less a personage than the Japanese ambassador to the U.S. proclaimed this "the most beautiful and authentic Japanese garden in the world outside of Japan." Ambassador Matsunaga was merely confirming what loyal visitors have long suspected: The Japanese Garden is a spiritual oasis.

The feeling is serene, quiet and meditative on this Washington Park promon-

EVERYTHING'S COMING UP ROSES

Portland isn't called the Rose City for nothing. In addition to the International Rose Test Garden, two other public rose gardens are well worth visiting:

* Peninsula Park Rose Garden

N Ainsworth between Kerby & Albina St.
503-823-3636

This rose garden features more than 8,800 roses in a sunken garden with a early-20th century design.

* Ladd's Addition Rose Garden

SE 16th & Harrison
503-823-3636

Ladd's Addition Rose Garden is a small and intimate garden located in a historic southeast Portland residential area. It contains some 3,200 roses. More are planted in precise designs in four blocks surrounding the garden.

---

tory, with views out over downtown Portland and on to Mount Hood. Among the pristinely manicured shrubs, deftly raked pebbles and artfully designed bamboo fences, children may subconsciously sense an indefinable otherness.

Within the 5.5-acre spread are representations of five separate formal garden styles: Strolling Pond Garden, Tea Garden, Natural Garden, the Dry Landscape Garden and Flat Garden. Ask your kids to identify them (without reading the plaques!).

There is much that appeals to children here: peekaboo pathways along a cascading stream, creaky boardwalks through a marsh and mysteriously intriguing koi. But parents should be aware that this is not a place for a free-for-all: Adults and children alike must stay on the pathways.

If you have a particularly rambunctious child, perhaps the best time to visit is Children's Day, celebrated each year in early May. Bring the kids then, and they'll be caught up in origami workshops, tea ceremonies, dancing and martial-arts demonstrations.

Willamette Park

SW Macadam & Nebraska, Portland
503-823-PLAY (7529)
Hours: 5 am-midnight
Fees: Free except in summer; $2/vehicle, $3/vehicle plus trailer 7 am-7 pm from Saturday of Memorial Day weekend through Monday of Labor Day weekend

Relatively flat and smooth, the park's Willamette Greenway Trail traces the west side of the river from just south of the park through Johns Landing and is great for strollers, toddlers and still-wobbly bicyclists. Plans are under way to extend the footpath north to the downtown waterfront and south to the Sellwood Bridge. But at present, just about a mile of trail is negotiable by foot or bicycle. Park near the playground at Willamette Park and watch the activity at the boat ramp, then follow the trail north as it meanders past condominium apartments and office buildings.

Popular with runners and cyclists, the narrow, paved footpath gets crowded on sunny weekend afternoons; give your kids a wide berth if their steering and braking are uncertain. Take time to skip stones and watch the boats at one of the rocky "beaches" and then retrace your steps to the playground for a picnic.

When you're ready, follow the path south from Willamette Park, through the adjoining neighborhood, and emerge in Butterfly Park. In spring and summer the native shrubs, trees and meadowlands here are particularly attractive to butterflies and other colorful flying insects.

Wildlife Areas

Jackson Bottom Wetlands Preserve
Hwy 219, south of Hillsboro
Hours: Daily, dawn to dusk
503-681-6278
www.jacksonbottom.org

Located within the city limits of Hillsboro, the 680 acres of Jackson Bottom Wetlands Preserve provide a tranquil sanctuary for both people and animals. The quiet open waters, rolling meadows, and upland ash and fir woods provide homes to thousands of ducks and geese, deer, otters, beavers, herons and eagles. Songbirds and small mammals, as well as salamanders and rare wetland plants, are also dependent on the marshes of the preserve.

At the north end of the preserve, a covered viewing shelter is both wheelchair and stroller accessible. There, one of the major attractions recently has been a nesting pair of bald eagles. The south end of the preserve features 3 miles of hiking trails. These trails, which wander along the Tualatin River and past ponds and marshy areas, are level and therefore easy for kids to negotiate. But beware: They are not necessarily stroller friendly; backpacks are best for the littlest members of the family.

Interpretive signs throughout the preserve, designed by Hillsboro schoolkids, make for easy self-guided tours. Every Wednesday at noon, from September through June, a preserve volunteer shows up at the north end's viewing site for a free "Lunch with the Birds" program. The first Saturday of each month also features family-friendly events, such as bird walks in the morning or night hikes appropriate for the entire family. Call for details.

A wetlands education center is planned for the near future. But take note: Only portable toilets are currently available.

Oaks Bottom Wildlife Refuge
SE Seventh & SE Sellwood Blvd
Portland
503-823-PLAY (7529)
www.portlandparks.org

Covering 163 acres, Oaks Bottom Wildlife Refuge started out as simply a wetland on the east bank of the Willamette River. Now its hiking trails are favored by bird-watchers aplenty. Some 100 species have been identified here, with hawks, pintails, quail, coots, woodpeckers, kestrels and mallards all known to make appearances. But the bird that draws many people to Oaks Bottom is the great blue heron, the official bird of the city of Portland. Because it's near one of the rookeries on Ross Island, the refuge is a favorite place for many of these impressive birds.

For rest rooms, go to nearby Sellwood Park.

Smith and Bybee Lakes Wildlife Area

2.5 miles west of I-5 on Marine Dr
Portland
503-797-1850
www.metro-region.org/parks/
smithbybeepage.html

Metro's Smith and Bybee Lakes Wildlife Area, taking in nearly 2,000 acres, is the largest protected wetland within an American city. Tucked away in an industrial-looking area of Portland, the wildlife area is also one of the city's best-kept secrets. Here, just minutes away from downtown, quiet visitors may spot beavers, river otters, nutria, black-tailed deer, ospreys, bald eagles and western painted turtles.

At this point, there's not much in the way of developed amenities here, just a small parking lot adjacent to the Interlakes Trail, which is a paved, level half-mile path. Hikers can check things out from two different wildlife viewing platforms. Plans call for more trails to

FOR A BIRD'S-EYE VIEW . . .

The Backyard Bird Shop (503-635-2044) hosts an impressive variety of guided walks, workshops and presentations year-round, many of which are ideal for families and youngsters. It also operates a summer day camp for schoolchildren interested in nature. Call for details.

be added and for an interpretive center to be built.

If you have access to a canoe or nonmotorized boat, you might have the upper hand when it comes to seeing wildlife. Boats can be launched from a location near the parking lot.

For the best bird viewing, go during the winter or spring, which is when the area has the most water—and therefore the most birds. During the summer, a naturalist offers free weekly programs at the area for school-age children accompanied by a parent. Program themes vary, with birds, bugs, mammals and turtles each targeted in turn.

State Parks

Champoeg State Heritage Area

Champoeg Rd, St. Paul
503-678-1251
www.oregonstateparks.org
Fee: $3/vehicle

To an outsider, 615-acre Champoeg (pronounced "Sham-poo-ee") State Park looks like any other park. The Willamette is slow and wide here, the trees dangle lichens and ferns, and the frogs offer a serenade. But Champoeg wasn't always so serene.

On this site on May 2, 1843, farmers who had settled the area voted 52 to 50 to establish a provisional government, the region's first. With its strategic location on the river, Champoeg became a regular stop for stagecoaches and steamboats, and was a thriving village (population 200), until a record flood washed out the town in 1861. Visitors today can peek in at the Manson Barn, which was salvaged from the flood. Two other structures are open to the public in sea-

ON THE WING

Cousins of the hummingbird, Vaux's swifts migrate up from Central and South America in spring to mate and to hatch their young before returning south when the weather gets colder. Like the swallows who return each year to California's San Juan Capistrano, these tiny birds have established a traditional communal roosting place in the chimney at Chapman School (NW 25th Ave & Pettygrove).

Sometime in late August (the timing is not predictable), as many as 25,000 swifts begin a bedtime ritual that continues nightly until the cold season arrives in late September. Come as dusk approaches and sit on the hillside by the baseball diamond (bring a blanket, as the grass is prickly). Then look up.

At first they look like tiny watermelon seeds dancing against the sky, chirping a singsong melody. Then, as quickly as they came, they are off to swoop over Forest Park, collecting friends. The tiny birds return as an ever-larger group, circle the chimney, flutter away, come again. The chimney whirlpool intensifies until, one by one, the swifts drop inside, where they cling by their claws, en masse, to the brick flue. Sleep tight!

The entire performance can last about 45 minutes. If you're lucky, the Audubon Society of Portland will be on hand with informational flyers, examples of swifts' nests (they stick twigs together with spit), binoculars and volunteers who can answer questions.

According to PAS, swifts roost together for several reasons: to avoid predators, to keep warm, to provide role models for their young and to locate one another before the long migration.

---

son: the Pioneer Mothers Cabin Museum (503-633-2237), a massive log structure built in 1931; and the Robert Newell House Museum (503-678-5537), which was reconstructed by the Daughters of the American Revolution.

Many are content instead to enjoy the setting. Hike in the woods near the river, or bring bikes for a ride along the 4-mile paved trail (it's wheelchair accessible). There are three picnic shelters here, and expansive meadows and lawns on which to spread out. The campground features 57 electric hookup sites, six walk-in tent sites, six yurts and six camper cabins. To reserve, call Reservations Northwest at 800-452-5687.

If you're a Frisbee fan, don't miss the 12-hole disc (Frisbee) golf course. Located near the Oak Grove Day-Use Area, the field is equipped with 12 baskets into which players try to launch their flying discs. There is no fee to play, but you must bring your own equipment. Pick up a course map at the visitors' center on entering the park.

Also, between Memorial Day and Labor Day, the park runs special junior ranger programs on the weekends for kids ages 6 to 12 in the campground program area. Check flyers in the park for details.

Silver Falls State Park
20024 Silver Falls Hwy, Sublimity
503-873-8681
www.oregonstateparks.org
Fee: $3/vehicle

At 8,700 acres, Silver Falls, the largest of Oregon's state parks, is aptly named. From the main day-use parking lot it's just a short, flat walk to a viewpoint that looks directly down on the 177-foot South Falls. But the park has nine other hidden treasures, which are visible from the popular 7-mile Trail of Ten Falls. (This hike is arduous, so think twice about embarking on it with small children.)

Stop by the visitors' center for trail maps and advice. The lodge also features a snack bar, fireplace (a great place to warm up), nature displays and a small gift shop.

Few children (or adults) can pass up an opportunity to stand behind a waterfall, so you'll likely want to descend into the canyon and slog through the mud and mist to crouch under the massive rock outcropping, sheltered from the spray and deafening rush.

Bring bikes for the paved, 4-mile loop trail, or rent horses or ponies (from Memorial Day through Labor Day: $25/hour per person) and explore 14 miles of equestrian trails. Picnic tables and shelters are scattered throughout the park, as are rest rooms.

In summer the river is dammed south of the parking lot for swimmers. The beach is rocky, not sandy, and the water is cold—but that doesn't seem to discourage children.

The Silver Falls campground is outfitted with 51 tent sites and 54 sites with electrical hookups. To reserve, call Reservations Northwest at 800-452-5687.

Tryon Creek State Park
11321 SW Terwilliger Blvd, Portland
503-636-4398
www.tryonfriends.org or
www.oregonstateparks.org

Nestled in a shady canyon between Lewis & Clark College and Lake Oswego, Tryon Creek State Park is a 645-acre forest with 14 miles of trails for hikers, bikers, runners and equestrians. Ask for a trail map at the nature center, and for advice on activities

TAKE A HIKE

The Portland Parks and Recreation Department offers Ladybug Nature Walks for preschoolers and their caregivers at parks throughout the city, including Hoyt Arboretum. Beginning around May 1 and running through October, the series appeals to all of a toddler's senses and encourages involvement. During a walk, participants might stop to touch a slug's slime, smell the bark of a fragrant tree, feel the veins of a leaf or listen to the sound of rushing water. Each walk costs $1 per child and is free for an accompanying adult. For details, call 503-823-3601.

STATE PARKS

appropriate to your family's stamina.

Shorter legs are happy enough with the 0.35-mile Trillium Trail, a paved, all-abilities loop. Older children may prefer to venture farther into the wilderness to explore the creek and its bridges. Bicyclists stay on a 3-mile paved path that runs parallel to Terwilliger Blvd (this is not a loop trail). Horseback riders have two packed-gravel loops to choose from, for a total of 5.2 miles.

Rest rooms are found in the nature center. A large pavilion shelter is equipped with benches.

The park is known for its Winter Solstice celebration and for the Trillium Festival, which occurs in spring. In summer, watch for details on the park's concert series, Forest Music. And if you haven't heard about them already, check out the park's popular after-school programs, as well as its summer day camp and winter- and spring-break camps. Recently, the park has also become a hit as a birthday-party site.

Chapter 3

ACTIVE PLAY: OUTDOOR FUN

Psst! Can you keep a secret? It doesn't always rain in the Portland area. But when there's a break in the clouds, everyone takes a break—outdoors. The Portland metro region is one of the country's most scenic. The wilderness is relatively unspoiled: Mount Hood is snow-capped year-round, the rivers run fast and clear or slow and sure, the lakes are well stocked with fish and rental boats.

When the weather is fine, head outside and get moving. Go for a paddle on a lake, head to the hills for some sledding or skiing, or enjoy an outdoor amusement park. It's all here, just waiting for you.

The Log Ride is a popular attraction at Enchanted Forest.

Amusements

Enchanted Forest
Exit 248 off I-5 in Turner (7 miles south of Salem)
503-363-3060 or 503-371-4242
www.enchantedforest.com
Hours: March 15-September, 9:30 am-6 pm (weekends only in April and September) $8.50
Admission: $6.95/adult, $6.25/senior (62+), $6.25/child 3-12, free/child 2 & under $7.50
Extras: Additional tickets (at 65 cents 75¢ each) required for Log Ride, Ice Mountain, Haunted House, Kiddie Bumper Boats, Frog Hopper, Kiddie Ferris Wheel and Pan for Treasure

Lovingly constructed on a wooded hillside near Salem, Enchanted Forest is a dream come true for little kids. Roger Tofte, a grandfather now, has been crafting storybook castles, village huts and amusement park rides for more than 30 years. And he's probably still not completely satisfied, though

many of his customers are. The most recent additions are the English Village and the Big Timber Log Ride, a tour-de-force attraction.

Preschoolers enjoy romping along the twisty trails, peering into the Seven Dwarfs' cottage, wiggling into a bunny hole near Alice in Wonderland's toadstool and slipping down a bumpy slide at the Old Woman's Shoe.

This is no Disneyland, though, so the challenge is to amuse older children. The scary haunted house, log ride and bobsled roller coaster may do that job. But nobody should miss Fantasy Fountains, a charming water-and-light show in the English Village.

Snack and lunch foods are available, as well as picnic tables if you pack your own. The steep, winding pathways can be slippery and muddy in poor weather, and the dense trees keep the temperature cool. Come on a hot, sunny summer afternoon for a welcoming patch of shade.

Family Fun Center

29111 SW Town Center Loop W
Wilsonville 97070
Exit 283 off I-5 (20 miles south of
Portland)
(503) 685-5000
www.fun-center.com
Hours: Summer: Fri-Sat, 9 am-11 pm;
Sun-Thurs, 9 am-10 pm. Fall/winter: Sun-
Thurs, 11 am-9 pm; Fri-Sat, 9 am-11 pm.
Admission: Mini-golf: $6/adult (13 &
over), $4/children and seniors (55 &
over). Go-karts: $5/driver, $2/passenger.
Bumper boats: $4.50/driver, $2/passen-
ger. Batting cages: $2/25 pitches

You'll find it all at this six-acre
amusement park: Kidopolis (see Active
Play: Indoor Fun, Indoor Playgrounds),
Bullwinkle's Family Restaurant, arcade
games, outdoor miniature golf, go-karts
and bumper boats.

Miniature-golf fans can choose from
one of two 18-hole courses—a castle
theme with cave and waterfall, or a
Western town with totem poles and
sawmill. Putters come in three sizes.

Go-kart drivers must be at least 57
inches or taller, and passengers must be
at least 3 years old and ride with someone 18 or older. Cars race each other
on the 1,000-foot road course, which
features dips and hairpin turns.

With 20 boats and a cascading
waterfall at the bumper-boat pond,
everybody's bound to get soaked, so
plan accordingly. Drivers must be at
least 44 inches or taller, and passengers
must be at least 3 years old and ride
with someone 18 or older.

The eight batting cages offer a range
of pitching speeds, from slow-pitch
softballs to 70-mile-an-hour fastballs.
Bats and helmets are provided.

Teens especially will enjoy chal-

OFF THE BEATEN TRACK

If you have a race-car fan who's
also a remote-control car buff, be
sure to check out the uncovered,
outdoor track at Aero Sports Hobbies, 17941 NE Glisan, Gresham; 503-
669-7665. Rarely vacant, especially
during the summer, this 80-foot-
by-60-foot track located next to a
hobby shop (not surprisingly, it specializes in remote-control everything) attracts many local families.
Lit by floodlights after dark, the
track is especially busy in the
evening. From mid-May through the
first of October (depending on the
weather), it's open round-the-
clock. Parents provide the supervision, and admission is free except
during organized races.

lenging each other in the laser tag
arena or challenging themselves at the
center's new 10-foot-high climbing
wall. Another new addition is the Max
Flight Cyber Coaster, a simulator pod
where two riders can dictate whether
the unit flips, turns, rotates or spins.

Malibu Grand Prix

9405 SW Cascade Ave
Beaverton 97008
503-641-0772
Hours: Winter: Mon-Thurs, 11 am-9
pm; Fri, 11 am-11 pm; Sat, 11 am-11

AMUSEMENTS

Malibu Grand Prix features two racetracks and three different go-kart models.

pm; Sun, 11 am-8 pm. Summer: daily, 11 am-11 pm
Racetrack: $3.25 per lap (price comes down some with purchase of multi-lap packages)
Batting cage: $1/12 pitches, $5/72 pitches; or reserve a cage, $18/half hour, $30/full hour

A popular birthday-party destination, Malibu Grand Prix showcases two racetracks and three different go-kart models. The larger, half-mile road course accommodates the Virage (a three-quarter-scale, gas-powered formula Indy car) and the Sprint racer. Equipped with brake and gas pedals (the transmissions are automatic), the cars can reach speeds of up to 30 miles an hour in races against the clock.

The small, oval racetrack accommodates a simpler go-kart called the Slick. On this track, drivers race each other. All drivers wear helmets and are strapped in using a four-point harness. On-track supervisors monitor the activity at all times. The tracks are least crowded after school, on weekend mornings and during dinner hour.

Not all children are tall enough to man the steering wheels at Malibu

Grand Prix. Drivers must be at least 4 feet 6 inches tall to drive the Slick and Sprint cars, and 3 feet 6 inches to accompany an adult driver. To drive the Virage without a driver's license, kids must complete the Car Control Clinic and be at least 14 years old.

In addition to the tracks, Malibu Grand Prix offers eight outdoor batting cages where players can practice using a variety of balls and speeds. Bats and helmets are provided.

Indoors, the 100 video games and mechanical kiddie rides do good business in poor weather. Snack foods are available.

Mount Hood SkiBowl Action Park
Government Camp 97028
503-272-3206, ext. 234; 503-222-BOWL (2695) (24-hour information line)
www.skibowl.com
Hours: Late May to mid-September, Mon-Fri, 11 am-6 pm; Sat-Sun, 10 am-7 pm (east side/additional attractions open one hour later)
Admission: Adventure Pass: $20/half day, $25/full day. Action Pass: $39/person. Check Web site for à la carte activity prices

The question isn't what's here; the question is, what isn't here. In summer, Mount Hood SkiBowl hosts legions of revelers—many of them no doubt the very same daredevils who schuss down the slopes in winter. They are drawn to the mountain by the region's only Alpine slide (a half-mile, side-by-side model) and more than a dozen other amusement-park activities, many of which defy description.

There are the obvious attractions: a scenic chairlift ride to the summit; Indy go-karts; pitching and batting machines; Kiddie Jeeps (tots steer the miniature gas-powered vehicles themselves); 18-

hole miniature golf and nine-hole Frisbee golf courses; a kids-only fun zone complete with ball bin and giant inflatable slide; horseback rides; hay-wagon rides; and 40 miles of rugged trails for mountain biking.

Then there are the downright outrageous: motorized skateboards (wear protective gear and closed-toe shoes); the Velcro Fly Trap (dress in a Velcro suit, jump on an air mattress, and hurl yourself onto a Velcro wall); a bungee trampoline (do flips and other gymnastic moves with the aid of a belt attached by bungee cords to poles on either side of a trampoline); and a 100-foot bungee tower. Get the picture? It's the kind of extreme stuff an adventurous teen will love.

Spread over 960 acres, the park is divided into west and east sides. The west features the chairlift, which provides access to the Alpine slide and upper bike trails. A half mile east lies the bulk of the action. The nature of most of these attractions precludes the participation of small children. Kids older than age 6 begin to have a fiendishly good time, however. (Be aware that some activities such as the Alpine slide and the bungee tower do have height and weight restrictions.)

To avoid crowds, come on a Monday, Tuesday or Wednesday. A full cafeteria is available, but picnics are also welcome (barbecuing is prohibited). Corporate picnickers swarm the grounds on weekends, so call ahead to ensure the entire park hasn't been reserved for a private party. Check also on weather conditions, which can close the Alpine slide and chairlift.

If you've only got a little time to spend at this amusement mecca, you may want to pay for selected activities on an à la carte basis. For instance, you can play a round of mini-golf for just $3 or take a hay-wagon ride for $1 per person.

Otherwise, the Adventure Pass ($25/full day, $20/half day) is SkiBowl

HOW TO GET AN (ALMOST) FREE RIDE

As summer approaches, watch for Multnomah County Library to announce details of its summer reading program. For the past several years, the popular program has kicked off with a big party, complete with free rides, at Oaks Park. This is a great, albeit hectic, way to start a kid's fun summer.

Watch, too, for midweek specials offered throughout the summer at the park. With coupons or receipts from local sponsors, you can often get ride bracelets at a price reduced by a couple of dollars. Past participants have included Wendy's, Safeway and Bi-Mart. Call the park or check the Web site for program details.

If you have small children, take advantage throughout the summer of the park's Chipper's Pre-School Mornings. Kids age 6 and under can enjoy unlimited rides in Kidland (with adults riding free) on Tuesdays and Thursdays, from 9:30 to 11:30 am, for $4.50. After enjoying the rides, your little one will love sitting down with milk and cookies for story time, too.

AMUSEMENTS

Action Park's best ticket package for die-hard thrill-seekers. The pass entitles each visitor to unlimited rides on the Alpine slide and unlimited use of all east-side attractions, except the batting cages, go-karts, bungee activities, horses and helicopter rides. Discounted tickets for these attractions are available to all Adventure Pass holders.

If you're interested in mountain biking and little else, call the park (503-272-3206) to assess the trail options in your skill-level range, and ask for a trail map. Many of the trails are gravel service roads; others are even more rugged. Helmets and permits ($3/day) are required of all riders. Should you decide to try the upper trails, you'll also need to purchase chairlift tickets ($5/round trip).

Oaks Amusement Park

Foot of SE Spokane St
Portland 97202
503-233-5777
www.oakspark.com
Hours: Spring break & Sat-Sun until mid-June: noon-5 pm. Mid-June-early September: Tues-Thurs, noon-9 pm; Fri-Sat, noon-10 pm; Sun, noon-7 pm. September-mid-October: weekends, noon-dusk.
Admission: $9.75/5-hour limited bracelet (excludes roller coaster, bumper cars and Scream 'N Eagle); $12.25/5-hour deluxe bracelet; go-karts, miniature golf and carnival games priced separately

Built in 1905, Oaks Park is one of the nation's oldest continuously operating amusement parks, and as such it has entertained generations of Oregonians at its rambling facilities on the banks of the Willamette River. Home to one of the West Coast's largest roller rinks (see Active Play: Indoor Fun, Roller Skating),

in addition to a full complement of rides, this place may lack high-tech razzmatazz, but it serves up generous portions of old-fashioned charm.

Spread over 44 acres, the amusement park is operated as a nonprofit community resource, and it teems with young children (teens don't find too much of interest here). Corporate picnics fill the amusement park on summer weekends. Bring lunch from home, or feast on snack foods from the concession stands. Dozens of picnic tables overlook the river, and shelters that are booked by groups on weekends are vacant on weekdays and in the evening.

The park is continually reevaluating its mix of rides. The miniature train, bumper cars and Ferris wheel remain favorites, but some of the park's newest rides, such as Scream 'N Eagle, the Tea Cups and the Frog Hopper, are gaining a following. Kiddieland features a historic wooden carousel, Skyfighters, Jump Cycles and Toon Cars. Height restrictions apply to rides that are excluded from the limited-bracelet package.

Thrill-Ville USA

Exit 248 off I-5 in Turner
503-363-4095
www.thrillvilleusa.homestead.com
Hours: Spring break & Sat-Sun until Memorial Day: 11 am-6:30 pm. Memorial Day-Labor Day: 11 am-6:30 pm daily Labor Day-October 1: 11 am-6:30 pm weekends (hours extended summer weekends)
Admission: Max Pass: $14.95/person 48 inches and over, $9.95/person 47 inches and under (go-karts, Turbo Force and Skycoaster extra); families of 4 or more pay $12.95/person (with same restrictions as Max Pass)
Extras: Ripper, bumper cars, go-karts

and Blaster Boats require separately purchased tickets.

If you haven't been to Thrill-Ville USA in a while, it's worth another look. Virtually every year since opening in 1990, this small amusement park adjacent to Enchanted Forest has installed a new ride or made another improvement.

New in 2001 were bumper cars and another ride called Turbo Force. Clearly aimed at the brave-hearted, Turbo Force claims to spin at more than 60 mph, at a height of more than 140 feet.

Other attractions include a go-kart track, Ferris wheel, Tilt-a-Whirl, Sidewinder and Octopus, plus bumper boats, side-by-side water slides and the Ripper roller coaster, Oregon's largest. Kiddieland features the Little Ripper roller coaster, an old wooden carousel and Bulgy the whale, as well as helicopter, car, and train rides.

Purchase snack foods or bring a picnic to enjoy in the covered grove near Kiddieland or on the lawn by the water slides.

Biking

Learning to ride a two-wheeler is a child's first true accomplishment—and first true taste of freedom. Because kids often have more stamina biking than hiking (they're just so excited to be going fast!), bike rides are sometimes a better option for families. And in Portland, undoubtedly one of the nation's most bicycle-friendly cities, there's no dearth of places to ride.

These are just a few of the area's many parks that feature paved bike trails (see Parks for details):
Blue Lake Park
Champoeg State Park

Eastbank Esplanade
Forest Park
Oxbow Park
Silver Falls State Park
Tryon Creek State Park
Willamette Greenway Trail
(See also Amusements, Mount Hood SkiBowl Action Park; and Fishing, Henry Hagg Lake and Sauvie Island.)

Springwater Corridor

The major southeast segment of the 40-Mile Loop (see Parks, Blue Lake Regional Park), Springwater Corridor was originally an interurban electric railway corridor that carried passengers between

NEED A LIFT?

All Tri-Met buses and MAX trains are equipped with bicycle racks. To use one, a cyclist must watch a short video and purchase a special permit (with no expiration date) that costs $5. Regular permits are issued to anyone 12 years or older. Youth permits are issued to children ages 8–11, and these young riders must be accompanied on buses and trains by adults with permits.

Permits are available at the Tri-Met customer service office in Pioneer Courthouse Square or at several area bike shops. For more information about the Bikes on Tri-Met program, including MAX restrictions, call 503–239-3044 or check online at www.tri-met.org/bpermits.htm.

BIKING

Portland and Estacada from 1903 to 1953. Today its smooth, 16.8-mile paved path makes it ideal for bikers and equestrians. Acquired by the city of Portland in 1990, the trail parallels Johnson Creek and travels from just east of SE McLoughlin Blvd to Boring, passing wetlands, farmlands, nature parks, and residential and industrial neighborhoods en route.

Trailheads with parking, rest rooms and picnic tables are found near SE Johnson Creek Blvd at 45th Ave., and in Gresham at SE Hogan Rd. Eventually this trail is set to connect to the Pacific Crest Trail through Mount Hood National Forest. To obtain a copy of a trail map, call Portland Parks and Recreation at 503-823-2223.

Bike Rentals

These shops rent bicycles and trailers by the hour or day. Kid-size bikes are harder to come by. One option is a tandem bicycle; another is a trail-a-bike. This bike attachment designed for kids features a seat, handlebars and back-wheel unit that hooks to a rack at the rear of an adult bicycle. Call ahead for availability. Helmets are usually included, but if you already own helmets that fit, use them.

Citybikes Workers' Cooperative

734 SE Ankeny, Portland 97214
503-239-6951
Hours: Mon-Fri, 11 am-7 pm; Sat-Sun, 11 am-5 pm
Fees: Bicycles, trailers, trail-a-bikes: $17.50/day, $35/weekend (helmets included)

The bikes in this shop's fleet go down to about 15 inches. No children's bikes available.

BIKING RESOURCES

For more on bicycling in Portland, be sure to check out the Portland Transportation Department's Bicycling in Portland Web site at www.trans.ci.portland.or.us/Traffic_Management/Bicycle_Program/. Here you'll find news about current and upcoming bicycling projects, bicycle safety tips and a wealth of resources. Among those resources are family-friendly bicycle maps for the southeast, north and northeast parts of the city. View PDF files of the maps online, call 503-823-2925 for a free map or send an e-mail request to geller@trans.ci.portland.or.us.

Keep an eye out at bicycle shops and recreation centers for a comprehensive citywide map of existing and planned bike lanes called Bike There! ($6), which was produced in 1999 by Metro.

Also available:

- Clackamas County bike map: $3.50; 503-353-4538.
- Multnomah County bike map and brochure: Free; 503-988-5050
- Washington County bike map: $2; 503-846-3960
- Oregon Coast Bike Route map and Oregon Bicycling Guide statewide maps: Free; 503-823-2925

Fat Tire Farm
2714 NW Thurman, Portland 97214
503-222-3276
www.fattirefarm.com
Hours: Mon-Fri, 11 am-7 pm; Sat, 9 am-6 pm; Sun, 10 am-5 pm
Fees: Bicycle or trailer: $20/1-2 hours, $30/4 hours, $40/day (helmets included)

Rentals of adult mountain bikes in various sizes down to 16 inches are on a first-come, first-served basis. The shop's location, just a few blocks from Forest Park's Leif Erickson Dr, puts you close to Portland's cycling heaven.

Gateway Bicycles
11905 NE Halsey St, Portland 97220
503-254-0800
www.gatewaybicycles.com
Hours: Mon-Fri, 10 am-7 pm; Sat, 10 am-6 pm; Sun, 11 am-4 pm
Fees: Tandems: $30/day, $45/overnight ($25/each successive day)

Gateway rents only tandems. They come in three different sizes and in two styles (mountain bike or road bike). The shop often has a waiting list for its bikes, especially on weekends, so call ahead to check on availability and make a reservation.

Northwest Bicycles
916 NW 21st Ave, Portland 97209
503-248-9142
Hours: Mon-Sat, 10 am-6 pm; closed Sun
Fees: Bicycles, trailers, tag-alongs: $25/first day, $5/each successive day

This shop rents children's as well as adult city bikes. In addition to the equipment listed above, it also has one tandem for rent. Call in advance to check on what's available.

Boating

Poised at the confluence of two rivers, Portland made its mark early as a significant seaport. Though the River City now relies less on the shipping industry for economic vitality than it once did, the rivers continue to be a focal point of tourism and recreation, which suits kids just fine.

Take a sightseeing cruise on a sunny afternoon and marvel at a new perspective. Children may have little patience for scenery, but they'll enjoy tossing crumbs to the seagulls, counting bridges, waving to passing watercraft and watching the captain navigate.

Choose a smaller vessel for a more intimate and vivid boating experience, and test the waters first with a shorter excursion. The atmosphere aboard larger yachts leans toward floating restaurant, and their exotic, gourmet dinner cruises are not particularly suitable for children. How would you like to share your romantic anniversary date with a stranger's bored (and hungry) brood?

Call ahead to check on availability and to make reservations.

Cascade Sternwheelers
1200 NW Naito Pkwy, Ste 110, Portland 97209
503-223-3928, 800-643-1354
Season: Year-round (mid-June-September on the Columbia; October-June on the Willamette)
Fees: Vary by cruise; see below for example

Authentic replicas of sternwheelers from a previous century, the Columbia Gorge and Cascade Queen are Portland's most distinguished vessels. The latter, the smaller of the two, is patterned after paddleboats of the Mississippi, with two decks and double smokestacks. The former resembles local sternwheelers of the 1890s—specifically, the Bailey Gatzert—and can accommodate 600 passengers.

With two docks downtown and one in Cascade Locks, these boats maintain an active schedule of narrated cruises on the Willamette and the Columbia in summer. Narrated excursions on Saturdays and Sundays ($14.95/adults, $8.95/children, free/children 2 & under) include historical narration, facts and trivia delivered by the ship's captain about Portland and the city's harbor.

Canby Ferry

Mountain Rd, Stafford
Holly St, Canby
503-650-3030
www.co.clackamas.or.us/dtd/trans/htmls/ferry.html
Hours: Daily, 6:45 am-9:15 pm
Fee: $1.25/car or pickup

There's no food on board (except for whatever snacks you may have stashed in the glove compartment), and it's not particularly romantic, but the Canby Ferry has been in operation almost continuously since 1914 and it has a loyal following. The ferry is a small, simple platform that holds nine vehicles and stays on course by means of an underwater cable. It receives power via an overhead line and shuttles cars across the Willamette from Mountain Rd in Stafford to Holly St in Canby. In nice weather, families out for a drive in the country often complement a train ride at Flower Farmer (see Farms, Special Farms) with the short trip on the Canby Ferry. There may be a wait on such afternoons. Bring a few toys, books and travel games just in case.

Portland Spirit

842 SW First Ave, Portland 97204
503-224-3900, 800-224-3901
www.portlandspirit.com
Season: Year-round
Fees: Vary by cruise; see below for example

Scenery takes a backseat to food aboard the three-story, 350-passenger yacht Portland Spirit. Operating from a dock at Front Ave and SW Salmon, the vessel focuses on dinner cruises, with live entertainment and an attractive menu of excursion options and special events.

Best for families is the two-hour champagne brunch cruise ($36/adults, $10/children 4-12, free/children 3 & under) to Lake Oswego, which features an impressive spread and an array of finger foods favored by kids. Passengers may forgo the meal to concentrate on the sights ($15/adults, $9/children 4-12, free/children 3 & under).

Sternwheeler Rose

6211 N Ensign St, Portland 97217
503-286-7673
www.sternwheelerrose.com
Season: Year-round
Fees: Vary by cruise; see below for example

This jaunty little red-and-white sternwheeler accommodates up to 130 passengers on two levels. Available for charter, the Rose also offers a regular schedule of public cruises south to Lake Oswego from its dock at OMSI. Families might prefer the hour-long harbor tours that run June, July and August ($12/adults, $6 child 3-9, free/children 2 & under) to the more formal, two-hour dinner ($35/adults, $17.50/children, free/child 2 & under) and brunch cruises ($25/adults, $12.50/children, free/children 2 & under).

Willamette Jetboat Excursions, LLC
1945 SE Water Ave (behind OMSI),
Portland 97214
503-231-1532

www.jetboatpdx.com
Season: Late April-mid-October
Fees: $25/adult, $15/child 4-11,
free/child 3 & under

Since 1997, this company, with its U.S. Coast Guard-certified pilots, has been showing visitors 37 miles of sights in the Portland metropolitan area on its

EDUCATION AND BOATING

For boating experiences with an environmental, educational bent, check into these organizations:

Headwaters To Ocean (H2O)
3945 SE Hawthorne Blvd
Portland 97214
503-228-9600
www.h2ocean.org
Season: March-late November
Fees: Prices vary

Up the Columbia River from Astoria to the Columbia Gorge, down the Willamette River from Oregon City to Portland, H2O (Headwaters to Ocean) uses fun, boat-based learning to acquaint people of all ages with the wonders and woes of the Columbia/Willamette River system. The goal is to inspire them to protect these rivers through thousands of small, simple actions. A nonprofit organization, H2O uses a 65-foot classic wooden vessel, the Captain Conner, to offer educational field trips, youth after-school programs, teen overnight voyages, dockside programs suit-

able for kindergarteners through third-graders and summer day camps.

Tualatin Riverkeepers
16340 SW Roy Rogers Rd
Sherwood 97140
503-590-5813
www.tualatinriverkeepers.org
Season: March-October
Fees: See below

Tualatin Riverkeepers, a citizen-based, nonprofit waterway-preservation organization, leads half-day guided canoe trips on the Tualatin River from March through October, in cooperation with other local nature groups. The group's aim is to build watershed stewardship through public education, access to nature, citizen involvement and advocacy. Limited space is available on their trips for participants without boats, so you're strongly encouraged to bring your own canoe and equipment. There is a trip fee of $5 for members or $10 for nonmembers. Some canoes are available to members at no cost; nonmembers may rent one for $20.

Discovery Day, begun in 1990, generally attracts as many as 300 boaters to a normally inaccessible, scenic stretch of the Tualatin River on the last Saturday in June.

BOATING

Join the Tualatin Riverkeepers for half-day guided canoe trips on the Tualatin River.

PHOTO COURTESY OF THE TUALATIN RIVERKEEPERS

two-hour trips. Giant cargo and military ships, elegant riverfront homes, majestic Willamette Falls, and bald eagles and osprey are all par for the course on one of these trips. Reservations are recommended.

Boat Rentals

You can sail the Columbia, canoe the Tualatin, raft the Sandy. The metro area offers any number of recreational boating opportunities on the rivers that crisscross the region. But before you rent a vessel with your children, be sure you feel comfortable in the skipper's seat.

Ask for pointers from the rental agents; most offer instructional programs for all ages and abilities. Discuss your planned route as well, especially if you're going rafting, and pick up a map of the river or harbor to help you navigate. Check the craft for appropriate safety equipment before setting out. Life jackets are required for all passengers and should be provided, but not all outfitters offer a wide selection of sizes. If your children are small, it's wise to bring life jackets you know fit them.

Pack a picnic and tie up at an island or beach, or pull up and dock at a waterfront restaurant. After a few hours in a cramped boat, everyone will welcome the opportunity to stretch their legs.

The following outfits rent vessels and provide tips to beginners. Call well ahead for reservations on summer weekends. (See also Parks, Blue Lake; and Fishing, Henry Hagg Lake.)

Alder Creek Kayak & Canoe

250 NE Tomahawk Island Dr.
Portland 97217
503-285-0464
www.aldercreek.com
Hours: Summer: Mon-Wed and Fri, 10 am-7 pm; Thurs, 10 am-9 pm; Sat-Sun, 8 am-7 pm. Winter: Mon-Fri, 10 am-6 pm; Sat, 8 am-7 pm; Sun, 10 am-6 pm.
Fees: Canoe: $10/hour, $40/day.
Double kayak: $20/hour, $60/day

Put in at a harbor on the Columbia. Paddlers must have prior experience. Shop must approve itinerary.

Ebb and Flow Paddlesports

0604 SW Nebraska, Portland 97201
503-245-1756
www.ebbnflow.citysearch.com
Hours: Tue-Fri, 10 am-6 pm; Sat, 9:30 am-5 pm; Sun, noon-5 pm
Fees: Canoe: $25/4 hours, $35/full day. Sea kayak (single): $25/4 hours, $35/full day; sea kayak (double): $40/4 hours, $50/full day

Cross the street and put in at the Willamette Park boat landing near Ross Island. Call to check on availability and make reservations.

Island Sailing Club

515 NE Tomahawk Island Dr
Portland 97217
503-285-7765
www.islandsailingclub.com
Hours: Daily, 9 am-6 pm
Fees: Sailboat: $140/half day, $175/full day; $25/reservation deposit

Knowledge of sailing and certification is required to rent the club's 23-foot sailboat.

REI

1798 Jantzen Beach Center
Portland 97217
503-283-1300
7410 SW Bridgeport, Tigard 97224
503-624-8600
Fees: Canoe: $30/day for members, $38/day for nonmembers (three- and seven-day packages offered also)

No roof racks, but REI supplies foam pads and straps for mounting on cars.

River Trails

336 Columbia River Hwy
Troutdale 97060
503-667-1964
Hours: April-October, daily, 9 am-6 pm
Fees: Canoe: -$30/day. Raft: $55-$95/day

Shuttles transport crafts and passengers to and from the Sandy River at 9:30 am and 11:30 am daily in season. Rafts are outfitted with oars or paddles, ice chests and river bags at no extra cost. No guides provided. There are two designated excursions: Dodge Park to Lewis and Clark State Park (Class III whitewater, no children under 5 years permitted), and Oxbow Park to Lewis and Clark State Park. Reserve well in advance for summer weekends.

Sportcraft Marina

1701 Clackamette Dr
Oregon City 97045
503-656-6484
Hours: Tues-Fri, 9 am-5 pm; Sat, 9 am-4 pm
Fees: Canoe or kayak: $30/day. Skiff: $60/day

Sportcraft has 30 canoes in its fleet. Put in at the floating shop, 1 mile below Willamette Falls. No reservations by phone; boats are provided on a first-come, first-served basis.

Fishing

Bait a hook with a wiggly worm, drop it in the water and you'll have a child's attention, if not a bite. Grown men and women have been known to spend countless hours trying to outsmart fish in lakes, rivers and oceans—only to come up empty-handed and, in the process, lose the interest (and respect) of their kids. Go fishing, not to catch a record-breaker, but to have fun outdoors.

If you're a novice angler, do a little

FISHING

research first, and you and your kids will get more out of the experience (and probably more fish, too). Where do fish bide their time? When, what and how do they eat? Fishing is a living, breathing science lesson that goes way beyond guts and gore.

In Oregon, children under 14 can fish for warm-water pan fish, such as trout and bass, without a license. Youths ages 14 through 17 are required to purchase an annual juvenile angling license ($6.75). An adult license costs $19.75 per year. Special annual tags are issued to all anglers who fish for salmon, steelhead, halibut and sturgeon ($6.50 to $16.50). Licenses and tags are sold at local sporting goods stores, including G.I. Joe's and Fred Meyer, and at Department of Fish and Wildlife offices. When purchasing licenses, ask for a copy of Oregon Sport Fishing, a booklet of information and regulations that's updated each December.

The best fishing for kids occurs at lakes. Rivers with fast-moving currents are much more dangerous. Choose lakes that are flushed and cleaned naturally, either by tidal action or by in-flowing rivers. Fish from a raft or canoe only if your child knows how to swim. Otherwise, find a spot on the bank where your child can nab frogs, skip rocks and hunt for snakes, should your patience and persistence outlast his or hers (and it will).

The following lakes and ponds are among the region's finest for families:

Henry Hagg Lake
Off Hwy 47 near Gaston, south of Forest Grove (about 30 miles southwest of Portland)
503-359-5732
Hours: Late April-late October, sunrise-sunset daily
Fees: $4/vehicle, $5/with boat
Seasonal pass: $30/vehicle, $35/with boat

Watercraft rental: Electric motorboat: $12/hour, $40/day. Other watercraft: $8/hour, $30/day

Owned by the U.S. Bureau of Reclamation, and maintained and operated by Washington County, Hagg (pronounced "Haig") Lake (a reservoir) is stocked with rainbow trout each spring. But small mouth-bass anglers are lured by the prospects of nailing a record-breaker.

The best thing about Hagg Lake may not be the fishing, however. This park is a recreational paradise. Divided by a buoy line that designates allowed boat speeds, the lake is popular with water-skiers and other boaters in summer. Rent a canoe, kayak, paddleboat or small fiberglass boat with electric motor, and cruise the slow zone. The grassy banks that sport picnic areas are especially hospitable to young anglers. You'll also find drinking water, rest rooms—and lots of other little fishermen.

Swimming is allowed, though there are no lifeguards on duty. A 15-mile hiking/biking trail follows the forested shoreline, and adjoining Scoggins Valley Park boasts a 10.5-mile bicycle lane. Disabled visitors are catered to as well, with a short, accessible trail, and special picnic sites and boat ramps.

Horning's Fishing and Picnic Hideout
21277 NW Brunswick Canyon Rd
North Plains 97133
503-647-2920
Hours: Daily, 8 am-dusk
Admission: $2/person 6 & over, which can be applied toward either fish or paddleboats
Paddleboats: $3/half hour, $5/hour
Fish: $4/lb.

Promontory Park's wooded picnic facilities provide shelter from the warm summer sun.

Admire the peacocks as you fish in a pond brimming with trout, barbecue in one of the many covered pavilions, play on the playground or just wander around and take in the pretty surroundings. You'll also find horseshoe pits and paddleboats at this little-known hideaway, which opened in 1983. Several times during the year, the amphitheater here attracts local grassroots festivals, such as the KBOO Pickathon.

Portland General Electric Recreational Areas

www.portlandgeneral.com

PGE has made available to the public nine recreational areas that are in the vicinity of some of the utility's hydroelectric facilities. The following two parks feature fine fishing for local families.

Promontory Park

Hwy 224, 7 miles east of Estacada
503-630-5152
Season: June-October
Fishing boats: $30/3 hours, $65/day.

Pontoon (20-foot) boats: $45/3 hours, $120/day

Located on the 350-acre North Fork Reservoir, behind North Fork Dam, Promontory Park features campsites, picnic facilities, boat rentals and docks, and rest rooms. Like Hagg Lake (see above), the reservoir is divided into two speed zones, with the upper portion more conducive to angling. However, kids have an even better reason to come to Promontory Park to fish: Small Fry Lake, a shallow, 1-acre pond developed and stocked for the exclusive use of young anglers up to age 14. The daily catch limit per child is three fish.

Roslyn Lake Park

From Sandy, north off Ten Eyck Rd (3.5 miles north of Sandy)
503-668-5690
Season: Late April-early September
Fee: $3/vehicle on Sat, Sun & holidays
Boats: $5-$10/hour

FISHING

Roslyn Lake is annually stocked with rainbow trout.

The forebay of PGE's Bull Run Hydroelectric Project, Roslyn Lake is stocked annually with rainbow trout. A day-use area with six picnic areas (three with shelters), in addition to playing fields, horseshoe pits, a concession store and boat rentals, the park is particularly suited to families. No motorboats or alcoholic beverages are permitted on the premises. Wheelchair-accessible features include a fishing dock, picnic area, sunbathing area and rest rooms.

Rainbow Trout Farm
52560 E Sylvan Dr, Sandy 97255
(7.5 miles east of Sandy)
503-622-5223
Hours: March 1-October 15, daily, 8 am-dusk
Fish priced by size

Nobody leaves the Rainbow Trout Farm without catching a fish. With 10 ponds full of ravenous trout and years of experience helping school groups land the big ones, the owners virtually guarantee you'll get lucky, and they supply lessons in fish physiology at cleaning time. Bring your own equipment and bait, or borrow from the farm at no charge. Bring a picnic, too, to enjoy in the parklike setting.

Sauvie Island
Off Hwy 30, north of Portland

A popular destination for fruit pickers in summer and fall (see Farms, Special Farms), Sauvie Island boasts nice beaches along the Columbia River, hiking and biking trails, and lakes, rivers and sloughs for anglers. For a map, stop at the Wildlife Area Office (18330 NW Sauvie Island Rd; 503-621-3488; Mon-Fri, 8 am-noon and 1-5 pm). The kiosk outside is well stocked for weekends.

Visitors to the wildlife area are required to purchase parking permits ($3.50/day, $11/year), which are available from the Cracker Barrel store on the island, near the bridge, or anywhere hunting and fishing licenses are sold, including G.I. Joe's and Fred Meyer stores. Bring a picnic blanket if you plan to lunch outside; there are no picnic facilities in the wilderness, though many farm stands have tables.

Sauvie Island offers several good fishing options for families. Gilbert River is accessible via two fishing piers: one on the west side at Big Eddy, off Sauvie Island Rd; the other on the east side on Gilbert River Boat Ramp Rd, off Reeder Rd. Expect to catch bullhead and channel catfish, walleye, crappie and perch. The following two ponds are also recommended for kids:

*Haldeman Pond
Take Reeder Rd to Oak Island Rd.
Season: April 16-September 30

This 2-acre pond on Oak Island is stocked with rainbow trout several times in early spring. Stay on the south side of the pond, where the bank is less steep, and for insurance have the kids wear life jackets. Rest rooms are found at the parking lot.
*Webster Pond
Take Reeder Rd to Oak Island Rd.

Season: April 16-September 30

The Oregon Bass and Panfish Club has adopted this 5-acre pond, and is developing and improving its population of warm-water fish species.

Miniature Golf and Golf

Once the kids stop arguing over who gets the blue ball, who gets to keep score and who gets to putt first, you can start having fun. After all, isn't that why you came?

All Golf at Sunset
16251 SW Jenkins Rd, Beaverton 97006
503-626-2244
Hours: Daily, 9 am-10 pm
Fee for 18 holes: $4/adults 14 and up, $3/children 13 & under
Driving range: $4/half bucket of balls, $7/bucket

Family Fun Center
(See Amusements.)

Mount Hood Skibowl Action Park
(See Amusements.)

Oaks Amusement Park
(See Amusements.)

Scappoose Mini Golf
50418 Columbia River Hwy, Scappoose 97056 (about 20 miles from Portland)
503-543-6500
Hours: Late April-October (weather permitting), Mon-Fri, 10 am-10 pm; Sat-Sun, 10 am-11 pm
Fees: $4.50/adult, $4/senior and child 12 & under

This 18-hole course features a series of challenges (good for ages 5 and up) amid a natural landscape.

Had enough of windmills, castles and loop-the-loops? Perhaps your child is ready for something a bit more challenging.

Frontier Golf Course
2965 N Holly St, Canby 97013
503-266-4435

TIE ONE ON

Be among the throngs of beginning anglers to hook a trout at the statewide Free Fishing Weekend, held annually in early June. The metro-area event occurs at Bonneville Hatchery. Children work their way through activity stations, learning about fish identification, water safety and knot tying, before "graduating" to Mitchell Creek—which is dammed and stocked for the occasion. Equipment and instruction are provided. For more information, call the Oregon Department of Fish and Wildlife, 503-657-2000. (See also Excursions, Columbia Gorge.)

Hours: March 1-October 31, opens at 8 am with last tee time at 7 pm
Greens fees: Mon-Fri, $6.50/adult and child, $5/senior; Sat-Sun, $7/adult and child, $5.50/senior

This countryside course is a mom-and-pop operation that has been open since 1964. Lovingly maintained, the course offers a mix of short and long holes that make it fun for all ages.

Meriwether National Golf Club
5200 SW Rood Bridge Rd
Hillsboro 97123
503-648-4143
Hours: Daily, dawn to dusk (weather permitting)
Greens fees: Vary depending on day and time of play.

This club offers three full-length sets of nine holes as well as a short course and an 18-hole, all-grass putting course ($3/person). All courses are open for all players. The best deal for young players (those 17 and under) is Monday through Thursday, when the price is $7 for nine holes.

The Children's Course
19825 River Rd, Gladstone 97027
503-722-1530
Hours: Summer: daily, 6:30 am-dusk.
Winter: daily, 7:30 am-dusk
Fees: $5-$9/9 holes; $8-$14/18 holes

Opened in July 1996 to provide children—particularly underprivileged and at-risk youths—with the opportunity to learn golf, the layout of this nine-hole, par-3 course is ideal for youngsters. Holes range from 130 to 165 yards, and a third set of tees provides further advantages to kids. Junior golfers are encouraged to enroll in lessons and

special clinics. Those who pass a written rules-and-etiquette test receive greens-fee discounts.

The Pub Course
2126 SW Halsey, Troutdale 97060
503-669-8610
Hours: Daily, 8 am-dusk
Greens fees: Mon-Fri, $8/9 holes, $13/18 holes; Sat-Sun, $9/9 holes, $14/18 holes

This 18-hole pitch-and-putt course set at McMenamin's Edgefield Brewery is hilly and picturesque. Holes range in length from 40 yards to 80 yards, wrapping precariously around the Edgefield estate. All ages and skill levels are welcome as long as course rules are followed and players keep pace. Take your own clubs or rent some there.

Tualatin Island Greens
20400 SW Cipole Rd, Tualatin 97062
503-691-8400
www.tualatinislandgreens.com
Hours: April-September: daily, 8 am-10 pm. October-March: daily, 8 am-9 pm
Fees: 18-hole putting course: $6/adult, $4/child 17 & under. Driving range: $5-$10/bucket of balls

The putting course here consists of 18 famous golf holes that were copied and reduced to scale (30 to 50 yards each), including an island green that's accessible only by bridge. Many of the 62 driving-range tees are covered and heated for year-round play on a synthetic surface. The facility features a pro shop, restaurant and junior golf programs.

Horseback Riding

Horseback riding isn't for everyone. Some people exude the scent of anxiety, which tips off horses to their vulnerability. The very riders who are praying not to trot are the first to veer off the trail in a cloud of dust. But for true horse lovers—the kids who collect plastic horses, wear cowboy hats and walk bow-legged—there's no rest until they've had a chance to handle the reins of a real beast.

The following ranches rent horses and ponies for use on their property. When you call to arrange a ride, provide information regarding your group's equestrian experience. Children must be about 6 years old to ride solo; doubling up with an adult is typically not allowed.

Dress appropriately in long pants (blue jeans are best) and lace-up shoes or boots. Leave pocketbooks and purses in the car, and stow valuables in a backpack or fanny pack.

Beaverton Hill Top Riding Stables
20490 SW Farmington Rd
Beaverton 97007
503-649-5497
Season: Year-round (as weather permits)
Fee: $25/hour per horse

Choose a guided trail ride through Hill Top's 50 scenic, wooded acres (trotting and cantering allowed), or exercise your horse in the indoor corral. Pony rides are available for children under 5 if parents are willing to lead the animals ($15/half hour, $25/hour). Hill Top accepts same-day reservations for individuals and families only. Larger groups are asked to provide advance notice.

Mount Hood Ski Bowl Action Park
(See Amusements.)

Mountain Shadow Ranch
690 Herman Creek Rd
Cascade Locks 97014
Exit 51 off I-5, 45 minutes from Portland
541-374-8592
business.gorge.net/mtshadow/
Season: Year-round (weather permitting), except Thanksgiving and Christmas
Fees: $30/person for 1-hour ride, $55/person for 2-hour ride, $10/person pony ride

This ranch is tucked between the river and the mountains. Guided rides wind up through Douglas firs, allowing riders beautiful views of the river as well as an up-close opportunity to see the area's wildlife. Children age 3 and up are allowed on the hour ride, but those 3, 4 and 5 share a horse with a guide who rides behind them. A pony ride gives little ones an up-close view of the ranch's emus, ducks, geese and llamas.

Equestrian Trails
There are many options locally for horse owners looking for new trails to blaze. Each of these parks allows horseback riding on some of its trails (see Parks, Nature Parks for details):
Forest Park
Oxbow Park
Silver Falls State Park (also rents horses for $25/person per hour; 503-873-8681)
Tryon Creek State Park
(See also Biking, Springwater Corridor.)

Snow Play

Portland's wet weather is legendary. But there is a silver lining to all those winter clouds: the snow. Just enough of it falls in town to remind us that Mother Nature still has the upper hand. And within a little more than an hour's drive, at Mount Hood, there's enough snow to ski on all year long.

Even before your kids are ready to ski (or you're brave enough to teach them), the Mount Hood area offers ample winter recreation opportunities. For toddlers it's often enough just to taste a snowflake, make snow angels and launch a few snowballs.

Whatever your intentions, always check the weather conditions before heading up to the mountain. Call the Oregon Department of Transportation's road condition report (800-977-6368) for an update, check the DOT Web site at www.tripcheck.com or call any of the resorts' dedicated snow phone lines (see below).

Be prepared with traction devices and emergency supplies (including snacks). And dress children appropriately: in multiple layers, starting with long underwear or tights and two pairs of socks, and finishing with a wool or fleece sweater, a warm hat, gloves and a thick winter parka. Pack a change of clothes for each family member; everyone's bound to be cold and soggy after an hour or two in the snow. Sunscreen is another necessity. In fine weather the sun reflects off the snow and burns unprotected skin.

Before You Go . . .

To park in many of the western states' winter recreation areas from November 15 through April 30, drivers are required to purchase and display in their vehicles valid Sno-Park permits. Available at Department of Motor Vehicles offices, sporting goods stores, some gas stations and ski resorts (which usually tack on a service fee), permits come in three sizes: one-day ($3), three-day ($7) and 12-month ($15). For more information, check the state Department of Transportation's Web site at www.tripcheck.com.

Alpine Skiing

People who learn to downhill ski as adults will tell you they wish they had learned when they were younger. It goes without saying that a child's body—with its supple bones and low center of gravity—is better designed for the slopes than an adult's. So if your kids show even the slightest interest in skiing or snowboarding, let them try it before they're old enough to creak and ache.

Mount Hood, the state's highest peak, boasts some of the nation's most extensive ski resorts, and some runs are groomed for skiing even in summer. Several local resorts make it especially affordable for parents to introduce their little kids to the sport by allowing youngsters under age 7 to ski free with a paying adult. And various resorts offer packages that allow you to cut costs some, for instance, by buying a pass early in the season.

If alpine skiing is not your idea of a good time, wait a few years until your kids are a little more self-sufficient. Schoolchildren are eligible to participate in special weekend ski-lesson packages that include bus transportation to and from the slopes.

Rentals

Depending on your circumstances, it might make sense to lease ski equipment in Portland, not at the mountain. Of course, your vehicle must be equipped

COOL DEALS ON HOT EQUIPMENT

Once you and the kids get hooked on skiing, you'll want to own your own gear. Many local families are as addicted to ski swaps as to the sport. In fall, high school ski teams often host weekend sales to raise funds for their endeavors. Sellers bring outgrown skis and related equipment (already priced), then donate a portion of their proceeds to the ski team. For news of such sales, watch your local community newspaper or call your neighborhood high school to inquire.

The granddaddy of all ski sales takes over the Expo Center (2060 N Marine Dr) during the first weekend of November. Sponsored annually by the Oregon Snowsports Industries Association (www.oregon-ski.org), the Subaru Ski Fever & Snowboard Show features representatives from local ski resorts, dozens of vendors selling new equipment and lots of used equipment for sale as well. For more information, call 503-249-7733 or check www.portlandskifever.com.

to carry a family's worth of gear, and you have to plan ahead to get outfitted. But with a little forethought you can circumvent the resort rental shops' frustrated and frantic early-morning crowds, and likely save money.

Several outdoor retail stores in the Portland area, as well as in Sandy, Welches and Government Camp, lease alpine and Nordic ski equipment, snowboards and even snowshoes. Expect to pay about $14/day for adult alpine equipment, $12/day for child alpine equipment and $25/day for snowboards. (For comparison, Mount Hood Meadows charges $22/adult and $15/junior (ages 7-12) for alpine rentals, and $28/adult and $21/junior for snowboards.)

Call in advance to inquire about children's gear and availability. Then take your time to ensure that the ski boots really fit.

Resorts

Cooper Spur Ski and Recreation Area

11000 Cloud Cap Rd, Mount Hood
541-352-7803
www.cooperspur.com
Season: Winter only
Hours: Thurs-Fri, 5:30-9 pm; Sat-Sun, 9 am-4 pm (closed Mon-Wed except Martin Luther King Jr. Day, Presidents' Day)
Lift tickets: $10-$15/adult; $7-$10/child 11 and under, free/child 5 & younger; $5/night skiing; $5/day for rope tow only

Popular with families since the 1940s, Cooper Spur still markets itself primarily to families and novice skiers and snowboarders. Because it's small—a T-bar provides access to just 10 runs—it's easy to keep tabs on the kids.

And the price is right: Cooper Spur is the most inexpensive resort around. First-time beginner group lessons (10

SNOW PLAY

Dress appropriately for a day on the slopes, where all that's predictable about the weather is its unpredictablility.

a.m. and noon on Saturdays) cost $30/person for downhill and $40/person for snowboarding, and include a lift ticket, lesson and rental equipment. (If you plan to go with a bunch of people, call ahead to ask about discounts for groups of 10 or more.)

For those who want to tube instead of ski, $10 includes the tube rental and a rope tow ticket, so you can ride both ways on the mountain!

Mount Hood Meadows Ski Resort

Hwy. 35, Mount Hood
503-337-2222, 503-227-SNOW (7669) (snow phone)
www.skihood.com
Season: Mid-November-late April
Hours: Mon-Tues, 8 am-4 pm; Wed-Sun, 8 am-10 pm
Lift tickets: $44/adult, $25/child 7-12, $6/child 6 & under; $20/night skiing; discounts in late spring and for tickets

focused on beginner chairs

With 10 chairlifts (including four high-speed quads) and 2,150 acres, Mount Hood Meadows is the largest ski resort on Mount Hood. Equipment rentals, lessons and groomed slopes and tracks are available for alpine and Nordic skiers and for snowboarders.

The Mount Hood Meadows Ski School oversees a variety of youth lesson packages.

KidSki/KidRide: Children 4 through 12 are grouped by age and ability in daily, supervised KidSki or KidRide programs. Choose a half-day ($50, plus $5 for rentals) or full-day ($70, plus $5 for rentals; lunch included) session. Reservations are recommended.

Learn to Ski or Snowboard Guarantee: This package ($75) includes two 90-minute lessons, equipment rentals and a lift ticket for both the Buttercup and Easy Rider chairlifts. By the end of the second lesson, the resort guarantees, you'll be able to ski or snowboard comfortably and in control on the Mitchell Creek Trail or the next lesson is free.

For details or reservations about either of the programs above, call (503) 337-2222, ext. 419.

For a different kind of fun, young skateboarding fans may want to check out the resort's snow-skate park, which is open on weekends. A snow skate is a skateboard without wheels that slides across the snow, and the park consists of a series of boxes, rails and tracks that riders slide across and balance on while executing tricks. No bindings or special boots are required. Admission is $5, and snow-skate rental is additional $5.

You can save money on lift tickets, lessons and rental equipment by planning your ski trips in advance and enrolling your children in one of the following multiweek ski-school packages, offered in January and February only.

Sno-Blasters: Children in grades 1 through 8 are eligible to participate in Sno-Blasters, a supervised, all-day ski-school program that meets for four consecutive weekend sessions ($245, plus $50 for rentals for either skiers or snowboarders).

Middle School Program: Children in grades 6 through 8 who no longer require supervision can enroll in the Middle School Program, which includes four half-day lessons in alpine skiing or snowboarding ($150, plus $50 for rentals).

Charter bus service: For kids who are really gung-ho about skiing (and parents who are not), Mount Hood Meadows has arranged a charter bus service that operates from many local schools on weekends in January and February, and is ideally suited to those who are enrolled in multiweek ski-school programs. Children in grades 1 through 12 are grouped with their peers on chaperoned private buses that depart from designated sites early on Saturday and Sunday mornings and return from the resort late in the afternoon. Expect to pay about $75 per child for a four-week session. For details about the route in your neighborhood, call the Mount Hood sales office: 503-BUS-LIFT(503-287-5438).

Bus-Lift, another charter service that transports skiers to Mount Hood Meadows on weekends in season, makes five stops in the metro area. Children 13 years and older may travel unaccompanied. Tickets are available from Ticketmaster ($25/bus ride; $50/bus ride plus adult lift ticket; $40/bus ride plus youth lift ticket). For details, call 503-BUS-LIFT(503-287-5438).

If you're the one driving to the mountain, remember that there is an alternate route to Mount Hood Meadows. Take I-84 east along the Columbia River to Hood River, then take Hwy 35 south to the resort. Traveling this way may add about 15 minutes to the 90-minute trip, but you'll avoid the congestion that typically clogs Hwy. 26.

Mount Hood SkiBowl
Government Camp
503-272-3206, 503-222-BOWL (snow phone), 503-254-0847 (ski school)
www.skibowl.com
Season: Winter
Hours: Mon-Tues, 3:30-10 pm; Wed-Thurs, 1-10 pm; Fri, 9 am-11 pm; Sat, 8:30 am-11 pm; Sun, 8:30 am-10 pm
Lift tickets: $19-$32/adult; $13-$18/child 7-12, free/child 6 & under

Mount Hood SkiBowl, the resort

Timberline Lodge was built in the 1930s as a WPA project.

nearest Portland, is one of the last to get snow. But when it does, SkiBowl offers the nation's largest night-skiing area, with night skiing on 34 lighted runs beginning daily at 3:30 pm. Sixty-five day runs with 960 skiable acres, including a 300-acre outback, are served by four chairlifts and five surface tows. The resort also features a snowboarding half-pipe and terrain garden. (See Amusements for details regarding the summer season's Mount Hood SkiBowl Action Park.)

A variety of ski and snowboarding packages are available for kids. Mogul Busters is an intensive, four-session program for children ages 4 through 13. Two instructors share responsibility for leading groups of six to eight children in two two-hour lessons each day ($220; $65/one-day session; rentals extra).

Ski and snowboard lessons for beginners are offered daily. Students are grouped by ability, not age, in these 90-minute sessions ($28/skiing, $36/snowboarding; rentals and surface-tow

pass included).

While your kids are in ski school, you can be, too. Parents whose children are enrolled in a four-session Mogul Busters program are treated to a special, concurrent lesson package at Mount Hood SkiBowl: four 90-minute lessons and all-day lift passes ($95, regularly $160).

Summit Ski Area
Government Camp
503-272-0256
www.summitskiarea.com
Season: November-April
Hours: Skiing: Sat-Sun & holidays, 9 am-4 pm. Tubing: Mon-Fri, 9 am-4 pm; Sat-Sun, 9 am-5 pm
Lift tickets: $20/full day, $13/half day (1-4 pm); $10 all day for tube rental

Opened in 1927, the Summit Ski Area is the oldest developed ski area in the Pacific Northwest and the first area developed on Mount Hood. It is a good option for beginners with its single chairlift that provides access to two runs. It also offers one rope tow and a small lodge with a café and a rental shop.

Summit's ski-lesson packages include a lesson, all-day lift ticket and rental equipment ($50 for alpine lesson, lift ticket and equipment rental; $55 for snowboard lesson, lift ticket and equipment rental). Groups of 10 or more buying a lift ticket and making an advance reservation get free lessons.

Summit may not be the glitziest mountain resort, but for families trying to satisfy skiers of varying abilities, it may be the best choice. Enroll the older kids in snowboarding classes and the younger ones in ski school, then take nonskiers tubing on the nearby slope (see also Sliding Areas below) or on a trek in snowshoes (available for rent for $15). Nordic skiers—and their babies—may prefer a cross-country sled ($15) to an infant backpack.

Timberline
Hwy 26, Timberline
503-231-7979 (ski area), 503-222-2211 (snow phone), 503-231-5402 (ski school)
www.timberlinelodge.com
Season: Year-round (upper lifts open September-October only, weather permitting)
Hours: 9 am-4 pm (may vary according to season); night skiing available Sat-Sun & holidays
Lift tickets: Daytime: $38/adult, $22/child 7-12, free/child 6 & under. **Nighttime:** $18/adult. $16/child 7-12

Grand, historic Timberline Lodge, built in the 1930s as a WPA project, sits near the summit of Mount Hood and watches over the activity on six chair-lifts and 32 trails. Timberline hosts the nation's most extensive spring/summer skiing season.

Lesson packages are available for alpine and Nordic skiers as well as snowboarders. Bruno's Children's Learning Center, a lesson program offered daily to children ages 4 through 12, includes rental equipment and lunch ($79/full day, $65/half day). Snowboarding instruction is available for youths 6 and older.

If you have an avid skier or snowboarder between the ages of 7 and 15, you might consider buying a junior pass good for the season at a cost of $119.

Timberline sells adult lift tickets through Ticketmaster at a discount. Good for any day of the week in season, 9 am to closing, each ticket costs $35 (that's a savings of $3). Junior tickets are not available through Ticketmaster.

Ticketmaster outlets also offer the Bus & Ski Package. This round-trip, chartered bus service to Timberline makes stops on weekends and holidays in season at G.I. Joe's stores in Beaverton, Eastport and Gresham. Passengers pay $49, lift ticket included. It's also possible to purchase four bus rides only for $80 or a one-time ride for $25. (The trip is not chaperoned, and there is no discount for children.) For information, call 503-231-7979.

Nordic Skiing
Whereas many Mount Hood resorts feature groomed trails for cross-country skiing, as well as Nordic rental equipment and ski lessons, their emphasis is on alpine and snowboarding customers, who purchase lift tickets. At Mount Hood Meadows, where Nordic skiers are treated to 15 kilometers of tracks, the trail fee is $10/adult and $5/child 7 through 12.

If you'd prefer a more backwoods experience, the Mount Hood region is a maze of trails for all abilities. To receive a comprehensive list of Nordic ski trails near Government Camp, call the Mount Hood Information Center (503-622-4822) or check at the Forest Service's Web site (webwww.fs.fed.us/r6/mthood).

The trails below are short, sweet and relatively flat and easy—good for youngsters just learning.

■ **Summit Trail:** This flat, 2-mile marked road begins at the east end of the SkiBowl parking lot.

■ **Snow Bunny Trail:** A more difficult, marked 2-mile road begins at the Snow Bunny Sno-Park.

■ **Pocket Creek Trail:** The first mile of this 4.5-mile trail is relatively flat. It begins on the east side of Hwy 35, 3 miles north of Mount Hood Meadows.

■ **Meadows Creek Tie Trail:** This easy, 1.2-mile trail branches off the Pocket Creek Trail (see above).

■ **Clark Creek Trail:** This easy, 2-mile marked trail begins at the Clark Creek Sno-Park on Hwy 35.

Sliding Areas

Sliding on saucers, inner tubes, sleds and toboggans may look like child's play, but on a crowded, unsupervised hill it can be more dangerous than skiing.

Teach your children the basic rules:

1. Know your abilities and stay on appropriate slopes.

2. Only one slider on the hill at a time.

3. Ascend along the sides of the slope, not up the middle.

4. Don't build jumps.

5. Clear out from the bottom as soon as you stop. (Most accidents occur there.)

The following designated areas are the only spots in the Mount Hood region where sliding is allowed.

Little John Snow Play Hill
Hwy 35, 31 miles south of Hood River
541-352-6002
Season: Winter
Hours: No limit
Fee: None (Sno-Park pass required)

Built by the U.S. Forest Service, Little John Snow Play Hill has two open slopes—one easy, the other more difficult. Bring your own discs, saucers or inner tubes; sleds, toboggans and snowboards are prohibited. Outhouses and a wooden shelter outfitted with a stove are open to the public. Haul some firewood from home so you can prepare a warm snack.

Little John Snow Play Hill is located on the edge of the snow zone, so it's wise to call ahead for snow conditions before planning an outing.

Snow Bunny Snow Play Area
Government Camp
503-272-0256
Season: November-April
Hours: Sat-Sun & school holidays, 10 am-4 pm
Fee: $10/tube rental

Monitored by the ski patrol, Snow Bunny Snow Play Area, just 2 miles from Summit Ski Area, features two hills with five lanes each, a small snack bar and an outhouse. Personally owned sliding devices are not allowed; all patrons must use (and pay for) Snow Bunny inner tubes. Kids are also allowed to tube on a designated slope at Summit Ski Area (9 am-5 pm daily; $10/tube).

Skateboard Parks

It's official: Skateboarding is not a crime.

At least it's not in Portland, where it became legal to skateboard on the city's downtown streets in 2001. And with the ever-increasing popularity of the sport, many communities have pulled out the stops in the past few years to create—with kids' help—skate parks where fans can practice their ollies, grinds and other moves.

For an updated list of the area's skate parks, including tips on the skill levels required for fun skating at the various parks, check out the Skate Oregon Web site at www.skateoregon.com.

Following is a sampling of some of the area's most popular places to skateboard:

Beaverton Skatepark

15707 SW Walker Rd (north end of the Howard Terpenning complex), Beaverton
503-645-6498 (Tualatin Hills Athletic Center)
Hours: Mon-Sat, 10 am-11 pm; Sun, 10 am-10 pm
Fees: Free; helmets required.

This is a big park and it's open year-round. Like many other outdoor facilities, though, it closes when it rains. Bicycles, blades and skateboards are all welcome.

Burnside Park

East end of Burnside Bridge, Portland
Hours: Dawn to dusk
Fees: None

Built, managed and operated by local skaters for skaters, this challenging concrete course, sheltered under the Burnside Bridge, has quite a following, but few hard-and-fast rules. (If your child is young and not so experienced, it's best to try this park early on a weekend morning before the more experienced skaters turn out.)

Canby Skate Park

At the most westernmost point of NW Third Ave, Canby
503-266-4021 (Canby Parks and Recreation Department)
Hours: Daylight
Fees: Free

Open since September 2000, this 12,000-square-foot park was designed, at least in part, by local skateboarders. It includes a couple of bowls and a pyramid.

Chehalem Skate Park

1201 Blaine St, Newberg
503-538-7454 (Chehalem Park and Recreation District)
Hours: Dawn to dusk, weather permitting
Fee: Free

This huge skate park, designed and built by Dreamland Skateparks Design and Construction, is hailed by skaters as one of the world's best. Helmets are required. Bikes are not allowed, but there's a BMX track right next to the skate park.

Davis Park

NE 194th Ave & Glisan, Gresham
503-618-2485 (Gresham Parks Department)
Hours: Dawn to dusk
Fee: Free

Developed and managed by the Gresham Parks Department, which recommends that all users wear safety equipment, this small, concrete skate park is ideal for beginners. Situated in a quiet neighborhood and bordering an elementary school, Davis Park features two benches and a low mountain.

Lake Oswego Skate Park
Pilkington & Willow, Lake Oswego
503-636-9673
Hours: Spring/fall: Mon-Fri, 3 pm-dusk; Sat, 10 am-dusk; Sun, noon-dusk. Summer: Mon-Sat, 10 am-8 pm; Sun, noon-8 pm (Park closes in mid-November and reopens around spring break, weather permitting.)
Residents: $10/term
Nonresidents: $15/term

Helmets are required at this supervised park. First-time registrants under 18 must have a parent sign the registration form; those over 18 are required to show identification.

Oregon City Skate Park
Clackamette Park, 1955 Clackamette Dr, Oregon City
503-655-7898 (Oregon City Parks and Recreation Department)
Hours: Dawn to dusk, year-round
Fee: Free

A 9,000-square-foot area with half-and quarter-pipes and some street-skating aspects as well, this park opened in January 2001. Helmets are strongly recommended.

Scappoose Skate Park
City Hall, 33568 E Columbia Ave, Scappoose (near corner of Hwy 30 & Columbia Ave)
503-543-7184
Hours: Dawn to dusk, year-round
Fee: Free

Helmets and pads are required. Bikes are not allowed.

St. Helens Skate Park
McCormick Park, 475 S 18th St
St. Helens
Hours: Dawn to dusk, year-round
Fee: Free
503-397-5520

Helmets and pads are strongly recommended.

INDOOR SKATING

When the weather turns bad, many kids make their way to this indoor facility.

Skate Church
Central Bible Church
8815 NE Glisan St, Portland
503-252-1424
Skateboarding: Grades 6-8, Mon, 6:30-9 pm; grades 9-12, Tues, 6:30-9 pm; 18 & over, Thurs, 6:30-9 pm
Girls skate: Fri, 5:30-8 pm
PeeWee Skate Church: 5th grade & under, Sat, 9:30 am-noon
In-line skating: Grades 6-12, Tues, 6:30-9 pm

Fees: $8/year; $2/visit

Open since September 1996, the warehouse building at Central Bible Church is equipped with a skate park made of wood and masonite that features a mini-half-pipe, vertical half-pipe and bowl. As many as 100 teens show up at designated weekly skate sessions to use the warehouse and basement street course and participate in half-hour Bible classes (attendance is mandatory). Other church rules: To register, skaters must present a current school ID card and waiver form signed by a parent, and all participants are required to wear safety gear when skating in the warehouse.

St. Johns Skate Park
In Pier Park, at N Bruce Ave & Central St, Portland
503-823-PLAY (7529) (Portland Parks and Recreation Department)
Hours: Dawn to dusk, year-round
Fee: Free

Portland's first official outdoor skate park, this 10,000-square-foot facility opened in August 2001.

Tualatin Skate Park
8515 SW Tualatin Rd, Tualatin
503-692-2000 (Tualatin Parks and Recreation Department)
Hours: Dawn to dusk, year-round
Fee: Free

Open since 1998, this park sees lots of action, especially on the weekends. Pads are required.

Wilsonville Skate Park
Memorial Park, 8100 SW Memorial Dr, Wilsonville
503-570-1522 (Wilsonville Parks and Recreation Department)
Hours: Dawn to dusk
Fee: Free

A smaller though well-used park, the Wilsonville Skate Park includes two quarter-pipes, a pyramid and a grinding rail. It opened in 1999. Helmets are required; only skateboards and in-line skates are allowed.

Trains and Trolleys

Like the effect of a high-pitched whistle on dogs, the clickety-clack of trains and ding-dong of trolleys elicit visceral reactions in children. Take them on a ride. It doesn't have to be a big-deal, all-day affair. Sometimes

Built in 1910, Mount Hood Railroad has been designated a National Historic Site.

TRAINS AND TROLLEYS

ALL ABOARD . . .

If you have a train buff in the family, you'll want to head south on I-5 to Brooks (about 40 miles from Portland) to visit the Oregon Electric Railway Museum (503-222-2226) housed at Western Antique Powerland (3995 Brooklake Rd. NE, Brooks 97303; 503-393-2424). Here you can see trolley cars from around the world: an Australian open car circa 1912, a Canadian Urban Car circa 1910, a Council Crest car circa 1904 and San Francisco trolleys from the 1950s. The museum is mostly outdoors.

A cooperative venture of a dozen clubs dedicated to the preservation of antique farm machinery, Western Antique Powerland has been in operation on its farmland acreage for about 26 years. Various groups display representative equipment. The Willow Creek Railroad offers rides aboard its miniature train. The Pacific Northwest Truck Museum features antique trucks, parts and memorabilia, including a 1917 Maxwell I-T Peddler—a farmstand on wheels—and a Portland-built 1949 Freightliner cab. The Powerland Museum houses a collection of tractors.

Powerland's days and hours vary (admission is $2/person), and much of the equipment is kept outdoors, so call ahead before scheduling a visit. Or plan to attend the Great Oregon Steam-up. Held on two consecutive weekends in late July and early August, the annual event showcases antique farm equipment at work. See threshing, log sawing, flour milling, tractor pulls and a farmyard parade, then hop aboard a historic trolley for a short ride. Admission for the Great Oregon Steam-up is $7/adult, free/child 12 and under.

spontaneous afternoon treats are the most fun.

Molalla Train Park
31803 S. Shady Dell Dr, Molalla 97038
503-829-6866
Hours: May-October, Sun & holidays, noon-5 pm
Fare: Donation

This 4-acre park is equipped with eight operating one-eighth-scale trains (engines are gas, steam and electric) and just under a mile of rails. Trains leave approximately every 15 minutes. Climb aboard and make tracks through woods, over bridges, across a pond and along a canal. Bring your own picnic or buy something to eat at the park's snack bar.

Mount Hood Railroad
110 Railroad Ave, Hood River 97301
800-872-4661
www.mthoodrr.com
Season: Late March or early April-December
Departures: 10 am & 3 pm daily (mornings only in winter)
Fares: $22.95/adult, $14.95/child 2-12, free/child under 2

You don't need to love trains to love this ride. A four-hour, 44-mile round-trip excursion from Hood River to Parkdale snakes through orchards and along country back roads. With its restored railcars from the 1910s and '20s, locomotives from the 1950s, a refurbished depot from 1911 and original tracks laid in 1906, the entire railroad is designated a National Historic Site. Events, including train robbery reenactments, seasonal specials and holiday festivities, are scheduled monthly.

In spring and autumn, you'll see the orchard landscape at its peak. The trip to Parkdale takes about 90 minutes, and time passes quickly, especially if younger children have brought along a few favorite travel games and lap activities. Ask to sit in the Timberline car, where banquettes face tables. Let the kids walk the aisles to get a feel for the dimensions of the train, and they'll likely make friends among the other young passengers. There's an open-air car at the rear, and a snack bar.

If you take the morning train, plan to eat lunch during the hourlong layover in Parkdale, where there are a few cozy cafés, a general store and picnic tables.

Reservations are strongly advised, and you are encouraged to arrive at least a half hour before departure to pick up tickets.

Phoenix & Holly Railroad
(See Farms, Special Farms, Flower Farmer.)

Willamette Shore Trolley
Depot 311 N State St
Lake Oswego 97034
503-222-2226
www.trainweb.org/oerhs/wst.htm
Season: January-February, Sat-Sun; March-May & October-December, Fri-Sun; June-September, Thurs-Sun
Departures: From Lake Oswego: even hours, 10 am-4 pm (also 6 pm on Fri-Sat, Memorial Day-Labor Day). From Portland (RiverPlace): odd hours, 11 am-5 pm (also 7 pm one-way trip on Fri-Sat, Memorial Day-Labor Day) May & October-December, Fri-Sun; June-September, Thurs-Sun
Fares: $8/adult, $7/senior (55 & over), $4/child 3-12, free/lap sitters 2 & under

This sightseer's delight boasts two cars (a double-decker from England that was "modernized" in 1921 and a Portland Broadway trolley from 1932) that trace the Willamette River between Lake Oswego and RiverPlace four times daily in summer. The round trip lasts an hour and 45 minutes. Stop at Willamette Park or at either terminal for window-shopping, and return on a later trolley.

Watch, too, for special runs, including ones during Christmas ships and

DINNER TRAIN TIPS

Planning a trip to central Oregon? Check out the Crooked River Railroad Company Dinner Train (PO Box 387, Redmond 97756; 541-548-8630; www.crookedriverrailroad.com; dintrain@coinet.com), an 1800s Western-theme train that runs along the scenic Crooked River Valley. This company offers a variety of trips, each featuring characters from the Wild West. Sign up for a Western murder-mystery trip or for a Sunday brunch or supper during which Jesse James holds up the train. Fares range from $20 to $38 for children and $59 to $71 for adults.

lights season and during Fourth of July fireworks celebrations.

Zoo Train
(See Kid Culture, Go Wild!, Oregon Zoo.)

Up in the Sky

Pearson Air Museum
(See Kid Culture, Exploring the Past.)

The Portland Rose
18965 SW Olson Ct
Lake Oswego 97034
503-638-1301
http://portland-rose.virtualave.net
Season: March-October

SPRUCE GOOSE

Commonly referred to as the Spruce Goose, the Hughes Flying Boat (or H-4 Hercules) now resides in the newly completed Evergreen Aviation Museum, 1 mile east of McMinnville on Hwy 18.

Constructed in the early 1940s of

The Spruce Goose is in the newly completed Evergreen Aviation Museum.

laminated wood (birch, not spruce), a "nonessential" material in wartime, the single-hull, eight-engine aircraft weighs approximately 400,000 pounds. Surmounting increasing skepticism about the viability of the project, Hughes and his team

of engineers labored on, and in late 1947 Hughes himself piloted the Flying Boat in a successful trial flight. The plane lifted 70 feet off the water, flew 1 mile in less than a minute at a top speed of 80 miles an hour, then made a perfect landing.

The new museum, occupying a 121,000-square-foot facility, offers aviation fans the opportunity to see not only the Spruce Goose but 29 other world-famous aircraft as well. The museum is open daily, from 9 am to 5 pm, except Thanksgiving, Christmas and New Year. For information, check out the Web site at www.sprucegoose.org; or call (503) 434-4180. Admission: $9/adult, $7/seniors, veterans and active duty military members, $5/student with ID, free/child newborn-5; special prices for veterans and service members.

KIDS AT PDX

It's not worth a special trip, but Kids' Flight Deck, a 1,200-square-foot, interactive play area at Portland International Airport (aka PDX), is a welcome diversion for traveling families in limbo. Similar in concept to a popular structure at the San Jose airport, Portland's features a mock airplane, air-traffic control tower and weather center—all connected by intercom.

In the cockpit, "pilots" steer; in the cabin, "passengers" watch in-flight movies. The jet engine is a slide. The control tower has a radar map of air traffic and computer monitors that supervise incoming planes and control runway lights. The weather center is equipped with a computerized barometer that measures current conditions in Portland.

In designing the miniature airport, Portland-based Sienna Architecture Company gathered ideas from the Children's Museum, OMSI and airport employees. Kids' Flight Deck is located near the Delta and United terminals. For more information, call 503-460-4234.

Fee: $159/person

Panoramic views of the Willamette Valley and breathtaking scenes above Lake Oswego are the order of the day when you sign on for a tour with this hot-air balloon company. The adventure begins just before sunrise and ends approximately three hours later. Layered clothing, a warm jacket, comfortable shoes and slacks are recommended. Passengers are invited to participate with the inflation and launching process under the guidance of the pilot and ground crew. A light champagne picnic follows touchdown.

Vista Balloon Adventures Inc.
701 SE Sherk Pl, Sherwood 97140
503-625-7385
www.vistaballoon.com
Season: April-late October, daily (weather permitting)
Fees: $185/person, $179/person for group of two or three; $160/person for group of four or more

Arrive before dawn, when the air is cool and still, to help set up and inflate the hot-air balloon. Climb into the basket and find a comfortable spot in which to stand. Glide for an hour, wherever the wind takes you—over the rolling vineyards, orchards and farmlands of the Willamette Valley. Then touch down in an open field and await the ground crew. Return to the launch field for a picnic of tasty gourmet hors d'oeuvres, desserts and sparkling cider. It's a special-occasion outing, to be sure, but one you won't soon forget.

In business since 1989, the company recommends this trip for children 8 and older only. (For one thing, the basket is 4 feet high.) Reservations are required.

Chapter 4

ACTIVE PLAY: INDOOR FUN

Cabin fever. It's a dreaded chronic malady known to cause irreparable damage to the nervous systems of otherwise healthy mothers and fathers. How can you avoid falling victim to this perplexing and disabling condition? Get out of the house!

You don't have to be a skier to enjoy winter weather. There's plenty of fun to be had out of the cold weather and rain.

Bundle the kids up in rain slickers or warm coats, head out to the car or bus, and go looking for fun. There's plenty of action indoors at these local establishments.

Indoor Playgrounds

On a long, wet winter day, there's nothing better than taking the kids—especially young ones—to an indoor playground.

Indoor playgrounds vary from the commercial variety—filled with tube slides and ball pits—to the programs run by Portland's Parks and Recreation Department.

If you head to a commercial establishment, be ready for a crowd, especially on weekends or bad-weather days. It can get warm with all that energy being expended. Come prepared with a hand towel to mop your child's brow and a water bottle to slake his or her thirst.

Discovery Space at OMSI
(Oregon Museum of Science and Industry)
1945 SE Water Ave, Portland 97214
503-797-OMSI (6674)
www.omsi.edu
Hours: Summer: Daily, 9:30 am-5 pm (museum open until 7 pm). Winter: Tue-Sun, 9:30 am-5:30 pm (closed Mon except Portland Public Schools holidays)
Admission: $7/individual 14-62, $5/child 3-13 and senior 63 & over

Though it's not exactly a playground, the Discovery Space allows children 6 and under (accompanied by an adult) to delight in playing in the sand, splashing in the water and building with giant Legos.

You'll also find a small menagerie of animals (such as zebra finches and fish) for children to experience up close, and a mechanic's deck where kids can search for answers to the question "How do things work?"

In addition, there's a toddler space for children 24 months and younger, a nursing room for moms, changing tables in the rest rooms and a bulletin board full of information about events at OMSI and in the Portland area.

Kidopolis
Family Fun Center
29111 SW Town Center Loop W, Wilsonville
Exit 283 off I-5 (20 miles south of Portland)
503-685-5000
www.fun-center.com
Hours: Summer: Fri-Sat, 9 am-11 pm; Sun-Thurs, 9 am-10 pm. Fall/winter: Fri-Sat, 9 am-11 pm; Sun-Thurs, 11 am-9 pm
Fee: $5/child 3 & up, free/child 2 years & under, free/adult with child

Open since 1994, the Wilsonville Family Fun Center likes to remind you that "Fun" is its middle name. They're on to something here. Besides the attraction of the indoor playground, the center also offers redemption games and a video arcade; a full-service restaurant with animated, computerized entertainment and fountain water show; and the outdoor facilities—miniature golf, bumper boats, go-karts and batting cages. It's a winning formula, especially when it's sunny.

Take the whole family and the oldest will disappear (do you really want to know where?), leaving you to focus on the youngest. Set a time to rendezvous at Bullwinkle's Restaurant. The kids can have pizza; there are better options for you, including barbecued ribs and a salad bar. (See also Active Play: Outdoor Fun, Amusements.)

Indoor Park Programs

Portland Parks and Recreation offers indoor park programs—and often art programs, too—at several of its facilities. Typically these programs take place in a gym filled with balls, bikes and portable play structures. Sometimes trampolines are available. Parents supervise their own children and help with setup. Hours vary according to location and season, with most taking the summer off or at least cutting back hours. Drop-in fees are minimal.

- **Dishman Community Center**, 77 NE Knott; 503-823-3186
- **East Portland Community Center**, 740 SE 106th; 503-823-3450
- **Fulton Park Community Center**, 68 SW Miles St (off Barbur Blvd); 503-823-3180
- **Hillside Community Center**, 653 NW Culpepper Terrace; 503-823-3181
- **Montavilla Community Center**, 8219 NE Glisan; 503-823-4101
- **St. Johns Community Center**, 8427 N. Central; 503-823-3192
- **Sellwood Community Center**, 1436 SE Spokane; 503-823-3195
- **Southwest Community Center**, 6820 SW 45th; 503-823-2840

Following is a sampling of other indoor parks located throughout the Portland area. Most are cooperatives, which means that parents agree to pitch in and help with administrative tasks as well as with park setup and cleanup. Look for an indoor park in your neighborhood and call for details.

Portland

- **Buckman Indoor Park:** Basement of gymnasium at Child Services Center, SE 14th & Stark; 503-775-2575
- **Friendly House Indoor Park:** Friendly House Preschool, 2617 NW Savier; 503-228-4391
- **Garden Home Indoor Playground:** Garden Home Recreation Center, 7475 SW Oleson Rd; 503-244-1101.
- **Happy Place Indoor Park:** Northminster Presbyterian Church, 2823 N Portland Blvd; 503-289-0318
- **Kids' Town, USA:** Bethany Baptist Church, 4545 NW Kaiser Rd; 503-645-2106
- **Northeast Indoor Park:** Central Lutheran Church basement, NE 21st Ave & Schuyler; 360-883-6778
- **Rose City Indoor Park:** Faith Lutheran Church basement, 6140 NE Stanton (off Sandy Blvd); 503-283-7857
- **Southeast Indoor Park:** Trinity United Methodist Church, SE 39th Ave & Steele; 503-788-7194

Tigard/Beaverton/Hillsboro

- **Athletic Center Indoor Playground:** Howard M. Terpenning Recreation Complex Athletic Center, 15707 SW Walker Rd, Beaverton; 503-649-0307
- **Cedar Hills Indoor Playground:** Cedar Hills Recreation Center, 11640 SW Park Wy, Beaverton; 503-644-3855
- **Conestoga Gym Fun:** Conestoga Recreation & Aquatic Center, 9985 SW 125th, Beaverton; 503-524-3941
- **Tiny Tykes Indoor Play Park:** Tigard United Methodist Church, 9845 SW Walnut Pl, Tigard; 524-8794
- **Tyson Recreation Center Indoor Park:** Tyson Recreation Center, 1880 NE Griffin Oaks St, Hillsboro; 503-615-6552

INDOOR PARK PROGRAMS

Lake Oswego/West Linn
- **Lake Oswego Indoor Park:** 332 First St (Wizer's Shopping Center), Lake Oswego; 503-635-7132
- **West Linn Indoor Park:** Sunset Fire Hall, 2215 Long St., West Linn; 503-557-4700

Newberg
- **Newberg Indoor Park:** Newberg Friends Center, 708 E Second St., Newberg; 503-538-1808 or 503-554-0051

Milwaukie/Oregon City
- **Indoor Playground:** Oregon Institute

CAROUSELS

If you're looking for a change of pace, one where you just might have as much fun as your child does, check out the following carousels. With their tinkly, old-time music and lovingly carved animals, they'll transport you and your kids to a simpler time.

Carousel at Jantzen Beach SuperCenter
1405 Jantzen Beach Center, Portland
503-289-5555
Hours: Mon-Sat, 10 am-9 pm; Sun, 11 am-6 pm
Admission: $1/ride, free/child 2 & under

This 1921 C.W. Parker carousel has recently been restored and is now the centerpiece of the SuperCenter's new food court. Listed on the National Register of Historic Places, the carousel includes 72 elaborate, hand-carved, one-of-a-kind animals.

Herschell-Spillman Carousel
Oaks Amusement Park
Foot of SE Spokane St, Portland
503-233-5777
www.oakspark.com
Hours: Spring break & Sat-Sun until mid-June: noon-5. Mid-June-

early September: Tues-Thurs, noon-9 pm; Fri-Sat, noon-10 pm; Sun, noon-7 pm. September-mid-October: Sat-Sun, noon-dusk
Admission: $1.50/ride

This carousel isn't exactly indoors, but it is covered. Nicknamed "Noah's Ark," it features brightly colored wooden animals, each with a mate opposite it on the machine. Animals include horses, roosters, frogs, pigs, dogs, cats, kangaroos, storks, lions, goats, dragons and giraffes.

Salem's Riverfront Carousel
101 Front St, Salem 97310
503-540-0374
www.salemsriverfrontcarousel.org
Hours: Summer: Mon-Thurs, 10 am-7 pm; Fri-Sat, 10 am-9 pm; Sun, 11 am-6 pm. Winter: Mon-Thurs, 10 am-5 pm; Fri-Sat, 10 am-7 pm; Sun, 11 am-5 pm.
Admission: $1/ride

The paint's still fresh on the area's newest carousel. An Old World-style machine, it stands next to a playground (and within walking distance of A.C. Gilbert's Discovery Village) in a building on the banks of the Willamette River. This beauty features 42 horses and two "Oregon Trail" wagons, lovingly hand-carved and hand-painted by community

of Technology, 7726 SE Harmony Rd, Milwaukie; 503-794-8080

- **Oregon City Community Schools' Indoor Playground:** Eastham Community Center, 1404 Seventh St, Oregon City; 503-657-2434

Clackamas County

- **Healthy Start Playgroups:** Healthy Start sponsors free playgroups throughout Clackamas County, including ones in Wilsonville, Oregon City and Molalla. To find the one closest to you, call 503-655-8601, ext. 3.

Multnomah County

For the past 10 years, Multnomah County has funded parent-child development service programs throughout the area, aimed at families with children ages newborn through 5. They offer parent-education opportunities as well as free playgroups. Several offer groups in different languages. Call for more information.

- **Together Program**, North Portland; 503-240-8138
- **Common Bond**, Northeast Portland; 503-280-1616

- **Portland Impact**, Southeast Portland; 503-988-6000
- **Nurturing Families**, East Portland; 503-254-1772
- **Eastwind**, Gresham; 503-491-3300
- **Neighborhood House**, West Portland; 503-768-4461
- **Asian Family Center Parent Child Development Service**, all of Multnomah County's Southeast Asian population; 503-234-1541

Washington

- **Battle Ground Indoor Playpark:** Bethel Lutheran Church, 12919 NE 159th St, Brush Prairie; 360-687-1189

- **Clark County Indoor Play Park:** Elks Lodge, 11605 SE McGillivray Blvd, Vancouver; 360-253-7943
- **Little Critters Indoor Play Park:** First Congregational Church, 1220 NE 68th St, Vancouver; 360-737-0326

Swimming Pools

It's true that Oregon may not be blessed with many months of swimming-pool weather. But as the list below indicates, it's not hard to find a pool close to you where your child can discover the joys of swimming both outdoors and in.

North Clackamas Aquatic Park

7300 SE Harmony Rd, Milwaukie 97222
503-557-7873
Season: Year-round; call for hours
Fees: $9.99/adult, $6.99/youth 9-17, $4.99/child 3-8, free/child 2 & under, $1/spectator

A Disneyland of the deep, this place has it all: a wave pool, lap pool, shallow wading pool, diving pool, whirlpool and three water slides. The noise level and commotion on weekends turn some away, but for many the chaos is part of the fun.

Children under 8 years old must be accompanied in the water by a responsible person 13 or older. Snack foods are available from the on-site café; food and beverages from home are not allowed.

To beat sticker shock at the admission desk, plan your visits carefully. Arrive during the last hour of open swim and receive $2 off each admission. Or come on a Friday or Sunday during open swim, when special family rates ($12/resident family, $24/nonresident family) are avail-

SWIMMING POOLS

North Clackamas Aquatic Center is a state-of-the-art swim playpark.

able. (Family rate includes two parents and up to four children in the immediate family.) Take note: Diapers are not allowed in the pools, so bring swim diapers or purchase one from the center. Call for a complete schedule of lesson and open-swim times.

Portland Parks and Recreation Pools
503-823-SWIM (7946)
Fees: $2.50/adult, $1.50/child 17 & under

Portland Parks and Recreation manages five indoor and eight outdoor swimming pools, each of which offers a variety of programs, including swimming lessons, water-exercise classes and special open-swim hours. Suited to waders and beginning swimmers, most Portland pools have shallow ends that begin at 1.5 feet. Indoor pools are open year-round; outdoor pools are open from mid-June through Labor Day. Call your neighborhood pool for a schedule or to reserve the facility for a party.

Indoor Pools
- **Buckman Swim Pool**
  320 SE 16th Ave, Portland
  503-823-3668
- **Columbia Swim Pool**
  7701 N Chautauqua, Portland
  503-823-3669
- **Dishman Community Center and Indoor Pool**
  77 NE Knott, Portland
  503-823-3165
- **Metropolitan Learning Center Swim Pool**
  2033 NW Glisan, Portland
  503-823-3671
- **Portland Community College/Sylvania Swim Pool** (lessons only)
  12000 SW 49th Ave, Portland
  503-823-5130
- **Mount Scott Community Center and Swim Pool**
  5530 SE 72nd, Portland
  503-823-3183

- **Southwest Community Center and Swim Pool**
  6820 SW 45th, Portland
  503-823-2840

Outdoor Pools
- **Creston Park Swim Pool**
  SE 44th Ave & Powell, Portland
  503-823-3672
- **Grant Swim Pool**
  2300 NE 33rd Ave, Portland
  503-823-3674
- **Montavilla Community Center and Swim Pool**
  8219 NE Glisan, Portland
  503-823-3675
- **Peninsula Park Community Center and Swim Pool**
  6400 N Albina, Portland
  503-823-3677
- **Pier Swim Pool**
  N Seneca & St. Johns, Portland
  503-823-3678

MICHAEL CLAPP

Kids enjoy Creston Park Pool.

- **Sellwood Park Swim Pool**
  SE Seventh Ave & Miller, Portland
  503-823-3679
- **Wilson Swim Pool**
  1151 SW Vermont, Portland
  503-823-3680

DIVE IN FOR FUN

The Portland Parks aquatics team deserves credit for dreaming up some of the region's most creative summertime activities. No doubt many parents find themselves fighting the urge to dive in, too.

To kick off each summer session, Portland pools offer one week of free swimming lessons. Be sure to reserve in advance. Scholarships are available to those who wish to continue but find the costs prohibitive.

A free, open-swim time is scheduled at each pool weekly. Call your local pool for a schedule. The turnout is considerable; best to come only if your kids thrive on noise and splashing.

Dive-in Movies feature second-run flicks shown on a big screen poolside. The audience, equipped with inflatable rafts and inner tubes, watches from the superheated water. Hosted at local pools on weekend evenings in late July and August, the films are rated G or PG, and the lifeguards carry flashlights.

At Fun Days, staff members lead splash fests, water games and penny dives. Itty Bitty Beach Parties are held at the Grant, Montavilla, Sellwood and Creston pools for kids ages 6 months through 6 years and their parents. Call for dates and details.

Admission for both Dive-In Movies and Fun Days is the regular swimming fee ($2.50/adult, $1.50/child 17 & under).

Tualatin Hills Park and Recreation
503-645-7454
Resident: $2/adult, $1.50/child 3-17
Nonresident: $4/adult, $3/child

The Tualatin Hills Park and Recreation District manages six indoor pools and two outdoor pools, where swimming and diving lessons and family open-swim times are offered throughout the season. Indoor pools are open year-round; outdoor pools are open from mid-June through early September. Call your neighborhood pool for a schedule.

Special programs for individuals with handicaps include disabled and physically limited swimming at the Beaverton and Harman swim centers, hearing-impaired and deaf instruction at the Aloha Swim Center and drop-in swims at the Harman and Sunset pools.

Indoor Pools
- **Aloha Swim Center**
  18650 SW Kinnaman Rd, Aloha
  503-642-1586
- **Beaverton Swim Center**
  12850 SW Third Ave, Beaverton
  503-644-1111
- **Conestoga Recreation/ Aquatic Center**
  9985 SW 125th Ave, Beaverton
  503-524-3941
- **Harman Swim Center**
  7300 Scholls Ferry Rd, Portland
  503-643-6681
- **Recreation Complex Swim Center**
  15707 SW Walker Rd., Beaverton
  503-645-7454
- **Sunset Swim Center**
  13707 NW Science Park Dr, Portland
  503-644-9770

Outdoor Pools
- **Raleigh Outdoor Pool**
  3500 SW 78th Ave, Portland
  503-297-6888

- **Somerset West Outdoor Pool**
  NW 185th & Parkview Blvd
  Beaverton
  503-645-1413

Other Pools

Three suburbs also maintain indoor, public swim centers that host swimming lessons and open-swim hours year-round:

Lake Oswego High School Pool
2455 Country Club Rd, Lake Oswego
503-635-0330
Resident: $4/adult, $3/child, $2/senior
Nonresident: $5/adult, $4/child, $3/senior

Mount Hood Aquatic Center
26000 SE Stark St., Gresham
503-491-7243
Fee: $3.50/adult, $2.50/child 18 & under, $2.50/senior

Located on the campus of Mount Hood Community College, this swim center may be the metro area's best-kept secret. Its two indoor pools are open year-round; the Olympic-size outdoor pool is open in summer only. Call for family swim times and hours.

Tigard Swim Center
8680 SW Durham Rd, Tigard
503-431-5455
Fee: $3/adult, $2/child

Climbing Walls

Constructed from concrete, wood and a variety of other materials, and punctuated by bolted-on handholds, carabiners and dangling ropes, climbing walls are a big hit with fitness fanatics who are forced indoors during inclement weather. And it's no surprise that many kids are intrigued as well, especially those who were climbing (living room bookcases, neighbors' fences, brick chimneys . . .) before they could walk.

Rock climbing is a highly technical sport, and experienced climbers take their hobby seriously, so newcomers are advised to visit first when the gym isn't busy (i.e., right after school and in summer) and to come with an adult.

Safety is of primary importance when your life is dangling at the end of a rope. Children under 18 must produce a waiver form signed by a parent or guardian in order to use the equipment. It's strongly recommended that children enroll in an introductory class to start with, and parents are encouraged to learn to belay so they can supervise.

Another option for beginners is to reserve a group session with several friends. Typically scheduled during off-hours, group parties include a brief instruction period and lots of practice time with a staff belayer. Call for details.

CLIMBING SHOES

Don't throw away old tennis shoes. An uncomfortably tight pair of sneakers worn without socks makes a decent substitute for rock-climbing shoes and saves a few dollars in rental fees. For bouldering (technical climbing without ropes), however, it's worth springing for the real thing. Appropriate clothing for rock climbing is anything that's comfortable and roomy.

ClubSport
18120 SW Lower Boones Ferry Rd
Tigard
503-968-4500
www.clubsports.com
Hours: Mon-Fri, 10 am-11 pm (gym opens 6 am on Tues); Sat, 10 am-10 pm; Sun, 10 am-8 pm
Nonmember fees: $18/person; $8/equipment rental for shoes and harness

ClubSport is the biggest rock-climbing gym in Oregon, with 11,500 square feet of climbing space. Walls reach up to 45 feet high and feature top roping, leading and bouldering. During the school year, the club offers special kids' climbing times on Fridays from 6 to 9 pm and on Saturdays and Sundays from 10 am to 1 pm.

Mount Hood Aquatics and Rock Wall Center
26000 SE Stark St, Gresham
(on the Mount Hood Community College campus)
503-491-7243
Hours: Mon-Fri, 3-8:30 pm; Sat, noon-4:30 pm
Fees: $2.50/MHCC students, $6/adult, $4/child 18 & under; $5/equipment rental

This facility boasts an 1,800-square-foot rock wall. To use the structure, young climbers must be at least 12 years old and accompanied by an adult. In fall 2001, the college launched children's rock-climbing classes; call for details.

Portland Rock Gym
2034 SE Sixth Ave, Portland
503-232-8310
www.portlandrockgym.com
Hours: Mon-Fri, 11 am-11 pm; Sat, 9 am-7 pm; Sun, 11 am-6 pm

CLIMBING WALLS

Kids scale the wall at Portland Rock Gym.

Nonmember fees: $14/adult, $7/child 11 & under; $5/shoe rental, $3/harness rental

Portland Rock Gym, open since 1989, features 8,000 square feet of climbing walls and prides itself on variety. Equipped with a 40-foot lead wall, 35- and 20-foot top ropes, and bouldering areas, including a "cave," the gym does its best to simulate real-life outdoor experiences.

Introductory classes are offered on Saturday mornings and Wednesday evenings. Each three-hour session costs $49 (rental equipment included). Groups of up to six people can receive private instruction and practice with a staff belayer for $35 an hour plus an additional $3/person; rental equipment is extra. Once parents or other adults have received instruction, they are permitted to visit the gym to belay their youngster for free.

Family-friendly sessions called Friday Night Heights are held weekly. These include three hours of climbing for all ages and abilities for $20/person (equipment included). Call ahead for reservations.

REI

Two locations:
1798 Jantzen Beach Center
Portland 97217
503-283-1300
Climbing wall public hours (subject to change): Sat, 10 am-1 pm
Fees: Free

7410 SW Bridgeport, Tigard 97224
503-624-8600
Climbing wall public hours (subject to change): Sat, 10 am-1 pm
Fees: Free

Each of the metro area's two REI outdoor equipment stores features a

modest-size climbing wall designed for novice rope climbers. The walls are open to the public during select hours.

An REI supervisor helps rope in and belay the climbers. Children are welcome to try scaling the wall, provided they fit into a harness (minimum weight: approximately 40 pounds). Arrive early, especially on Saturdays, and expect to wait.

Stoneworks Inc. Climbing Gym
6775 SW 111th Ave, No. 205,
Beaverton 97008
503-644-3517
www.belay.com
Hours: Mon-Thurs, 4-10 pm; Fri, 4-8 pm; Sat-Sun, noon-8 pm
Fees: $10/day pass; $4/shoe rental, $2/harness rental; also offers a punch-card option
Annual membership: $525/2 individuals, $80/ each additional family member

Stoneworks caters to children and fields a great junior climbing team. The handholds here have been purposely placed close together so kids don't have to stretch. Devoted mostly to bouldering, the facility has more than 5,000 square feet of climbing surface, including walls up to 30 feet. An introductory climbing class for $40 includes three hours of instruction plus a pass and rental gear for a month.

Kids are invited to join the junior program, which meets Wednesdays, 4 to 7 pm. Participants, who compete up and down the West Coast, range in age from 8 through 20.

Bowling

Once upon a time, bowling meant a night out for Mom and Dad.

Now bumper bowling, along with so-called extreme, cosmic or glow-in-the-dark bowling, has given new life to the sport.

Bumpers are pads, or in some cases rails, that deflect the ball away from the gutters and turn what was once a physically technical pastime into a forgiving one. In bumper bowling, even the weakest, meekest novice throws strikes. (Warning to adults: Use bumpers at your own risk; they are known to be addictive.)

The following alleys offer bumper bowling at various times. They also offer birthday-party packages for kids, and some even sponsor bumper-bowling leagues on Saturday mornings for children age 3 and up. Call ahead for hours of operation and to ensure lane availability. Call, too, to get the scoop on when cosmic bowling (popular even with older kids) takes place.

Rental-shoe sizes vary, but if your child's feet are too small, he or she is usually welcome to bowl in sneakers or socks. Prices for rental shoes vary (usually they cost about $1.75); some places offer free shoes for kids on weekdays.

AMF 20th-Century Lanes
3550 SE 92nd Ave, Portland
503-774-8805
Fees: $2.75-$3.75/adult, $2.25/child 18 & under

AMF Cascade Lanes
2700 NE 82nd Ave, Portland
503-255-2635
Fees: $3.75/adult, $2.75/child 17 & under

BOWLING / ROLLER SKATING

AMF Pro-300 Lanes
3031 SE Powell Blvd, Portland
503-234-0237
Fees: Mon-Fri until 5 pm: $2.75/adult,
$2.25/child; Mon-Fri after 5 pm and
Sat-Sun: $3.75/person per game

AMF Rockwood Lanes
18500 SE Stark St, Portland
503-665-2123
Fees: $2-$3/adult, $1.85/child

AMF Timber Lanes
2306 NE Andresen Rd
Vancouver, Washington
503-285-4340
Fees: Mon-Thurs, $2.75/person; Fri-
Sat, $3.75/person; Sun, $1.59/person

Gladstone Lanes
20100 McLoughlin Blvd, Gladstone
503-656-2668
www.gladstonelanes.com
Fees: $2.50-$3.50/adult, $2-3/child

Grand Central Bowl
808 SE Morrison St, Portland
503-232-5166
Fees: $15.95-$19.95/hour per lane;
Sun & Mon nights, $1/game

Hollywood Bowl
4030 NE Halsey St, Portland
503-288-9237
Fees: Mon-Sat., $2.75/adult before 5
pm, $3/adult after 5 pm, $2.50/child;
Sun, $1.50/person per game

Interstate Lanes
6049 N Interstate, Portland
503-285-9881
Fees: $3.25/adult, $1.75/child
Call for specials.

Kellogg Bowl
10306 SE Main St, Milwaukie

503-659-1757
Fees: $3/game

Sunset Lanes
12770 SW Walker Rd, Beaverton
503-646-1116
Fees: $2.75/person before 6 pm;
$3.50/person after 6 pm

Tigard Bowl
11660 SW Pacific Hwy, Tigard
503-639-2001
Fees: $22/hour for up to 6 people,
shoes included

Valley Lanes
9300 SW Beaverton-Hillsdale Hwy
Beaverton
503-292-3523
www.valleylanes.com
Fees: $2.25/game

Wilsonville Lanes
29040 SW Town Center Loop
Wilsonville
503-682-2346
Fees: $2.50-$3.25/adult, $2-$2.75/child
or senior

Roller Skating

Who would have predicted that roller skating could be so hip? The advent of in-line skates has forever revolutionized skating—and roller rinks 'round the country couldn't be happier. Easier than ice skating and a lot warmer, roller skating is fun for the whole family.

Skaters may bring their own (in-line skates are allowed as long as they don't have black brakes) or rent them. Call for information about times for information on family skate sessions, rates (they can vary according to day and time) and birthday-party packages.

Oaks Park Skating Rink
Foot of SE Spokane, Portland 97202
503-236-5722
www.oakspark.com
Fees: $4.50-$5.75, skates included

This rink is one of the largest on the West Coast. It has a well-maintained wooden rotunda floor and is equipped with a genuine Wurlitzer theater organ.

The rink offers special morning skating sessions each week for children 6 and under. These sessions include a short lesson. Parents can then go out on the floor with their street shoes to help their youngsters practice new skills. Call for details about this program and to find out more about special family night pricing.

Mount Scott Community Center
5530 SE 72nd Ave, Portland 97206
503-823-3183
Fees: $1/person, skates included

Opportunities for skaters of all ages to learn abound here. They even offer a Roller Hockey for Families class.

Skate Church
Central Bible Church
(See Skate Parks, Outdoor Fun.)

Skate World
1220 NE Kelly, Gresham
503-667-6543
Fees: $3-$5.50, skates included; $3 extra/in-line skate rental

A special session for home-schoolers ($3/person, skate rental included) takes place every Thursday, September through June, 11 am to 1 pm.

The rink also offers a Tiny Tots program for preschoolers and caregivers on Thursdays from 9:30 to 11 am during the school year. For $2.75 per child, youngsters receive 30 minutes of instruction, followed by games and playtime. Adults are welcome on the rink in street shoes

during these sessions, as are strollers.

Skate World
4395 SE Witch Hazel Rd
Hillsboro 97123
503-640-1333
Fees: $3-$6.75, skates included; $13/family of 4 (parent must skate, too); $3 extra/in-line skate rental

The rink is reserved for home-schoolers ($3/person, skate rental included) the first and third Friday of the month, September through June, 1 to 3 pm.

Here, the Tiny Tots program for preschoolers and caregivers is on Saturdays from 10 to 11 am during the school year. The cost is $2.75/child.

Ice Skating

Olympic skaters make it look easy, but anyone who has tried knows ice skating is a slippery proposition. You can expect your beginners to wibble-wobble on rubbery ankles and to cling to you for balance. Come prepared—both of you—with gloves and padding. You'll likely spend some time prone on the ice.

The rinks below offer lessons and birthday-party packages for children. Call for public skating schedules and other details.

Ice Chalet at Clackamas Town Center
1200 SE 82nd St, Clackamas
503-786-6000
Fees: $6.25/adult, $5.25/child 17 & under; $2.50/skate rental, $3.50/hockey-skate rental

Ice Chalet at Lloyd Center
2201 Lloyd Center, Portland
503-288-4599
Fees: $6.50/adult, $5.50/child 17 & under; $2.50/skate rental

ICE SKATING / LASER TAG ARENAS

Mountain View Ice Arena
14313 SE Mill Plain,
Vancouver, Washington
360-896-8700
Fees: $6/person 6 & over, $3/child 5 &
under or 55 & over; $2.25/skate rental

Sherwood Ice Arena
20407 SW Borchers Dr, Sherwood
503-625-5757
Fees: $6/person; $2.50/skate rental

Valley Ice Arena
9250 Beaverton-Hillsdale Hwy
Beaverton
503-297-2521
Fees: $7/person, skates included;
free/child 4 & under with paid adult

Laser Tag Arenas

"Capture the flag" meets *Star Wars*. This, in essence, is the concept behind the high-tech laser games that are so popular with kids—and many adults. Equipped with laser "guns" and computerized vest packs, players are divided into opposing teams whose mission is to disable the enemy and claim their home base.

Disappearing into dark, mysterious, cavernlike mazes obscured by fog machines and illuminated by black lights and special lighting effects, players are immersed in a three-dimensional video game in which stealth, cunning and quickness reap the biggest rewards. Games last about 25 minutes, and monitors on duty throughout the arena ensure there is no running or physical contact among players. Still, arena owners do not recommend laser tag for children younger than 6 or 7 years old.

Hard-core patrons, who tend to be young adult males, come dressed in black

and depart drenched in sweat. Weekdays, when the arenas are less crowded, are best for families. If you want to play on a weekend, call ahead to reserve.

Family Fun Center
29111 SW Town Center Loop W
Wilsonville
Exit 283 off I-5 (20 miles south of
Portland)
503-685-5000
www.fun-center.com
Hours: Summer — Fri-Sat 9 am-11 pm;
Sun-Thurs 9 am-10 pm; Fall/winter —
Sun-Thurs, 11 am-9 pm; Fri-Sat, 9 am-
11 pm.
Fees: $5/game

LazerXtreme is just one of the many activities available at this amazing six-acre amusement park. The arena here is filled with music, fog and strobe lights. (For more on the Fun Center, see Amusements, Outdoor Fun.)

Laserport
10975 SW Canyon Rd, Beaverton 97005
503-526-9501
Hours (subject to change): Mon-Thurs,
noon-9 pm; Fri, noon-midnight; Sat,
10 am-midnight; Sun, 11 am-9 pm
Fees: $7/first game, $5/each additional game

Laserport computers keep a running tally of game scores and relay that information to voice chips in players' equipment vests. There's also a full-service pizza kitchen, coin-operated video and simulation games, and a party room. Reservations are recommended for groups of 10 or more.

Ultrazone
Holly Farm Center, 16074 SE
McLoughlin Blvd, Milwaukie

503-652-1122
www.ultrazoneportland.com
Hours (subject to change): School
year: Tues-Thurs, 4-10 pm; Fri, 3 pm-
midnight; Sat, 11 am-midnight; Sun,
11 am-9 pm. Summer: Mon-Thurs,
noon-9 pm; Fri, noon-midnight; Sat,
noon-11 pm; Sun, noon-9 pm
Fees: $5-$6.50/game

Beyond its super sound system and
three-team format, Ultrazone has an
added wild card: an enemy robot sen-
tinel, programmed to fire randomly,
that roves the upper level.

Teens congregate here after school
and on weekends to play laser tag, as
well as video and simulation games. Ultrazone makes a point of maintaining a
wholesome atmosphere. On report-card
days, students form a long line to cash in
on discounts for A's and B's. Sunday is
Family Day, when parents play free with
paying children until closing. For a deal,
go on Fridays when you can play from
8 pm to midnight for $14 per person.

Reservations are required for large
groups and birthday parties only.

Tours

Their questions begin almost as
soon as they can talk: "Why?" "How
come?" At first you dutifully try to
answer, but before long these queries
don't even register. And that's OK. Like
the involuntary jerk of the lower leg after
the doctor taps that tender spot just
below the kneecap, toddlers can't help
themselves; their questioning is reflexive.

Not for long. Within a year or two,
you notice a change. Your ears prick
up; this could get interesting. "Where
does the mail come from?" "Why is

cheese different colors when milk's
white?" "Where do the police officers'
horses go when they're tired?" "Who
decides what's news?"

School teachers have long known
that one of the best ways to motivate
children is not to explain, but to show.
But why wait for a teacher to work a
field trip or group tour into the cur-
riculum? The locations below open
their back doors to the general public
for a peek at what really goes on.

The Candy Basket
1924 NE 181st Ave, Portland
503-666-2000; reservations required
Hours: Tues-Thurs, 9:30 am
Duration: About 45 minutes
Recommended ages: All ages
Group size: 30 maximum

Right out of *Charlie and the Chocolate Factory*, the tour of this 60-year-
old, family-run operation begins beside
a 20-foot chocolate cascade. Watch the
candy-making process up close, then
taste the results. Learn about fudge,
peanut brittle, chocolate molds, how
creams are dipped and how to package boxed candy.

Chevys Mexican Restaurant
Various metro-area locations
Hours: Times vary from store to store
Recommended ages: 3 & over
Group size: Some locations ask for a
minimum of 10; plan to have at least 1
adult for every 5 children

You have to feel good about a restaurant that's willing to let you in the
kitchen. Follow a patron's order from
computer to chef to table. The famous
El Machino tortilla press turns out 900
tortillas an hour—that's one every 53 sec-
onds! Leave with a goody bag full of fun
stuff, including a coupon for a free kid's
meal. (See also Basics, Restaurants.)

TOURS

Learn about the care and training of horses at the Mounted Police Horse Stables.

Franz Bakery

340 NE 11th Ave, Portland 97232
503-232-2191, ext. 365; reservations required
Season: Mid-September-June
Hours: Mon & Wed-Sat; times vary
Duration: 90 minutes
Recommended ages: 7 & over
Group size: 10 minimum, 40 maximum

From sifting flour to packaging loaves of bread to loading them on delivery trucks, visitors see it all. Try samples as you go. Sandals and jewelry are not allowed.

KGW Channel 8 News

1501 SW Jefferson, Portland
503-226-5000; reservations required
www.kgw.com
Hours: Mon-Fri, 9-11:30 am & 1-3:30 pm
Duration: 1 hour
Recommended ages: 7 & over

Begin the tour with a brief video, which explains what goes on in a newsroom, then see the real thing. Watch reporters and anchors gather facts and draft scripts. Visit the master control room, where the taping takes place; the director's control booth; and the weather center.

Mounted Police Horse Stables

1362 NW Front Ave, Portland
503-823-2100; reservations required
Hours: Winter/spring, Tues-Fri, 10 am; summer/fall, Tues-Fri, 2 pm
Duration: 30-45 minutes
Group size: 20 maximum

Follow an officer through the stables and learn about the care and training of the horses in the Portland police force. As one officer proudly says, "They're nine of the finest horses this side of the Mississippi."

Oregon Candy Farm

Hwy 26, Sandy 97055
503-668-5066
Candy-making hours: Mon-Thurs, 9 am-5 pm

While the Oregon Candy Farm doesn't actually offer a tour, it does offer a behind-the-scenes view of the candy-making process to visitors of all ages who line up to watch through large windows and to receive a free sample. While the store is open every day (Mon-Fri, 9 am-5 pm; Sat-Sun, noon-5 pm), candy making takes place Monday through Thursday only.

The Oregonian

1320 SW Broadway, Portland 97201
503-221-8336; reservations required
Hours: Wed & Thurs, 9:30-11:30 am
Duration: 2 hours
Minimum age: 12 years
Group size: 24 maximum

Begin at the Broadway building, where you'll watch a brief instructional video, visit the newsroom and see how the paper is laid out. Then move on to the plant, at 16th Ave. & Taylor, to watch the plate-making, printing and mail-room processes. The two Oregonian facilities are about 15 blocks apart, and tour groups must provide their own transportation.

Portland Center for the Performing Arts

1111 SW Broadway, Portland 97205
503-248-4335
www.pcpa.com
Hours: Wed, 11 am; Sat, 11 am-1 pm (every half hour); first Thurs of month, 6 pm
Duration: 1 hour
Recommended ages: 4 and up
Group size: No restriction

Visit the regal Arlene Schnitzer Concert Hall, built in the 1920s, and the Newmark and Dolores Winningstad

A tour of the Portland Center for the Performing Arts is as good as a backstage pass.

theaters in the contemporary New Theatre Building next door. Together with the Keller Auditorium, these buildings make up the Portland Center for the Performing Arts, one of the largest in the nation. Learn about the theaters' histories, art and architecture, and—if you're lucky—get a peek at a dress rehearsal.

Portland International Airport

7000 NE Airport Wy, Portland
503-944-7057
www.portlandairportpdx.com
Hours: Mon-Fri, 9 am-4 pm
Duration: one hour
Recommended ages: 8 & over
Group size: Varies

An expansion project at the airport on the B and C concourse has resulted in a new area that is incredibly creative. This tour will have you checking out a glass rocket, as well as an exhibit titled "The Mighty Columbia, River of Trade," which houses cases of artifacts, video and computer monitors filled with scenes of the Columbia and Willamette rivers, and a real tug pilothouse showing films of tugboats at work. You'll also see artist Larry Kirkland's bronze *Columbia River,* which is embedded in a blue terrazzo floor and snakes its way among whale benches. (Even if you don't have a group for a tour, call to ask about info that would allow you to take a self-guided tour.)

Tillamook Cheese Factory

Hwy 101, Tillamook 97141
503-815-1300
www.tillamookcheese.com
Hours: Fall/winter/spring, daily, 8 am-6 pm; mid-June-Labor Day, daily, 8 am-8 pm
Recommended ages: All ages
Duration: Self-guided
Group size: No limit

Begin the self-guided tour in the exhibit hall. Here a mechanical cow demonstrates the milking process and a short video provides a history of the Tillamook factory. Then move upstairs, where three videos help explain the cheese-making process on view on the factory floor below. End the tour with complimentary samples of cheese. (You may not be able to resist buying an ice cream cone, though it's hard to choose from among the 40 flavors.)

Other ideal destinations for school field trips and scout outings include the following, which offer group tours:

- **Bonneville Dam**, 541-374-8820
- **Fox 49 TV station**, 503-548-4949
- **OPB TV station**, 503-244-9900

Extras

Archers Afield
Tigard Plaza, 11945 SW Pacific Hwy
Tigard
503-639-3553
Hours: Mon-Fri, 9 am-9 pm; Sat, 9 am-6 pm; Sun, 10 am-6 pm
Fees: $3.75/day with your own bow; $10/recurve bow rental, $15/compound bow rental

Archers Afield, a carpeted indoor archery range and store, features 30 shooting lanes and 60 targets. Serious archers come here for lessons and practice. Curious beginners are welcome, but are encouraged to take a lesson before renting equipment. One of the most popular ways of learning for beginners of all ages is the Wednesday-evening Big Kids Little Kids League. During these six-week sessions (6:30-7:30 pm), a coach and equipment are provided for $28.50/person.

No unusual physical strength is required by the sport, so children as young as 5 years old are capable of mastering it. Archers Afield stocks rental equipment for kids this little, and rental fees may be applied toward equipment purchases at the store.

Patrons are allowed to bring snacks from home to enjoy at the diner booths.

Family Country Dance
Multnomah Art Center Gymnasium
503-357-5997
Season and hours: October-April, second Sat of every month, 5-7 pm; dance followed by potluck
Fees: $5/adult, $3/child under 16 years; free/infant; $15/family maximum

The motto of the Portland Country Dance Community, which organizes Family Country Dance potluck gatherings, is "If your kids can walk, they can dance. (So can you.)" This family dance series is designed for beginners—both adults and children.

A caller offers instruction in a variety of American folk dances, and the steps are purposely kept rudimentary. Kids like best the live folk bands, with their fiddles, guitars, mandolins and pianos.

Wear comfortable clothes and shoes, bring a dish for the potluck that follows and expect to meet new people; about 100 typically attend.

Chapter 5

FARMS

To many city kids, chicken nuggets might as well grow on trees. And potatoes—don't they spring from the ground precut and fried? When your kids begin to grow suspicious of their food—to dissect their peas, spit out tomato seeds, and refuse hamburger ("this is COW!!")—it's time to visit a farm.

Plan to get dirty and to return home with something fresh and exotic for supper. Let the children help prepare the new food (farm stands can often supply recipes), and make a pact over the meal to return at each new season for another day in the country and another dietary experiment.

Berries & Orchards

Portland's mild, damp weather grows more than moss, mold, and mildew. The metro area is blessed with an abundance of fresh-grown produce (chiefly apples, pears, peaches, cherries, berries, hazelnuts, and walnuts),

FREEZING BERRIES

When harvesting fruit, wear hats and sunscreen. Show children how to avoid thorns on berry bushes, how to maneuver among the bushes, and how to determine which fruits are ripe (perhaps the farmer will share his secrets). Some farms prohibit children from climbing ladders and trees; you may want to adopt strict rules yourself.

Pick only what you can reasonably use. Many fruits don't freeze well, but most berry varieties can be frozen if you follow this method: Remove stems, wash and drain berries on a towel. (Wash delicate raspberries by placing them in a colander first, then submerging the colander in a sink full of water. Raise the colander to drain.) Spread fruit in a single layer on a cookie sheet covered in wax paper. Place the pan in the freezer for two hours. Remove pan from freezer, scoop frozen berries into plastic bags, and return to freezer.

and dozens of farmers are glad for help at harvest time. Reservations are not necessary, but call ahead to determine the course of the season. Ideally you want to plan your picking early in the harvest and early in the day for the best selection. U-pick establishments often supply containers, but take some along just in case. (The long, flat boxes available at nurseries work best.) When you're finished, your haul is weighed and you pay by the pound.

The *Tri-County Farm Fresh Produce Guide*, published annually in the spring by an association of member farms, is a comprehensive guide to local orchards, nurseries, and farms. Copies are available at libraries, chambers of commerce, and local county extension offices. For additional information about regional harvests, call the Ripe & Ready Hotline: 503-226-4112 (updated weekly, mid-April-November).

Bulb Farms

In spring these three Willamette Valley bulb farms put on quite a show. Arrayed in neat rows, acres of flowers—a symphony of nature's purest colors—take their bows in unison. Children are welcome to explore the display fields, which are planted with hundreds of varieties so customers can select favorites to order, but farmers ask that they take care to stay in between rows to avoid damaging the flowers. There's no charge to visit these farms—unless, of course, you wind up going home with fresh flowers and bulbs.

Cooley's Gardens Inc.
11553 Silverton Rd NE, Silverton 97381
503-873-5463

MICHAEL CLAPP

Swan Island Dahlias features more than 40 acres of flowers.

www.cooleysgardens.com
Season/hours: Early to mid-June, 8 am-7 pm daily

Ten acres of iris display gardens and seedlings, weekend food booth, indoor cut-flower show.

Schreiner's Iris Gardens
3625 Quinaby Rd, Salem 97303
503-393-3232
www.schreinersgardens.com
Season/hours: Late May-early June, daylight hours

One-acre iris display garden, picnic tables. A gift shop is open, too, during bloom season.

Swan Island Dahlias
995 NW 22nd Ave, Canby 97013
503-266-7711
www.dahlias.com
Season/hours: August-September, daily dawn to dusk

The largest dahlia grower in the nation, this farm features more than 40 acres of the flowers for public viewing. Fresh cut flowers are available in season as well. Visit the farm for the Indoor Dahlia Show in late August/early September and view more than 250 arrangements with 30 varieties of the colorful bulbs and blossoms.

Wooden Shoe Bulb Co.
33814 S. Meridian Rd
Woodburn 97071
800-711-2006, 503-634-2243
www.woodenshoe.com
Season/hours: March 20-April 20, 9 am-6 pm

Fifty-acre daffodil display garden, 30-acre tulip display garden, entertainment, demonstrations, picnic tables, weekend food booth.

Pumpkin Harvests

Squirrels collect nuts. Birds fly south. People go to the pumpkin patch, another rite of autumn.

At last count, more than a dozen metro-area farms were featuring these colorful squashes in time for Halloween. Some make a month-long party of it, with hay rides, hay mazes, spooky trails, funny dioramas, and festive goodies. Call ahead to confirm dates and hours, then pray for a break in the clouds.

Fantasy Trail at Wenzel Farm
19754 S. Ridge Rd, Oregon City 97045 (10 miles east of Oregon City)
503-631-2047
Season/hours: October— Mon-Sat, 7-10 pm; December — Mon-Sat, 6-9 pm
Fees: $3.50/adult; $3/child 12 years & under

At Halloween, the lighted, wooded Fantasy Trail at Wenzel Farm may be full of spooky sights and sounds, but it's never too scary. All ages will enjoy the trail as well as the 40-foot castle, which is haunted at Halloween but turns into a winter wonderland at Christmas time. Return in December to experience the magical scene.

Fir Point Farms
14601 Arndt Rd, Aurora 97002 (20 miles from downtown Portland)
503-678-2455
Season/hours: April-December — Tues-Sun, 9 am-6 pm

The annual Pumpkin Fest packs this 75-acre spread every weekend in October, when special activities include a deep, dark hay maze (carry a flash-light just in case), corn maze, hay slide, pony and hay rides, half-mile haunted trail, and refreshments.

You can also pick your own flowers and vegetables here, examine the apiary and greenhouse, and gape at the goats who romp on ramps set amid the tree-tops. Your youngest will enjoy seeing the chickens, turkeys, and rabbits, too.

Flower Farmer
(See Special Farms.)

Lakeview Farms
31345 NW North Ave
North Plains 97133 (about 20 miles from downtown Portland)
503-647-2336
Season/hours: October — Mon-Sat, 9 am-5 pm; Sun, 10 am-5 pm. (Also open some days in September and December — call for specifics.)

Lakeview Farms' 15-acre spread has lovely views out over rolling agricultural land, but most visitors are too intent on finding the perfect pumpkin to notice. This is the place to come if you prefer literally "picking" pumpkins (bring a pocket knife or garden shears). The vines are tall and prickly, so you may opt instead to peruse the supply of prepicked pumpkins in the mown meadow.

The Lakeview theme is transportation. Take the four-car miniature train to the patch through a haunted tunnel. Return across the lake by barge, but beware of a pair of Loch Ness monsters.

The grounds—green grass punctuated by a grove of tall evergreens—also feature farm animals, a gift shop, snack shack (weekends only), hay maze, and educational displays about farming. There are no restrooms, just portable toilets.

Rasmussen Fruit & Flower Farm

3020 Thomsen Rd, Hood River 97031
(about one hour from Portland)
541-386-4622, 800-548-2243
www.rasmussenfarms.com
Season/hours: Mid-April-mid-
December, 9 am-6 pm daily

This 20-acre farm with u-pick sunflowers and pumpkins hosts several distinct harvest festivals. In July, there's a celebration surrounding cherries. In September, there's the Pear Party, with free samples, pear cider, pear pie, and live music. The Apple Express follows, with free samples, apple cider, apple pie, and "aebelskivers"—tiny, Danish apple pancakes. And in October, there's Pumpkin Funland, a holiday tradition. During the pumpkin festival, the greenhouse is decorated for fall with as many as 50 scenes with storybook characters as well as farm and zoo animals created from vegetables, squashes, and gourds. Other activities include a mildly scary Halloween Hut and a corn maze.

The Pumpkin Patch

16511 NW Gillihan Rd
Sauvie Island 97231 (about 10 miles
northwest of Portland)
503-621-3874
www.the pumpkinpatch.com.
Season/hours: June-October, 9 am-6
pm daily

Check out the bunnies, birds, bees and other animals in the Pumpkin Patch's 100-year-old red barn, which opens in mid-July. The farm's annual Harvest Festival on Labor Day weekend is a popular event. The farm is also busy during October when you can catch a free hayride out to the u-pick pumpkin fields to select your own jack-o-lantern-to-be from an assortment that comes in all shapes and sizes. Older children especially will enjoy the challenge of figuring out the farm's amazing MAiZE, carved out of a cornfield where the stalks are 9 feet tall. (Call or check the farm's Web site for details about the MAiZE's hours and admission; additional information can be found at www.cornfieldmaze.com).

PICKING TIPS

Even if the sun's shining on pumpkin-picking day, take boots along in the car for insurance. Though you'll likely have many shapes and hues to choose from, in most cases, the pumpkins will already have been cut from the vine. If wheelbarrows and wagons are scarce, be prepared to carry what you select to a scale for weigh-in (an old pillowcase works well). Most places charge by the pound.

Following is a sampling of still more area farms that offer pumpkin patches and harvest activities. Call for details:

- **Baggenstos Farms**, 16520 SW Beef Bend Rd, Sherwood 97140, 503-590-4301
- **Duyck's Peachy-Pig Farm**, 3480 SW Johnson School Rd, Cornelius 97113, 503-357-3570
- **Gramma's Place**, 21235 SW Pacific Hwy, Sherwood. 503-625-7104.
- **Hagg's Tree Farm & Pumpkin Patch**, 18175 SW McCormick Hill Rd, Hillsboro 97123, 503-628-1007
- **Hartnell Farms**, 8481 SE Jannsen Road, Clackamas 97015, 503-655-1297.

PUMPKIN HARVESTS / FARMERS' MARKETS

- **Hoffman's Dairy Garden**, 6815 S. Knightsbridge Rd, Canby. 503-266-4703.
- **Koch Family Farm**, 11350 SW Tualatin-Sherwood Rd, Tualatin 97062, 503-692-5749.
- **Kruger's Farm Market**, 17100 NW Sauvie Island Rd, Portland 97231, 503-621-3489.
- **Lee Farms**, 21975 SW 65th Ave, Tualatin 97062, 503-638-1869.
- **Oliphant Orchard**, 23995 SW Pacific Hwy, Sherwood 97140, 503-625-7705.
- **Peterson Farms Apple Country**, 4800 NW Glencoe Rd, Hillsboro 97124, 503-640-5649.
- **Plumper Pumpkin Patch**, 11435 NW Old Cornelius Pass Rd, Portland 97231, 503-645-9561.
- **Rossi Farms**, 3839 NE 122nd Ave, Portland 97230, 503-253-5571.
- **Three Rivers Farms**, 2525 North Baker Dr, Canby 97013, 503-266-8055.
- **Trapold Farms**, 5211 NE 148th Ave, Portland 97230, 503-253-5103.

Farmers' Markets

Visiting a farmers' market is the next best thing to getting muddy in your own garden. Besides, a parsnip gains personality when you've met its farmer. In summer and fall, produce-growers congregate in local squares and parking lots to display fresh-picked fruits, vegetables, and homemade treats and crafts. Colorful and personal, these scenes resemble the street markets that are still plentiful abroad.

The state's Agricultural Development and Marketing office (1207 NW Naito Parkway, Suite 104, Portland 97209-2832) produces a brochure annually called "Oregon Farmers Markets" that lists markets statewide. To receive one of these brochures, call 503-872-6600, or visit www.oda.state.or.us/Ag_Development/farmers_markets.html

Here is a sampling of some of the Portland area's most vibrant markets:

Beaverton Farmers' Market
503-643-5345
www.beavertonfarmersmarket.com
Off of Hall Blvd, between Third and Fifth avenues
Season/Hours: Mid May-late October: Sat, 8 am-1:30 pm; mid-July-late September: Wed, 3 pm-7 pm

The largest agricultural-only farmers market in the Northwest, this market features produce from 90 to 100 growers plus live music every Saturday.

Canby Growers' Market
503-632-4041
Railroad parking lot, First Avenue North and Grant Street
Season/Hours: Early May-late October: Sat, 9 am-1 pm

In addition to local produce, you'll find ornamental trees, ground covers and flowers as well as crafts and music.

Forest Grove Farmers' Market
503-359-7887
Corner of Pacific Avenue and Cedar Street
Season/hours: Mid-May-early October: Sat, 8 am-1 pm

Offers produce and garden-related products, but also features crafts and even a section devoted to kid-entrepreneurs. On the third Saturday of each month, you'll find crafts, a storytime and more fun activities for kids.

It's all about kneading at Summer Loaf, the annual celebration at Portland Farmer's Market.

Hillsboro Farmers Market
503-844-6685
Two locations:
Second and E. Main at
Courthouse Square
Season/hours: Early May-late
October: Sat, 8 am-1 pm
First to Third Streets on Main
beginning at Courthouse Square
Season/hours: Early June-late August:
Tues, 5 pm-8:30 pm
Includes produce, entertainment
and arts and crafts. Tuesdays usually
feature children's activities.

Hollywood Farmers' Market
503-233-3313
NE Hancock, between 44th and 45th,
Portland
Season/hours: Late May-late October:
Sat, 8 am-1 pm
Features produce, plants and food,
plus weekly music and entertainment.

Lake Oswego Farmers' Market
503-675-3983
www.ci.oswego.or.us/farmersmarket/
farmmart.htm
Millennium Plaza Park, corner of First
and Evergreen
Season/hours: Mid-May-late
September: Sat, 8 am-1 pm
Along with the produce, you'll find
kid-friendly activities just about every
week, including story and song sessions and craft activities.

People's All Organic Farmers Market
503-232-9051
3029 SE 21st Ave., Portland
Season/hours: Early April-late
November: Wed, 2 pm-7 pm
Features all-organic produce.

Portland Farmers Market
503-241-0032
www.portlandfarmersmarket.org

FARMERS' MARKETS / SPECIAL FARMS

Three locations:
South Park Blocks at Portland State
University, SW Park & Montgomery
Season/hours: Early May-late
October: Sat, 8 am-1 pm

Dowtown Park Blocks at Schmanski
Park, SW Salmon and Park
Season/hours: Late May-early
October: Wed, 10 am-2 pm

North Park Blocks in Pearl District
Season/hours: Early July-late August:
(weekday TBA), 4 pm-8 pm

Artichokes to zucchini, fresh bread
to flowers — it's all here. Local chefs
frequently host on-stage cooking
demonstrations using fresh, seasonal
ingredients purchased at the market.
Watch for special events like the Great
Pumpkin Festival in October.

Tigard Area Farmers' Market
503-244-2479
Parking lot at corner of Hall Boulevard
and Oleson Road
Season/hours: Late May-late October:
Sat, 8 am-1 pm

You'll find primarily produce, plants
and flowers here, but there are also crafts.
Weekly entertainment is scheduled.

Wilsonville Farmers Market
503-682-0411
Wilsonville Town Center Park,
Clackamas County Visitors Center
Season/hours: Selected Saturdays
throughout summer, 8 am-1 pm

Features produce and crafts.

Special Farms

Alpenrose Dairy
6149 SW Shattuck Rd, Portland 97221
503-244-1133

www.alpenrose.com
Season/hours: open on selected sum-
mer Sundays and for special events
Special events: Easter, summer, &
Christmas

In the 19th century, the rolling hillsides of southwest Portland were dot-
ted with dairy farms, which were
largely operated by Swiss immigrants.
One pioneering dairyman, Florian
Cadonau, owned a small farm at SW
35th Ave. and Vermont, and began
delivering milk in 3-gallon cans by
horse-drawn wagon in 1891. More
than a century later, Cadonau's ances-
tors are still in the dairy business.
Though no longer milking cows, the
Alpenrose operation purchases milk
from local Tillamook and Willamette
Valley farms for its lines of milk, ice
cream, cottage cheese, and sour cream.

Local families may not associate
Alpenrose with milk, however, because

YEAR ROUND FUN

Alpenrose deserves a blue ribbon for
community service. At Easter it sponsors the city's largest egg hunt. At
Christmas its flocked Storybook Lane
is a sparkling winter wonderland for
small children. (Bundle up, though; the
buildings aren't heated.) In summer the
Sunday afternoon Dairyville open houses
(1:30–4:30 pm) feature free pony rides,
balloons, candy and games. Many families' annual traditions encompass three
visits a year, and they're not sorry.

Flower Farmer's Phoenix & Holly Railroad attracts children eager to ride the rails.

the farm has evolved to include a unique array of entertainment facilities and an annual series of family holiday events.

Built by Florian's son and grandson, Dairyville is a replica of a Western frontier town. Its dozen false-front shops—among them a doll museum, old-fashioned ice cream parlor, harness shop, and music store—are filled with period antiques. The grand old opera house, with seats for 600, harbors the majestic pipe organ that once played in the old Portland Civic Auditorium. Elsewhere, an impressive collection of antique music boxes, nickelodeons, and victrolas is on public display.

No less impressive are the Alpenrose sports facilities: a baseball stadium, velodrome, and miniature racetrack. Initially built to provide athletic diversions for Cadonau children and cousins, it wasn't long before they were made available to the larger community. (See Sports, Nonprofessional Leagues.)

Flower Farmer
2512 N. Holly, Canby 97013
(about 25 miles from Portland)
503-266-3581
www.flowerfarmer.com
www.phoenixandholly.com
Hours: Vary by season and activity. Call for information.
Season: May-December

The Flower Farmer's main attraction isn't its many acres of colorful u-cut flowers nor its farm animals. Kids come in droves to ride the Phoenix & Holly Railroad, a half-size, narrow-gauge train with a 30-horsepower diesel locomotive named Sparky and a bright red caboose named Fred. All aboard for a half-mile loop through the fields, with a pit stop see the miniature donkey, chickens, turkeys and ducks ($3.50/adult; $3/child 3-12 and senior, free/child 23 months & under). The train's hours vary, so it's best to call ahead to be sure you're on schedule. In general, though, the train operates weekends and holidays through the summer 11 am-6 pm or by appointment. In October, the train runs Monday through Saturday 10 am-9 pm and Sunday 10 am-6 pm.

For Halloween, select pumpkins and check out the spooky railroad tunnel, hay maze, and straw mountain. Christmas features a special lighting display.

COUNTRY DRIVE

The drive to Flower Farmer is a lovely country outing no matter how you choose to come, but the favored route among children hooked on transportation includes a ride on the Canby Ferry (see Active Play: Outdoor Fun, Boating).

Magness Memorial Tree Farm
31195 SW Ladd Hill Rd
Sherwood 97140
503-228-1367
www.worldforestry.org
Season/hours: 9 am-5 pm; Memorial Day-Labor Day, 9 am-7pm

Donated to the World Forestry Center in 1977, this 70-acre forest on Parrett Mountain has been developed and maintained to demonstrate different methods of woodland management—from selective harvesting to clearcutting. View examples of the various techniques from one of the farm's two hiking trails (the third, a paved trail, is wheelchair-accessible), then scale the 60-foot fire tower for a panoramic view of the Cascades. Year-round on Sundays at 2 pm, a naturalist leads a free guided hike.

Facilities include a picnic shelter; rustic log cabins for outdoor schools, overnight camping, and retreats; and a visitors' center with restrooms.

Old McDonald's Farm, Inc.
Corbett 97019 (30 minutes from Portland)
503-695-3316
www.oldmcdonaldsfarm.org
Season: year round
Hours: casual — drop-ins encouraged

Hands-on, structured, educational experiences are at the heart of Old McDonald's Farm, a nonprofit, charitable organization that uses livestock, agriculture and natural resources as educational tools.

As the executive director explains, here the point is "not necessarily to teach children and youth to be farmers, but rather to use the farm to teach kids to be kind, caring, compassionate, capable, 'can-do' people."

Summer programs, day visits, Saturday workshops, after-school programs and more are offered. Children can learn such skills as how to feed and care for all types of livestock, how to ride a horse, and how to compost, plant, weed and cultivate a garden.

Philip Foster Farm
29912 SE Hwy 221, Eagle Creek 97022
503-637-6324, 503-630-5051
Season/Hours: June-August — Fri-Sun, 11 am-4 pm; September — Sat-Sun, 11 am-4 pm
Special seasonal events: May, August, & September
Admission: Free; donations appreciated

IT'S A MATTER OF TASTE

Portland Nursery's annual Gourmet Apple Tasting event (the second and third weekends of October) is fun for the whole family. More than 50 apple varieties are sliced and arrayed on a "U"-shaped table for sampling, and after you figure out which you like best, you can usually purchase them by the pound. Besides the tasty fare, you'll find balloon artists and craft activities geared for kids as well as live music. For details: Portland Nursery, 5050 SE Stark St., Portland 97215, 503-231-5050, www.portlandnursery.com.

This historic Eagle Creek farm—home to Philip Foster, one of Oregon's early entrepreneurs—was the first settlement some 10,000 emigrant pioneers and their wagon trains encountered after embarking on the Oregon Trail. Today a farmhouse, barn, pioneer store, and blacksmith shop highlight pertinent demonstrations. Children are invited to pump water, scrub clothes, cut wood with a bucksaw, and experiment with levers and pulleys. Tour the pioneer gardens and join in a treasure hunt.

Pomeroy Living History Farm
20902 NE Lucia Falls Rd
Yacolt (Washington) 98675
(about 45 minutes from Portland)

360-686-3537
Season/hours: 1st full weekend of month, June-October. Sat, 11 am-4 pm; Sun, 1-4 pm.
Fees: $3.50/adult; $2/child 3-11 years; free/child 2 & under
Special events: May & October

With an operating blacksmith shop, six-bedroom log house, and extensive herb and vegetable gardens, this historic farm in the Lucia Valley of northern Clark County, Wash., depicts life as it was in the 1920s. Guests are encouraged to participate in many of the daily chores: churning butter, scrubbing clothes, grinding coffee and grain, pumping water, and feeding chickens. In May, there's an annual herb festival with thousands of herb plants and live entertainment. October features a pumpkin festival with hayrides, scarecrow making, and pumpkin painting.

Sauvie Island
Off Hwy 30, north of Portland
This island in the Columbia River, just north of the city, is an agricultural oasis. A haven for bicyclists, bird-watchers, and sunbathers (there are four beaches along the northeastern shoreline), Sauvie Island also boasts some of the metro area's finest produce. Come in spring for fresh berries and peaches; in fall for pears, apples, and pumpkins; or just about anytime to pick and choose from the bountiful farmstand displays of fruits, vegetables, and homemade specialty goods. (See also Active Play: Outdoor Fun, Fishing.)

Modern-day farms give way to a historic Sauvie Island orchard at the Bybee House.

GROW FOR IT!

Portland Parks & Recreation maintains 26 community gardens throughout its district. Individuals and families lease 400-square-foot garden plots on an annual basis ($30, plus $10 deposit), then plant, tend, and harvest the produce for their own use. Participation in garden cleanups and other group events is required, and use of organic gardening methods is strongly encouraged. Community gardens average about half an acre in size, and still there are waiting lists for plots. Check with the Community Gardening Program, 503-823-1612, www.portland-parks.org/Parks/CommunityGardens.htm for more information. Or e-mail pkleslie@ci.portland.or.us.

Bybee House
Howell Park Rd, Sauvie Island
503-222-1741
Season/hours: June-August, noon-5 pm weekends
Suggested donation: $3/adult; $2/child

Built in 1858 by pioneers who arrived via the Oregon Trail, this nine-room Classic Revival dwelling was restored in 1966 by the Oregon Historical Society. Staffed only in summer on weekends, the site hosts guided tours, a series of special living-history events called A Day in the Country, and late September's Wintering-In harvest festival.

Behind the house and adjacent to the Pioneer Orchard is the Agricultural Museum, where children are welcome to explore horse-drawn farming equipment as well as harness and woodworking shops.

State/County Fairs

Q: What sounds like a farm and smells like a farm, but isn't a farm?
A: The Oregon State Fair.

Held each summer, this is the best place to get your fill of farm animals (see listing for details). You'll see barns full of cows, horses, goats, sheep, pigs, rabbits, and fowl, and exhibit halls full of farming displays. As the kids mature, they may grow less interested in livestock and more interested in carnival rides, but all generations agree that the Oregon Dairy Women's ice cream earns a blue ribbon.

The State Fair is the grandaddy, but local county fairs are fun, too, and can be more intimate. When arranging your visit, call ahead to ask about special admission and carnival-ride discounts.

Multnomah County Fair
Oaks Park, Portland
503-233-5777
When: Late July
Admission: $3/adult; $1/child 6-12 years; free/child 5-under

Washington County Fair & Rodeo
Washington County Fair Complex
Hillsboro
503-648-1416
www.faircomplex.com

When: Late July
Admission: $7/adult; $4/child 6-15
years; free/child 5-under

Clark County Fair
Clark County Fairgrounds
17402 NE Delfel Rd, Ridgefield, WA
360-397-6180
www.clarkcofair.com
When: Early August
Admission: $7/adult; $3/child 7-12
years; free/child 6-under

Clackamas County Fair & Rodeo
Clackamas County Fairgrounds, Canby
503-266-1136
www.co.clackamas.or.us/fair
When: Mid-August
Admission: $7/adult; $4/senior;
$3/child 8-15 years; free/child 7-under

Oregon State Fair
Oregon State Fairgrounds, Salem
503-947-FAIR (3247)
www.fair.state.or.us
When: Late August-early September
Admission: $7/adult; $4/senior;
$3/child 6-12 years; free/child under 6

Rufus, the mascot of the Oregon State Fair, gets a warm greeting from a young fan.

Chapter 6

EXPLORING DOWNTOWN

The best way to experience downtown Portland is on foot. Grasp your child's hand in yours, keep her against your right flank (sheltered from traffic) and slow to her speed. She'll sense immediately by your revised pace that this isn't errand-running, this is something special.

Make a pact: She'll forgo pebbles, dropped coins, and cracks in the sidewalk, and you'll forgo window-shopping. Now, look at the statues, fountains, and buildings (many boast intricate architectural features). You've never seen Portland like this before. This is a treasure hunt.

The Portland Streetcar follows a route that takes it past the Multnomah County Library.

Getting around

Portland's shorter city blocks lend themselves to walkers—and to shorter legs—but even the best hikers can grow weary and need a rest. A downtown walking tour can be especially ambitious, and even more fun, if you incorporate some public transportation into your adventure.

Get On Board

Portland Streetcar: The city's newest mode of public transportation, the Portland Streetcar, created quite a stir when it was inaugurated in July 2001. The Portland Streetcar is being hailed as the first modern streetcar in the U.S. These vehicles, each seating 30, run on a 4.7-mile L-shaped loop that goes north from the SW Fifth and Montgomery terminus at Portland State University (PSU), past the Portland Art Museum, the Multnomah County Library and Powell's Books, and turns west in the midst of the Pearl District to loop around Legacy Good Samaritan at NW 23rd before heading back downtown. Stops are located every two or three blocks. The entire loop takes 40 to 50 minutes, depending on stops and traffic. For more information, check www.portlandstreetcar.org.

Tri-Met (bus and light rail): If the streetcar doesn't get you where you want to go, Tri-Met can. Tri-Met (503-238-RIDE; www.tri-met.org) manages the rest of Portland's public transit system, which consists of Tri-Met buses, MAX (Metropolitan Area Express) light rail and the vintage trolleys, which run on the MAX lines.

In Portland, there is still such a thing as a free ride. Within a 300-block section of downtown called Fareless Square, passengers can ride Tri-Met buses and light-rail cars for free (trolleys are always free). The fareless area is bordered on the west and south by Interstate 405, and on the north by Irving St. In September 2001, it was extended on the east to cross the Willamette River and take in the Lloyd District. This extended area on the east side of town means that riders on MAX and on 10 bus routes can travel free in an area bounded by N Multnomah Blvd, NE Holladay and NE 14th.

For travel beyond Fareless Square, the basic fee is $1.25; longer rides cost $1.55. Youths ages 7 to 18 pay 95 cents, and as many as three children age 6 and under are permitted to ride free with each fare-paying adult. Day passes are available for $4. Tri-Met's latest fare innovation is the Quik Tik, a six-hour ticket that's valid on all buses and MAX. At $3, the Quik Tik's is cheaper than a day pass.

To ride, place exact change or a ticket in the fare box when boarding the bus. MAX tickets may be purchased and validated using the vending machines at each station. Though they are neither owned nor operated by Tri-Met, the streetcars conveniently use the same fare system as Tri-Met, but be aware that streetcar fare boxes accept only coins. (Remember to keep your transfer: It's good for 90 minutes.)

You can purchase Tri-Met tickets and find schedules downtown in a number of locations, including Portland State Bookstore (1880 SW Sixth Ave) and Oregon Stamp & Stationery (625 SW 10th Ave). Perhaps the best, and most central, place is Tri-Met's Pioneer Courthouse Square office (SW Sixth Ave & Yamhill), where you can also stop at the new visitors center for tips. Throughout the city, you can expect to find tickets at local Safeway, Albertsons and Fred Meyer stores. You can usually find different route schedules on racks near the front of buses.

Most of Tri-Met's 100 bus lines loop through the downtown transit mall on SW Fifth and Sixth avenues. Shelters line the broad brick sidewalks of these byways, and auto traffic is minimized and even eliminated along certain sections of the mall. Television monitors inside most shelters in the heart of downtown show schedules so you can figure out which bus to expect next.

The MAX light-rail route travels 15 miles east from downtown to Gresham, as well as 18 miles west from downtown to Beaverton and Hillsboro. The new MAX Red Line, opened in September 2001, has been touted as the West Coast's "first train to the plane." Dropping passengers just 150 feet from the baggage claim area, the train takes just 38 minutes to get from downtown to Portland International Airport. MAX trains typically run every 15 minutes, though some lines run more frequently during rush hour. For MAX schedule information, call 503-22-TRAIN (228-7246).

Vintage Trolleys: For sheer fun, the Vintage Trolleys still rank as one of the best rides in town. At the turn of the century, electric trolleys offered regular service throughout downtown and into the West Hills. In November 1991,

A ride on a vintage trolley is one of the best rides in town.

four working replicas of the original Council Crest cars were introduced along a light-rail route that links the downtown shopping district with Lloyd Center on the east side. Trolleys operate on a limited schedule, but the rides are free when you can catch one. Call the Vintage Trolley office for details at 503-323-7363, or check the Tri-Met Web site (www.tri-met.org).

FINDERS, KEEPERS . . .

If you have the misfortune of leaving something behind on one of the Tri-Met-operated lines, before you despair call Tri-Met's lost-and-found department at 503-962-7655. You might just get lucky!

Park It!

You can't count on finding vacant parking spaces when you need them in the downtown core. But when you do get lucky, be prepared with lots of quarters. On weekdays and Saturdays, 8 am to 6 pm, 25 cents will buy you 20 minutes from parking meters. Parking is free at night and all day on Sundays and holidays.

Even parking garages fill up with some regularity these days. The city's most affordable short-term parking is found at any of the six Smart Park locations downtown (look for their circular red-and-white signs). Expect to pay 95 cents an hour for the first four hours and about $3 for each additional hour. After 6 pm there is a flat rate of $2 for the entire evening.

If you're shopping downtown, ask the merchants you patronize about the FreePark program. Nearly 200 merchants, including some restaurants and offices (look for FreePark decals), validate the parking tickets of customers who make purchases of $25 or more. Each stamp is good for two hours of free parking at any downtown lot or garage. The merchants pick up the tab.

Landmarks and Public Art

An inscription on the city's oldest artwork, Old Town's Skidmore Fountain, erected in 1888, reads: "Good citizens are the riches of a city." In Portland, "good citizens" have turned the city into riches.

The Percent for Public Art ordinances, established in the city of Portland and in Multnomah County in 1980, require that 1 percent of major capital construction budgets be earmarked for public art. From a mammoth, hammered-copper statue to computerized water fountains to trompe l'oeil (fool-the-eye) murals—there's something interesting and curious around virtually every corner downtown.

A Portland trademark almost as recognizable as the rose, the **Benson Bubblers** that punctuate the downtown streetscape have come to symbolize Portland's free-flowing hospitality. In response to his workers' claims that they frequented the saloons in town because there was no fresh drinking water, teetotaling lumber baron Simon Benson donated $10,000 in 1912 to outfit the city with 20 bronze, four-bowl drinking fountains. The fountains were designed by A.E. Doyle, architect of the Multnomah County Library, Meier &

This colorful, authentic gate commemorates Portland's Chinese citizens.

Frank and U.S. National Bank buildings (see below). There are now 50 Benson Bubblers in Portland (plus another 75 single-bowl variations located around town). During the drought of 1992, the city installed push-buttons for use during periods of water shortage.

In 1890, Portland's **Chinatown** was the nation's second-largest. With the new Classical Chinese Garden, created by Chinese artisans practicing centuries-old craftsmanship, there's a new reason to explore this area of the city. Though Burnside tends to be rather shabby and not particularly hospitable to families near the great Chinatown Gate (NW Fourth Ave & Burnside), it's still fun to get a close-up view of the gate. Dedicated in 1986 to commemorate Portland's Chinese citizens, the authentic design features two fearsome bronze lions, five tiered roofs and 64 dragons.

Designed in 1917 by architect A.E. Doyle (see Benson Bubblers), the neoclassical **U.S. National Bank** building

nearby (SW Broadway & Stark), with its soaring Corinthian columns, looks like a bank should—imposing, elegant and, above all, permanent. The entrance on Sixth Ave is decorated with glazed, turn-of-the-century terra-cotta coins.

Affectionately referred to as the city's "living room," **Pioneer Courthouse Square** (SW Broadway & Yamhill) is another example of forward-thinking civic planning. Once a parking lot, the grand public space is now host to planned cultural events (concerts and festivals) and impromptu gatherings. Brown-bagging executives sprawl on its steps at noon, teens congregate to play hacky-sack, mothers bring their toddlers to romp and commuters line up for the ride home.

To fund the square's construction in 1984, more than 63,000 personalized bricks were sold. Read the names under your feet. Who can find "Wm. Shakespeare," "Sherlock Holmes," "Frodo Baggins" and "Bruce Springsteen"? Then hunt for the echo chamber.

Let the kids discover and explore the whimsical artwork in the square: *Allow Me*, a life-size bronze gentleman with umbrella; *Mile Post*; and terra-cotta

The umbrella man (also known as "Allow Me") overlooks Pioneer Courthouse Square.

LANDMARKS AND PUBLIC ART

REGIONAL ARTS AND CULTURE COUNSEL

"Portlandia" crouches on a ledge above the entrance to the Portland Building.

columns that pay homage to the city's architectural roots (to name a few). Plan your visit to coincide with lunch hour and you'll be treated to an electronic fanfare by the Weather Machine in the northwest corner. See the wrought-iron gate and fence? They once graced the Portland Hotel, which was built in 1890 on this spot. The elegant hotel played host to eight U.S. presidents and Portland's high society until 1951.

Recently the square has undergone a major $2.7 million renovation. The interior lobby is now a unique new public space, housing both the Portland Oregon Visitor Association (503-275-8355) and a Tri-Met customer-assistance office. The center is open every day (Mon-Fri, 8:30 am-5:30 pm; Sat, 10 am-4 pm; Sun, 10 am-4 pm), and among the many brochures you'll find here is the *City Kids Fun Book*. This colorful free guide is packed with kid-size bites of information about the city's landmarks.

Also located within the center is Ticket Central, where you can purchase Ticket-

Master, Fastixx, and Artistix event and theater tickets. Ask at Ticket Central also for a free ticket to the Theatre on the Square, a so-called "surround theater." Here, you can see *Perfectly Portland*, a 12-minute film about the people and places in and around Portland and Oregon (on the half hour, Mon-Fri, 10 am-6 pm; Sat, 10 am-3 pm; Sun, noon-3 pm).

Opened in 1875, **Pioneer Courthouse** (SW Sixth Ave & Yamhill; 503-326-5830) is the oldest U.S. courthouse on the West Coast. Still in use today, by the U.S. Court of Appeals and the U. S. Post Office, the building is open to the public on weekdays, 8 am to 5 pm.

Take the elevator to the third floor, then continue up the stairs to the glass-enclosed cupola for a view of the city and the mountains beyond. (If the door's locked, ask a security officer for assistance.) The aged and rippled glass and the historic photographs up here put it all in perspective.

Flanking the courthouse on SW

REGIONAL ARTS AND CULTURE COUNSEL

Few children can resist "Animals in Pools," which flanks Pioneer Courthouse.

Yamhill and Morrison is a series of concrete pools decorated with 25 native animals and birds cast in bronze—seals, bears, ducks, otters. Let the kids perch on a deer and pet a beaver.

The **Plaza Blocks** (SW Third Ave from Madison to Salmon), comprising Chapman and Lownsdale squares, are separated by Main St, which curves around a massive bull elk statue that was given to the city in 1900 by a former mayor. Elk from the West Hills are said to have grazed here before the parks were dedicated in 1852. The squares, which attracted orators and milling crowds of citizens, were segregated into ladies' (Chapman) and gentlemen's (Lownsdale) "gathering places" in the 1920s to encourage decorous behavior.

Nearby, Terry Schrunk Plaza (SW Third Ave & Jefferson) boasts an echo chamber (how does it compare to the one in Pioneer Courthouse Square?), a small replica of the Liberty Bell and shrapnel from the Oklahoma City bombing.

Michael Graves' controversial **Portland Building** (SW Fifth Ave & Madison) represents the nation's first major postmodern structure. What do your children think of it? Do they like the colors, the adornments? How is it different from and/or similar to some of its historic neighbors?

Stand in the shadow of *Portlandia*, which looms over the entrance, and look up. A jolly greening giant modeled after Lady Commerce, she is the nation's second-largest hammered-copper statue (her trident alone is longer than a Tri-Met bus). Who can name the largest? (Hint: She's in New York City.)

For a new perspective on *Portlandia*, enter the Portland Building and climb to the second-floor atrium. Here,

the Metropolitan Center for Public Art (open weekdays only) showcases a full-size plaster cast of the statue's head, in addition to photographs taken during her arrival via barge. Another vantage point can be had from the Standard Plaza building across the street. Take the escalator to the enclosed landing area for an unobstructed view.

From Portland State University at the south (Jackson St) to Salmon St at the north, the 12 grassy, shaded **Park Blocks** that form downtown's cultural core are punctuated by sculptures and benches. Look for statues of Abraham Lincoln and Theodore Roosevelt, and for *In the Shadow of the Elm* (Clay St), a granite pavement sculpture constructed in 1984. One of Benson's original bubblers stands at SW Park and Salmon. Who can spot *Salmon on Salmon?* (Hint: It's at the corner of SW

This trompe l'oeil mural, one of several, was commissioned by the Oregon Historical Society in 1989.

LANDMARKS AND PUBLIC ART / RESOURCES

"*Friendship Circle*" *marks the beginning—or is it the end?—of Tom McCall Waterfront Park.*

a focal point for fair-weather recreation and festivities. It's fun to bike or skate by the harbor and along the promenade, but if you walk you're more likely to enjoy the scenery.

Begin at the Steel Bridge. Friendship Circle, erected in 1990, commemorates Portland's 30-year association with sister city Sapporo, Japan. A collaboration between sculptor Lee Kelly and composer Michael Stirling, the stainless steel sculpture resonates with sounds that are reminiscent of the flutes and drums of Japan.

A maze of image and word pathways etched in granite paving stones, the Story Garden (just south of the Burnside Bridge) was commissioned in 1993 in response to citizens' requests for a children's playground in Waterfront Park. Move from slab to slab as you would on a game board, and create a story. Play King of the Hill on the massive granite throne. Or share your responses to the tough questions, e.g., "What is your sadness?" or "Why is there evil?"

Blink and you'll miss it. That's Mill Ends Park (SW Front Ave & Taylor), the world's smallest. It used to be a pothole below the office window of *Oregonian* journalist Dick Fagan, until he planted it with flowers. "Visit" so you can say you did, but use caution in this busy intersection.

Salmon St & Ninth Ave.) Continue north to the Studio Building (SW Ninth Ave & Taylor), whose frieze features the busts of famous composers.

Commissioned by the Oregon Historical Society in 1989, Richard Haas' *Oregon History Murals* use a trompe l'oeil technique. Adorning the Sovereign Hotel, the west (SW Park & Madison) and south (SW Broadway & Jefferson) murals depict historic personalities, panoramas and architectural details. Where does three-dimensional reality give way to two-dimensional art?

Portland has been called unsophisticated, provincial, sleepy—even backward. For instance, there was the time, in 1974, when the governor razed a freeway to build . . . a park! **Tom McCall Waterfront Park**, which stretches for 22 blocks along the west bank of the Willamette River, stands as a testament to progressive visions of civic development.

A riverside greenway first conceived in 1904 by the Olmsted brothers, Boston's landscaping gurus, the park is

Resources

The Regional Arts and Culture Council (620 SW Main St, Ste 420; 503-823-5111; www.racc.org) has developed *Public Art Walking Tour*, a 65-page guide to the city's art collection. Most recently revised in 1992, the booklet divides the downtown and Lloyd Center districts into eight zones. Numbered

REGIONAL ARTS AND CULTURE COUNSEL

The Ira Keller Fountain brings the sights and sounds of the wilderness to the downtown core.

artworks are located on zone maps and briefly described. Drop by the RACC office for a free copy of the guide.

The Portland Development Commission (1900 SW Fourth Ave, Ste 100; 503-823-3200; www.portlanddev.org), in cooperation with the Historic Preservation League of Oregon, created three walking-tour brochures in 1988. Still in circulation, each pamphlet emphasizes an architecturally historic downtown district: Yamhill, Skidmore/Old Town and Glazed Terra Cotta (the commercial core). The map/guides are available at PDC offices for $2 apiece.

Powell's Books (various locations) also publishes a free walking map of downtown with numbered highlights and descriptive information. Outlined on a simple fold-out leaflet, the complete tour is 7 miles long, so families are advised to design an abridged version. Pick up a map at any Powell's store, or call 503-228-4651 for more information.

Farther Afield: A Capitol Tour

When in Salem, get a free copy of *A Walking Tour: State of Oregon Capitol Grounds* at the Capitol information desk. The brochure highlights the plantings, fountains and monuments on the mall. For little kids, there's a sculptural metal play structure called *The Parade of Animals*. Older kids will appreciate the Peace Plaza (Commercial St, between City Hall and the public library). Decorated with colorful symbolic banners, the centerpiece is a concrete wall that features remarks on the subject of peace by renowned international figures and local citizens. For information, call 503-986-1388.

Wet and Wild

One sure way to get your kids interested in doing a bit of walking downtown, especially on a hot summer day, is to center the hike on the city's fountains.

Have them wear their swimsuits under their clothes, tuck a towel in a backpack and hit one or all of the following cool spots.

■ **Ira Keller Fountain**, SW Third Ave & Market (opposite Keller Auditorium). Named after an advocate of urban renewal, the park holds naturalistic brooks, terraces and cascading waterfalls that are suggestive of the Northwest landscape.

■ **Lovejoy Fountain**, SW Third Ave & Hall. Walk several blocks south from Ira Keller Fountain to visit another cascade. Ask the kids to comment on the two fountains' similarities and differences. Which is more realistic? Which do they prefer, and why?

■ **Salmon Street Springs**, SW Naito Parkway & Salmon. Here, the 185 water jets are programmed by computer to keep frolickers on their toes. Just when you've adjusted to the fountain's rhythms, they change, and the kids wind up drenched (and grinning).

■ **Skidmore Fountain**, SW First Ave & Ankeny. When this fountain was built, its placement marked the center of town. Made of bronze using funds designated for this purpose in druggist Stephen Skidmore's will, the fountain is now a centerpiece of Saturday Market, Portland's beloved arts and crafts fair that sprawls beneath the Burnside Bridge each weekend from March through December.

■ **Essential Forces**, the Rose Garden, 1 Center Court. This fountain makes Salmon Street Springs look like a romp through the backyard sprinkler. Constructed as a gift to the city by Paul Allen and sited at the main entrance to the Rose Garden, this impressive computerized fountain features 500 water jets and two towers that emit geyser-force blasts of water and gusting flames.

■ **Holladay West Park**, NE 11th & Holladay. Sandwiched between the MAX line and the Lloyd Center, this tree-filled park recently underwent quite a restoration. Now it sports an interactive water feature, where kids delight in the often-changing arc of various water jets. There are benches to rest on and three beautiful bronze sculptures to admire as well.

If the idea of a fountain tour really whets your child's enthusiasm, check with the Portland Water Bureau (503-823-7459) for a free brochure titled *Portland's Municipal Fountains* or ask about a newly developed lesson plan surrounding the fountains that could easily be used by parents as well as teachers.

Dining with Downtown Flair

Downtown Portland's dining options run the gamut from fast-food frenzy to gourmet grand, from healthful Mexican to eclectic Continental. If you want to eat on the go, consider buying something from one of the many streetside vendors who set up shop here and there, especially around Pioneer Courthouse Square. Snow White House Crepes to Go (SW Ninth & Yamhill) is great for satisfying a deep-down hunger with, say, a ham-and-cheese crepe, or a sweet tooth with a chocolate crepe covered with powdered sugar.

Cascades, the Pioneer Place shopping-mall food court (SW Fifth Ave &

DINING WITH DOWNTOWN FLAIR / TO MARKET, TO MARKET

Taylor; www.pioneerplace.com), is arguably the best bet for families. Its attractive setting, with cascading waterfalls and seating on several levels, showcases more than a dozen separate concessionaires who sell pizza, sandwiches, salads, gyros, corn dogs, ice cream—everything but the kitchen sink. Popular with the business crowd on weekdays at noon, the atrium gets very noisy. Come before or after the lunch-hour rush, or on weekends.

These downtown restaurants offer kids' menus and mostly conventional fare:

- **Harborside Restaurant**, 0309 SW Montgomery; 503-220-1865
- **Mayas Taqueria**, 1000 SW Morrison; 503-226-1946
- **McDonald's**, 1035 SW Sixth Ave; 503-295-1234
- **Newport Bay RiverPlace**, 0425 SW Montgomery; 503-227-3474
- **Pizzicato**, SW Alder off Broadway; 503-226-1007

The Saturday Market beckons visitors.

MICHAEL CLAPP

To Market, To Market

If you're out on a weekend March through December, a stop at Saturday Market (503-222-6072; www.portland saturdaymarket.com) can be fun for the whole family.

A sensory adventure, the market features more than 250 craft and food vendors who cluster beneath the west end of the Burnside Bridge to sell their handmade wares and homemade treats (Sat, 10 am-5 pm; Sun, 11 am-4:30 pm).

Depending on their age, kids with a little spending money in their pockets gravitate toward the balloon artists, the handcrafted wooden toys, the tie-dyed T-shirts, the scented candles or the racks of shiny earrings. The challenge is to keep tabs on them.

COMING SOON!

Within the next few years, the city of Portland is planning to replace approximately 5,900 single-space meters in the downtown core with approximately 850 pay stations that use new technology. The new stations are units that operate multiple parking spaces from a single location, usually in the middle of the block. Because they allow you to use credit and debit cards for parking fees, they eliminate the need to keep endless rolls of coins handy.

Locals and visitors can learn about bridges on the Portland Bridge Walk.

If you go fairly early, there's less of a crowd. And after wandering the craft booths, you can make your way to the food area, where the savory options range from fresh cinnamon-sugared elephant ears to peanut-sauce-covered pad thai. Instead of eating on the run, take the time to find a bench or chair near the stage to listen to the musicians. Young children revel in dancing to the live music. Or wander over to the Skidmore Fountain area to join the crowd surrounding such acts as a family of tap-dancing kids or a magician at work. (Scheduled entertainment is posted on the market's Web site.)

Guided Tours

Where were you in third grade? In Portland, that's the year schoolchildren study civics, learn about cities and explore their hometown. Classrooms sign up en masse with local tour oper-

ators to trudge the streets and pick up tidbits about the history and architecture of the sights many of us take for granted.

You don't have to be 9 years old to get something out of a guided walking tour, however. Families are welcome on these tours, though advance reservations are required. Tour guides are generally amenable to designing a tour to fit your special interests and requirements. Most guides cover lots of territory in upwards of two hours of fast walking and talking. If your children are younger than 5 years old, consider their attention spans and stamina before booking a tour.

Peter's Walking Tours
503-665-2558
Season: Year-round
Fees: $10/adult, free/child 12 & under (with paying adult); group rates available

A former elementary-school reading instructor, Peter Chausse knows how to captivate children. He stuffs his pockets with magnets, paper and crayons before a tour, then passes out the materials when the time comes to test the properties of the cast-iron Franz Building (SW First Ave & Yamhill) and make rubbings of the intriguing phrases in *Streetwise* (SW Third Ave & Yamhill). His entertaining, two-and-a-half-hour downtown walks highlight art, architecture, urban parks, fountains and local history. Call at least a day ahead to reserve. Tours are offered on both weekdays and weekends.

Portland Bridge Walk

Portland Parks and Recreation
www.portlandparks.org/outdoorrec.htm
503-823-5132
Season: Spring, summer, fall
Fees: $18/ person

Sharon Wood Wortman literally wrote the book (*The Portland Bridge Book*) on Portland bridges. She can quickly rattle off the three main bridge types (arch, suspension, beam), the three main moveable bridge types (vertical lift, bascule, swing) and local examples of each. Her Portland Bridge Walk, offered monthly in season for Portland Parks and Recreation since 1991, is made possible, she notes, by

the city's compressed layout: Portland has eight notable bridges in close proximity to one another.

Children are welcome on the three-and-a-half-hour outings, and Wood Wortman, who has lots of experience hosting school groups, can fashion a tour to meet the needs of her guests. Participants view and discuss the eight bridges, walk across two, learn how the city works and play games to simulate a bridge's balancing act. Reservations are suggested.

Urban Tour Group

503-227-5780
www.urbantourgroup.org
Season: Year-round
Fees: $25/group of 1 to 5 people, $5/each additional person

A nonprofit volunteer organization with 85 trained guides and more than 30 years of experience leading free downtown walking tours for school groups, the Urban Tour Group also offers customized guided tours to the public. Call two weeks ahead to schedule a tour. Weekdays are preferable to weekends, when accessibility to many buildings is limited. (For before-you-go fun, check out the virtual walking tour posted at the group's Web site.)

Chapter 7

SPECTATOR SPORTS

The greater Portland area offers plenty to cheer about in the sports arena. For years, Portland has been home to one major player—the National Basketball Association's Portland Trail Blazers. Now it's also home to a Women's National Basketball Association expansion franchise, the Portland Fire. With the updating of Civic Stadium—now known as PGE Park—and the addition of a San Diego Padres farm team, the Triple-A Baseball Portland Beavers, lots more fans are singing "Take Me Out to the Ballpark."

And don't forget about high school and college sports teams. Often these are the teams that put on the best show. From a seat in a bare-bones gym 10 feet from the action, you and your kids will observe lessons in fair play, cooperation, and persistence that are a visceral undercurrent. The players aren't superstars, they're superkids—athletes who play, not for millions, but for glory. They're role models you can feel good about. And what's more, the price is right.

PSU plays home games at PGE Park

Professional Leagues

Portland Beavers
PGE Park
503-553-5555 (ticket line)
www.pgepark.com/beavers
Season: mid-June-early September
Tickets: $2.99-$8.75

In partnership with the City of Portland, Portland Family Entertainment oversaw a $38.5 million renovation of the former Civic Stadium, renamed

TICKET PRICES

This may go without saying, but we'll say it anyway. Be sure to check current ticket prices with the appropriate sporting organization. Ticket prices often change each season, and some seasons were winding down as we went to press.

PGE Park, that was completed in 2001. In addition to an upgraded playing surfce that complies with Major League Baseball's field dimensions, the new PGE Park features brand-new corporate suites and lower bowl seats, new restrooms, a new menu and the Fred Meyer Family Deck, which has a vintage soda-fountain and open air grills.

Now the park is home to both the Triple-A Baseball Portland Beavers, a farm team of the San Diego Padres, and A-League Soccer Portland Timbers, both of which are owned and operated by PFE.

Perhaps one of the best deals in baseball throughout the nation are the Fred Meyer Family Fan Club seats. For $2.99, you can have a front-row seat on the third base line between the Beaver's dugout and bullpen for an incredibly upclose view of the action. These seats are limited in number, so get your tickets early.

Children never seem to tire of the side-show antics that take place in addition to the game that include the appearance of costumed characters and delivery of prizes such as peanuts or T-shirts by slingshot. Arrive early if your youngster is a real fan: A couple of players usually offer autographs prior to each game.

Portland Fire

Rose Garden, 1 Center Ct.
Portland 97227
503-797-9622
www.wnba.com/fire
Season: May-August
Tickets: $5-$75

Portland was awarded a Women's National Basketball Association expansion franchise in summer 1999, and the team, dubbed the Fire, played its first game in summer 2000. The team has caught on with sports fans, with some 8,500 showing up for each game. Many families appreciate the emphasis the WNBA places on the fans. Players routinely hold autograph sessions after games, and the team's mascot, Spot, an oversize Dalmatian, is a huge draw for kids. As an expansion team, the Fire is still finding its footing, but each season finds its stats improving. And with much young talent, including Jenny Mowe, who played for the University of Oregon, the games are fun to watch.

Portland Timbers

PGE Park, 1844 SW Morrison
Portland 97205
503-553-5555 (tickets)
www.pge.com/pgepark.com/timbers
Season: Late April-September
Tickets: $4.75-$14.25

An expansion franchise of the United Soccer Leagues' A-League, the Portland Timbers began playing at PGE Park in spring 2001. Typically, the Timbers play 30 games during their regular season, which kicks off in late April and runs through early September. In their first season at PGE Park, the Timbers made the fall playoffs, much to the delight of the team's growing number of fans.

Portland Trail Blazers

Rose Garden, 1 Center Ct.
Portland 97227
503-797-9600 (tickets), 503-234-9291
www.nba.com/blazers
Season: October-May
Tickets: $10-$127

The Portland Trail Blazers, a National Basketball Association franchise, are the town's big ticket. The team plays in one of the league's glitziest arenas, the Rose Garden, which is comfortable and roomy. And with all of the activities that go on in addition to the game—the BlazerDancers strutting their stuff out on the floor, the remote-control blimp adrift in the arena and dropping fast-food coupons—each game is truly a spectacle.

Consult with a ticket agent and ask about special discounts and ticket packages. For instance, the Blazers often have promotions that include family nights or "meal deals," when tickets are discounted or include free hot dogs or hamburgers. You also get a price break if you purchase tickets to multiple games, then divvy them up among friends.

If your child is a big fan, ask any Rose Garden employee to direct you after the game to the autograph sections that exist both for the Blazers and for the visiting team.

Portland Winter Hawks

Rose Garden, 1 Center Ct.
Portland 97227
Memorial Coliseum
1401 N Wheeler Ave, Portland 97227

503-238-6366
www.winterhawks.com
Season: September-March
Tickets: $14-$21.50/adult, $11-$18.50/student and senior

A fast-paced, rough game (yes, there are brawls), hockey draws capacity crowds in the Northeast and Canada. On the West Coast, where kids are less apt to grow up on ice skates, it's an acquired taste. Still, the Winter Hawks, a Portland fixture since 1976, have developed a loyal following. In the 1997-1998 season, the Western Hockey League team finished first in the Western Conference in the regular season and went on to win the Memorial Cup in the playoffs.

Nonprofessional Leagues

Portland State University
506 SW Mill St., Portland 97207
503-725-5635
http://goviks.fansonly.com
Football season: September-November
PGE Park, 1844 SW Morrison, Portland
Tickets: $9-$17
Basketball season: November-March
Stott Center, SW 10th and Hall
Tickets: Men's games, $6-$12; women's games, $4-$6

Playing at the Division I-AA level, PSU offers the best bet for watching football locally. PSU's team plays six home games at PGE Park. The university also fields men's and women's basketball teams, who play primarily in Stott Center but usually have a couple of games at the Rose Garden.

If your family loves sports, PSU's Family Pass is a good deal. For $150, two adults and up to four kids have access to every regular-season home game for women's basketball, volleyball, soccer and softball as well as for men's wrestling matches.

University of Portland
5000 N Willamette Blvd.
Portland 97203
503-943-7117, 503-943-7525 (box office, Wed-Fri, 1-5 pm)
www.portlandpilots.com
Soccer season: Fall
Merlo Field
Tickets: $4-$10
Volleyball season: Fall
Chiles Center Gymnasium
Tickets: $3-$6
Basketball season: Winter
Chiles Center Gymnasium
Tickets: $5-$10
Baseball season: Spring
Tickets: $2-$6

If your children really like soccer, taking them to a Pilots game is a must. Soccer is the big fall sport at the University of Portland. The east-side school consistently fields nationally ranked soccer teams, thanks in large part to coach Clive Charles. His women's team, especially, has amassed a sterling record. Players of the caliber of graduates Shannon MacMillan and Tiffeny Milbrett, who were instrumental in the Olympic women's team's gold-medal performance in 1996, continue to enroll at the university. Soccer season runs from September through late November, with games played on Merlo Field. Tickets range in price from $4 to $10, but if you arrange tickets for your child's own soccer team, you can get a discount. (Cool-ers and food from home are allowed; no glass bottles, please.)

Also in fall, women's volleyball (there is no men's team) competes for attention in the 5,000-seat Chiles Center gymnasium. Seating is by general admission, and the concession stands are open. Single tickets cost $3 to $6.

Basketball is also popular at the school. The women's team regularly competes in the National Collegiate Athletics Association postseason tournaments, while the men's team flirts with qualifying. Some reserved seats are available at Chiles Center for men's games. Seating at women's games is by general admission only. Expect to pay $5 to $10 per ticket.

The baseball team (men only) is a member of the West Coast Conference. Concession stands are available, but food from home is allowed. Single tickets cost $2 to $6 each.

Alpenrose Dairy

6149 SW Shattuck Rd., Portland 97221
503-244-1133
www.alpenrose.com

No longer a working dairy farm, Alpenrose remains a local fixture, known as much for its sprawling sports complexes and special holiday events as for its milk and ice cream (see Farms). Developed to accommodate the hobbies of the children and grandchildren of the founding Cadonau family, the athletic facilities include a 3,000-seat baseball stadium plus two smaller diamonds, an oval racetrack for quarter-midget cars and a velodrome for racing bicycles. In season, the place is crawling with families who've come to compete, watch or both.

Little League Softball World Series

www.softballworldseries.com
Season: Mid-August (12-15 games)
Admission: Free

Each August since 1994, more than 100 of the world's preeminent female youth softball players gather on the three grass Alpenrose diamonds to crown the world champions. Selected as all-stars from their respective regions, these 11- and 12-year-olds represent Europe, the Far East, Latin America, Canada and the eastern, western, southern and central United States. The players have already endured four grueling double-elimination tournaments to get here, and in six short days it's all over.

Spectators are admitted free, but are encouraged to purchase food and souvenirs from the concession stands to support the tournament. Food from home is allowed.

Alpenrose Velodrome

503-246-0330
www.obra.org/track
Season: May-September
Admission: Free

A banked, 268-meter concrete track that resembles a giant cereal bowl, this 500-seat velodrome (one of only 19 in the United States) is specifically designed for technical, Olympic-style events that feature fixed-gear bikes without brakes.

In season, races for experienced riders are held each Thursday at 6:30 pm. Juniors, masters and beginning women compete on Fridays at 6 pm. In addition, from May through August, anyone who wants to learn how to ride at the velodrome, including kids, can get special help on Wednesdays from 6 pm to dusk.

Spectators are admitted free to the races, where they can picnic in the bleachers (there are no concession stands). Children are encouraged to bring their own bicycles (trikes, training wheels, two-wheelers) for non-competitive, 1-kilometer races on the infield track that take place before Thursday events. All participants receive ribbons.

Quarter-Midget Racing

503-649-2404
Season: March-October, Saturday, 9 am; Sunday, noon
Admission: Free

Sponsored by the Portland Quarter-Midget Racing Association (PQMRA), these events feature competitive races among child drivers, ages 5 through 16. Seated at the wheel of a gas- or alcohol-powered miniature race car equipped with a one-cylinder engine, the driver can reach about 30 miles an hour on the banked, oval racetrack. To race, you must be a member of the PQMRA and bring your own vehicle and safety equipment.

Spectators are admitted free to the bleachers. A snack bar is available; food from home is allowed.

Support Your Local High School

Deafening bands and milling crowds of teens compete with the sports teams for attention at high school games, but it can be fun to follow the early career of a baby-sitter or other teen friend, or to play talent scout and try to spot incipient star power.

Call your local high school in the fall for a schedule of home games in your sport of choice. If you'd prefer to be more selective, plan to attend one of the state's all-star games. Held in June and July at venues throughout Oregon, these contests provide an opportunity to see the year's best crop of athletes. Each year Portland hosts various girls' and boys' all-star games. For a schedule, contact the Oregon Coaches Association (503-399-9132) or check the association's Web site (www.oregoncoach.org).

Introduced in 1997, the Great Northwest Shootout capitalizes on the regional rivalry between Oregon and Washington high schools with two seniors-only basketball games: one for men, one for women. Selected by the coaches' associations, most of the team's 12 graduating seniors have, until this night, been rivals. Here they must forget feuds and rivalry to work together as a team. Held in mid-June at the Chiles Center (University of Portland) and televised locally, the double-header is sponsored by the Multnomah Athletic Foundation. Call 503-223-6251 for ticket information.

Chapter 8
EXCURSIONS

Y ou can fill an entire book with suggestions of things to do as a family in the Portland area. Then you can fill an entire year doing them. But even if you never tire of the tried-and-true local parks, museums, and activities, the time will come when a couple of hours in the car with the kids won't sound so bad.

Perhaps it's the visiting in-laws who want to see Mount St. Helens, or the kids who are aching for a visit to the aquarium in Newport. Whatever the impetus, don't hesitate. Pack up the car and go.

There are numerous destinations within a few hours' drive of downtown that will provide your family with a deeper understanding of the region's culture and history. You'll know your neighborhood better for having gone away.

Columbia River Gorge

Though Portland straddles the Willamette River, it's the Columbia that gets more attention. And well it should. Just 40 miles east of the city is some of the state's finest scenery—fir-speckled basalt cliffs and granite outcroppings, bubbling brooks, cascading waterfalls and peaceful pastureland. Crown Point Vista House and Multnomah Falls attract crowds of tourists in season, but there are dozens of lesser-known natural spectacles just off the beaten path.

From Portland, take I-84 east—then, if time allows, follow signs for the Historic **Columbia River Hwy** (exit 17 at Troutdale). A masterpiece of engineering know-how when it opened in 1915, the 22-mile roadway winds along a high bluff past nine waterfalls and six state parks. Look for original Italian stonework walls that still line sections of the route, and stop for a panoramic view at the **Portland Women's Forum** overlook or at **Crown Point**, the site of Vista House (503-695-2230; www.vistahouse.com), which is one of the most photographed spots in the Columbia River Gorge. During the summer months, Vista House hosts folk-art demonstrations between noon and 4 pm on weekends. In 2000, VistaHouse, which holds an interpretive center and a gift shop, was named in the Save America's Treasures program by the White House, the National Trust for Historic Preservation and the National Park Service. It is currently undergoing restoration.

After you leave Crown Point, plan to get out of the car to explore at least one waterfall up close. The gently sloping lower trail at Latourell Falls is ideal for little kids. Wear hiking boots or other sturdy shoes, and tote rain gear. The trails are often muddy and damp from rain and mist, and the dense forest keeps the sun at bay. For trail maps and other information, contact the Columbia Gorge National Scenic Area Forest Service (541-386-2333).

You really must stop at **Multnomah Falls**—if you can find a parking space. Nearly 2 million visitors stop at the falls each year, making it the number-one public attraction in the state. At 620 feet, it's the second-highest year-round waterfall in the nation, and it's spectacular. Little kids can paddle in the stream. Older children will want to hike to the top. Take the steep, 1.25-mile paved trail at

LISTEN WHILE YOU DRIVE

Pam Vestal of Drive-It-Yourself Tours created *The Columbia Gorge* with families in mind. Both educational and entertaining, the 77-minute audiocassette begins in downtown Portland, then follows the Columbia River Hwy, with eight stops at waterfalls, scenic overlooks and landmarks. Even if you've been to the gorge before, a trip with a built-in soundtrack has lots to recommend it. Learn about volcanic explosions, political wrangling, a quest for gold and cataclysmic flooding.

Available for $14.95 at Powell's Books and other area bookstores, the self-guided driving tour can also be ordered by calling 503-730-7495.

your own risk; there are no railings, and several perilous drop-offs. Built in 1925, the historic lodge (503-695-2376; www.multnomahfallslodge.com) features a cozy restaurant, rest rooms, a snack bar and a gift shop. There's also a visitors center operated by the U.S. Forest Service (503-695-2372).

Rejoin I-84 at exit 35 and continue east to Cascade Locks (exit 44). This is the best place to break for a meal or snack. **The Charburger** (714 Wanapa St; 541-374-8477) grills made-to-order hamburgers to go with its spectacular view of the river and Bridge of the Gods, and the gift shop sells delicious home-baked cookies. Just down the street at the **East Wind Drive-in** (541-374-8380), indulge in a chocolate, vanilla or swirl soft-serve ice cream cone.

Cross the Bridge of the Gods into Washington, then head east on Hwy 14 to Stevenson, home of **Dolce Skamania Lodge** (800-376-9116). Open since 1993, the lodge sits regally on a rolling meadow facing the Columbia River. Constructed of heavy timbers, with a massive stone fireplace in the lobby and Mission-style furnishings throughout, this place is reminiscent of Timberline Lodge (see Mount Hood).

Come on a Sunday between 9 am

THE LEGEND OF THE BRIDGE OF THE GODS

While geologists believe a natural bridge spanned the Columbia at the present-day site of Bridge of the Gods some 1,000 years ago, Native Americans use an enchanting legend to explain the topography of this region.

Caught in a battle for the affections of Squaw Mountain, two brothers, Klickitat (Mount Adams) and Wy'east (Mount Hood), grew violent. They stomped their feet; spat ashes, fire and clouds of smoke; and hurled hot rocks at each other. When their stone-throwing destroyed the bridge, their father, the Great Spirit, intervened. Wy'east, the smaller of the brothers, graciously relented.

Squaw Mountain dutifully took her place beside Klickitat, but her heart was broken, for she had loved Wy'east best. Presently she sank into a deep slumber at Klickitat's feet. She is now known as the Sleeping Beauty, which lies just west of Mount Adams. On observing his squaw's countenance, Klickitat dropped his head in shame.

Meanwhile, Loo-Wit, an old woman who had been assigned by the Great Spirit to guard and protect the bridge, had been badly burned and clobbered during the brothers' fight. When the Great Spirit learned of her injuries and her faithfulness, he offered to grant her a wish. Loo-Wit asked to be made young and beautiful again. And so she took her place among the other great mountain peaks—but at a polite remove, befitting her aged spirit. Today she is called Mount St. Helens, the youngest of the Cascade Mountains.

and 2:30 pm to indulge in the sumptuous brunch buffet ($23.95/adult; $13.95/child 8-12 years; $7.95/child 4-7 years; free/child 3 & under; reservations encouraged). Then stay to work off the meal.

Three mile-long nature trails meander past golf courses and ponds. The fitness center and pool area are open daily ($10/adult, $5/child 12 & under). The rock-pool hot tub outside is fun for kids in nice weather. On a rainy day they can splash instead in the indoor whirlpool and lap pool. Locker rooms are equipped with saunas, hot tubs, showers and towels.

Don't return home before visiting the **Columbia Gorge Interpretive Center** (990 SW Rock Creek Dr, Stevenson, WA; 800-991-2338; www.columbiagorge.org). Designed to resemble the sawmills that sat here earlier in the century, this gem of a museum is located just below Skamania Lodge. Its manageable size and engaging exhibits, which trace the history of the gorge by underscoring its resources and inhabitants, make it particularly suitable for families.

Children are intrigued by the basalt cliff adornments, indoor waterfall, replica fishwheel, Corliss steam engine and logging truck. A short slide presentation examines the geologic formation of the gorge. (Open daily, 10 am-5 pm, except Thanksgiving, Christmas and New Year's Day; $6/adult, $5/senior or student, $4/child 6-12, free/child 5 &under.)

On the drive back to Portland on I-84 west, turn in at the **Bonneville Lock and Dam** (541-374-8820; www.nwp.usace.army.mil/op/b/) on Bradford Island. The glass-walled visitors center features an observation deck, historical displays and underwater windows that look out on fish ladders. Chinook, coho and sockeye salmon and steelhead migrate upriver to spawn in spring, summer and fall. Come in summer (June through September) for the best viewing. (If you really want to be organized, check the Web site before you go to coordinate your visit with one of the dam's many events geared especially for kids.) Take a guided tour of the dam powerhouse (call ahead for reservations), then, on your way out to the highway, stop to examine the Navigation Lock.

Adjacent to the dam is the **Bonneville Fish Hatchery** (541-374-8393), where approximately 20 million salmon fingerlings are raised for release into neighboring Tanner Creek each spring. The parklike setting features sculpture ponds, picnic tables and a gift shop (closed in winter). But the real draw is the fish.

Three natural-style rock ponds teem with rainbow trout and huge sturgeon, including a 10-footer named Herman. Purchase a handful of pellets (25 cents) to feed the trout. Adult salmon are housed in five outdoor holding ponds from September through December. Monitored indoors, fry and fingerlings are not on display.

Hood River

Hood River (just off I-84, 60 miles east of Portland) is a sailboarder's mecca. A walk down Oak St reveals shops that hawk every device necessary to equip a board and sailor—as well as the requisite souvenirs. The town is quaint nonetheless, with pretty bungalows, rolling lawns and views of the river.

If the wind is up, you can get a front-row seat at sporting entertainment down by the water. The grassy beaches at the **Hood River Event Site** (exit 63

On a trip to Hood River, don't miss the Columbia Gorge Discovery Center.

off I-84) and the sandy beaches near the **Port Marina Park** (exit 64 off I-84) afford accessible views of windsurfing. The **Expo Center** nearby houses the offices of the Hood River Visitors Center and local Chamber of Commerce.

The Hood River region is also famous for its orchards. A large percentage of the nation's pears (Anjou, Bosc, Comice and Bartlett) are grown here, as are the world's preeminent Newtown Pippen apples. Pick up a copy of the **Fruit Loop** map, an annual guide to local farm stands (available at shops and restaurants in town, or by calling the Hood River County Visitors Center at 800-366-3530), and take a drive in the country. Or board the historic **Mount Hood Railroad** for a four-hour, round-trip excursion along peaceful back roads (see Active Play: Outdoor Fun, Trains and Trolleys).

Plan your visit around a seasonal festival to see the valley at its best: Blossom Festival (third weekend in April), Gravenstein Apple Fair (late August), Pumpkin Funland at Rasmussen Farms (late September through late October) or Harvest Fest (early October).

From Hood River, if time and stamina allow, get back on I-84 and head 20 miles or so east to the Chenowith exit, where you'll find the **Columbia Gorge Discovery Center** and **Wasco County Historical Museum** (541-296-8600; www.gorgediscovery.org/). You can view exhibits devoted to the geology of the gorge and the early inhabitants of the region and see a 33-foot-long model of the Columbia from the Deschutes River to The Dalles, complete with running water. If you've brought your own food, you can picnic in the **Oregon Trail Living History Park**, outside the museum. If not, you can purchase snacks (including espresso drinks) at the museum's own cafe. (Mid-March-December, open daily, 10 am-6 pm, except Thanksgiving, Christmas and New Year's Day. January-mid-March, open Tues-Sun, 10 am-4 pm. $6.50/adult, $5.50/senior, $3/child 6–16, free/child 5 & under).

For a scenic drive back to Portland, from Hood River take Hwy 35 south. The 44-mile route begins in flat fruit orchards, then climbs steadily and winds past mountainous, glacial terrain. From this vantage point, Mount Hood looms gracefully to fill the windshield.

Continue to **Timberline Lodge** (see Mount Hood) at the summit, then descend via Hwy 26 and return to Portland. The Mount Hood Information Center in Welches (503-622-4822, 888-622-4822; www.mthood.org) carries free copies of *The Mount Hood Columbia Gorge Loop*, a brochure that details this scenic drive, plus trail maps, lodging guides and other tips for visitors.

Hood River At a Glance

Hood River County Chamber of Commerce and Visitor Center
405 Portway Ave, Hood River 97031
800-366-3530
www.hoodriver.org

Columbia Gorge Discovery Center and Wasco County Historical Museum
5000 Discovery Dr, The Dalles 97058
541-296-8600
www.gorgediscovery.org

Mount Hood Railroad
110 Railroad Ave, Hood River 97031
800-872-4661
www.mthoodrr.com

Mount St. Helens

On May 18, 1980, Mount St. Helens erupted with the force of several atomic bombs, dramatically changing the landscape for miles in all directions. The event itself is the stuff of history books. No less intriguing is the story of the environment's natural recovery process.

Mount St. Helens National Volcanic Monument (www.fs.fed.us/gpnf/mshnvm/) features five interpretive centers lining Hwy 504 east of I-5 near Castle Rock, Washington. Visitors here are treated to panoramic views of the mountain, video and slide presentations, and educational, interactive displays and exhibits that document the eruption and its aftermath.

Pick and choose among the options; to visit each one would be to experience sensory overload. Avoid crowds of tourists by avoiding summer weekends, but pray for a clear day for the best view.

Fuel up the car in Castle Rock (exit 49 off I-5). Also known as Spirit Lake Memorial Hwy, Hwy 504 makes a sinuous 60-mile climb to within 5 miles of the volcano, and there are no gas stations en route. Carry lightweight jackets and rain gear, as well as sunscreen and water. The temperature fluctuations are unpredictable near the peak, and with few trees, there's little protection from the elements. Pack a picnic to spread out on a table at one of the visitors centers or at Seaquest State Park near Silver Lake, or lunch in the Hoffstadt Bluffs restaurant (see below) or Coldwater Ridge cafeteria.

The U.S. Forest Service requires visitors to purchase a Monument Pass. The per person pass is good for one day at each of the following recreational fee sites: the Mount St. Helens Visitor Center at Silver Lake, the Coldwater Ridge Visitor Center Complex (including Coldwater Lake Recreation Area), Johnston Ridge Observatory and Ape Cave (a lava tube). Passes may be purchased at monument visitor centers and the Cascade Peaks Restaurant and Gift Shop on Rd 99. If you plan to visit just one center, the cost is $3 per adult and $1 per child 5 to 15. If you plan to visit more than one center, the multi-site pass is $6 per adult and $2 per child.

The Cinedome Theater
1239 Mount St. Helens Wy, Castle Rock (Washington)
360-274-9844
www.mtsthelenscinedome.com
Season: May-October
Hours: Daily, 9 am-6 pm
Admission: $6/adult, $5/senior or child 6-12, free/child 5 & under

Mount St. Helens erupts every 45 minutes in season on the giant 70-mm screen at the 174-seat Mount St. Helens Cinedome. An Academy Award-nominated, 25-minute documentary, *The Eruption of Mount St. Helens* is more experience than movie. The screen is three stories high, and three rows of special seats at the rear vibrate with the roar of the volcano. Children under 5 years may be overwhelmed by the sound system; older kids will surely be enthralled.

Mount St. Helens Visitors Center at Silver Lake
Hwy 504, 5 miles east of Castle Rock (Washington)
360-274-2100
Hours: 9 am-5 pm daily; start closing at 4 Nov 1-March 1

The exhibits at this U.S. Forest Service facility on the shores of Silver Lake provide an introduction to the eruption with a walk-through volcano mock-up, 16-minute film, plus views of the mountain (on a clear day) through telescopes. You can also wander along the 0.8-mile Silver Lake Wetlands Trail to discover how the lake was formed by a previous eruption and how the aquatic life continues to change the lake today.

Hoffstadt Bluffs Visitor Center
Hwy 504, 27 miles east of Castle Rock (Washington)
360-274-7750
Shop hours: Winter: Thurs-Mon, 10 am-4 pm. Summer: daily, 9 am-7 pm
Restaurant hours: Winter: Summer: opens at 11 am and last seating is at 5:30 pm

Built by Cowlitz County, this post-and-beam, alpine-style building houses a gift shop and full-service family restaurant with a view of the Toutle River Valley. Starting in mid-March, there's a free logging show each Saturday at 2 pm. In summer, helicopter tours ($99/person) depart regularly from the parking lot.

Charles W. Bingham Forest Learning Center
Hwy 504, 33 miles from Castle Rock (Washington)
360-414-3439
www.weyerhaeuser.com/sthelens/
Season: May 15-October
Hours: Daily, 10 am-6 pm

The "volcano" playground at the entrance to the Forest Learning Center is visible from the highway, so you'll probably have to stop at this free attraction to appease the kids in the backseat. Stretch your legs on the half-mile trail, then try to spot elk through the telescopes.

Inside there's a replica helicopter, presentations on the eruption and its aftermath, and a model forest. Exhibits stress the eruption's effects on private timberland and the timber industry's efforts to salvage, replant and recover lost acreage. Weyerhaeuser, the Rocky Mountain Elk Foundation and the state Department of Transportation collaborated on this facility.

Coldwater Ridge Visitors Center
Hwy 504, 43 miles east of Castle Rock (Washington)
360-274-2131
Seasons and Hours: winter, 9 am-5 pm starting Nov 1, closed Mon and Tues; hours expand in April; Summer, daily 10 am-6 pm daily

On a bluff directly opposite the mountain's lopsided crater, the U.S. Forest Service's Coldwater Ridge Visitor Center underscores the region's recovery process, with interactive exhibits that detail native life forms before, during and after the eruption. Take a walk along the paved trails beside Coldwater Lake (once a river) and scout for hummocks—the rocky mounds that were blasted from the volcano.

Johnston Ridge Observatory
Hwy 504, 52 miles east of Castle Rock (Washington)
360-274-2140
Season: Closed November 1-spring. Opening date depends on snowpack; call for information
Hours: Daily, 10 am-6 pm

This is the end of the road, and probably as close as you'll want to get to the still-steaming crater. Opened in May 1997, Johnston Ridge Observatory represents Mount St. Helens National Monument's crowning glory. The brand-new, $8.3 million U.S. Forest Service facility features a large formal theater; a 15-minute, wide-screen, computer-animated video program; and a jaw-dropping view right down the throat of the mountain. The engaging exhibits examine the geologic events surrounding the big eruption and subsequent eruptions, techniques used by scientists to monitor active volcanoes and eyewitness accounts from eruption survivors. During the summer months, look for a schedule of regular interpretive talks and guided walks posted at the front door.

Mount Hood

Native Americans called it Wy'east, and at 11,235 feet, it's the state's tallest peak. Ski lifts run year-round, but even if you don't ski, the 60-mile trip to the summit at 6,000 feet is rewarding.

At the end of the road to Mount Hood sits **Timberline Lodge** (503-231-7979; www.timberlinelodge.com). A National Historic Landmark, the lodge was built during the Depression (in 1937) as a showcase for the talents of local craftsmen and artisans. It is truly a masterpiece of hewed logs and great stone fireplaces—the quintessential Northwest mountain lodge.

Take I-84 east from Portland to Hwy 26. At Government Camp, watch for signs.

In ski season, special Sno-Park Permits are required of lodge guests and visitors, and parking spaces may be limited.

The **Magic Mile Express Chairlift**

Timberline Lodge at Mt. Hood is a National Historic Landmark.

to the base of the Palmer Snowfield is open to nonskiers in spring (daily, 10 am-1:30 pm) and summer (daily, 10 am-5 pm), weather permitting. Purchase a sightseer pass ($8/adult, $6/child 7-12, free/child 6 & under) for a view of the Oregon Trail's Barlow Road and on toward Mount Jefferson and the Cascades (bring quarters for the telescope).

Then, if you're game, return to the lodge on foot. A free trail map, available at the front desk, highlights points of interest along the 1-mile trail down.

The lodge interior manages to feel at once massive and cozy. Don't miss the 27-minute video, which highlights the handiwork and graphic themes that are echoed throughout. The Forest Service also offers guided tours of the lodge from mid-June through Labor Day. Check in the lower lobby across from the front desk for information.

Children with energy to burn after the drive have three lobby areas to explore. There's also a tabletop shuffleboard game (ask at the front desk for board games), a pub and a formal dining room. No doubt hungry kids will prefer the fast-food offerings at the adjacent **Wy'east Day Lodge**, which feeds crowds of skiers at lunchtime. Or you can eat outside on the deck at the **Market Cafe**, which serves barbecue fare.

Another good option for families is located in Government Camp. Managed by the same company that manages Timberline Lodge, the **Mount Hood Brew Pub** (87304 E Government Camp Loop; 503-272-3724; www.mthood brewing.com) serves wholesome pizza, hamburgers, salads, sandwiches and chili in an informal chalet setting.

Newport

From Portland, Newport (about two and a half hours by car) may not be the nearest coastal beach, but in fair weather, and especially in foul, it's surely among

PHOTO COURTESY OF TIMBERLINE LODGE

The Oregon Coast Aquarium is a favorite with visitors of all ages and a top attraction in Newport.

a child's top picks. And that's largely because of its first-rate aquarium.

When the **Oregon Coast Aquarium** (2820 SE Ferry Slip Rd; 541-867-3474; www.aquarium.org) opened to enthusiastic crowds in 1992, visitors raved about the innovative exhibits.

Today, the aquarium continues that tradition with its newest exhibit, "Passages of the Deep." After Keiko, the much-loved orca, was shipped to waters around Iceland to rediscover his aquatic roots, the aquarium was left with a large, empty tank. Extensive remodeling of that tank has resulted in the chance for visitors to experience life within the ocean by wandering through a 200-foot undersea tunnel. Visitors can watch leopard sharks, yellowtails jacks, big skates, Pacific halibut and thousands of other fish swim above, beside and below them in three large ocean habitats.

While "Passages of the Deep" is an aquarium highlight, kids still love seeing the mesmerizing jellyfish, the frol-

icking sea otters, and the tufted puffins and other birds in the aquarium's aviary, one of the largest seabird aviaries in North America. They can also search for a giant Pacific octopus that lurks in an undersea coastal cave and then explore the Crab Lab at the Ocean Exploration Stations for an up-close view of Dungeness and red rock crabs.

Short lecture presentations, called Keeper Talks, are offered twice daily year-round in the Qwest Theatre. Feeding times are on a set schedule as well. For instance, the otters are fed at 11:30 am, 1 pm and 3:30 pm daily. Look for schedules for both the Keeper Talks and feeding times in the lobby when you first enter.

Popular behind-the-scenes tours ($7.75/adult, $4.75/child 4-13) take visitors on 90-minute tours of off-exhibit areas. Highlights of these tours include stops at the jellyfish nursery and care facility, a visit to the seabird rearing and rehabilitation facility, and a visit to the shark and bat ray holding ponds.

The aquarium goes out of its way to accommodate patrons with special needs, families included. All of the rest rooms are equipped with changing facilities. Rental strollers are available ($4/single. $6/double), as are wheelchairs ($4), and the gift shop carries disposable diapers and one-size-fits-all rain ponchos ($1.95).

(Summer: open daily, 9 am-6 pm; winter: open daily, 10 am-5 pm, except Christmas Day. $10.25/adult, $9.25/senior, $6.25/child 4-13, free/child 3 & under.)

There's more than enough to do in Newport to fill a day, even without a visit to the aquarium. Stroll along the historic bay front to get a feel for the industry that built this town. Inspect the fishing boats, crab traps and shellfish steamers, then stop for incredibly fresh fish and chips at **Gino's Seafood and Deli** (808 SW Bay Blvd; 541-265-2424) or go to the original **Mo's Restaurant** (622 SW Bay Blvd; 541-265-2979), renowned for its clam chowder.

The Pacific Ocean roils, boils and explodes along the rugged coastline just north of Newport. For a scenic detour, take US 101 to **Otter Crest Loop Dr at Cape Foulweather**. Bring binoculars and a generous dose of patience in winter and spring to help you spot migrating gray whales.

During Whale Watch Weeks, in late December and again during spring break, 30 sites along the coast are manned by volunteers who are trained to help novices spy whales. For more information before you go, including a list of all the sites, check out the Web site *Whale Watching Spoken Here* (http://whalespo-ken.org). To receive Whale Watching Spoken Here, a free booklet with a site

map, contact Mike Rivers, program coordinator, at 541-563-2002.

Yaquina Head Outstanding Natural Area (541-574-3100; www.or.blm.gov/salem/html/yaquina/), operated by the Bureau of Land Management, boasts some of the coast's best tide pools. A popular attraction, the park (open dawn to dusk, 365 days a year; $5/car entrance fee) is on Agate Beach, just off US 101 at the north end of Newport. Concrete pathways and man-made pools are accessible to wheelchairs (and toddlers). The beach also features plenty of natural tide pools. During low tides, interpretive staff members give talks about the intertidal inhabitants. They also offer half-hour and one-hour environmental education talks and guided headland walks.

Tides are at their lowest daytime levels in spring, though any day with a tide below 2 feet uncovers a multitude of marine treasures: sea urchins, sea stars, anemones, chitons, sculpins, shore crabs and lots of kelp.

Bring rain gear and wear sturdy tennis or running shoes to help you maintain your footing on the slippery rocks, and keep a close watch on your children at all times. Collecting is not allowed, so leave buckets in the car.

At Yaquina Head Interpretive Center, which opened in 1997, you can see a video with details about the Yaquina Lighthouse as well as about Oregon's rocky intertidal life (summer: daily, 10 am-5 pm; winter: daily, 10 am-4 pm).

Less-developed tide-pool areas include Otter Rock Marine Gardens in Otter Rock State Park, 7 miles north of Newport; and Seal Rock State Park, 5 miles south of Newport.

The Yaquina area features two lighthouses: **Yaquina Head Light-**

house and **Yaquina Bay Lighthouse**.

At Yaquina Head Outstanding Natural Area, you can hike up into Yaquina Head Lighthouse, the tallest lighthouse on the Oregon coast at 93 feet (open noon-4 pm, weather permitting).

Yaquina Bay Lighthouse (May-September, open daily, 11 am-5 pm; October-April, open daily, noon-4 pm; closed holidays; donations accepted.) is at Yaquina Bay State Park, just west of the Yaquina Bay Bridge. Built in 1871, the refurbished lighthouse, Newport's oldest existing structure, was relit in the mid-1990s following 122 years of darkness. It is on the National Register of Historic Places.

Children are invited to imagine what life was like for a lighthouse keeper in the old days and to climb as high as the watch room, where the keeper spent the night. With its view of the open ocean, this is a great spot for whale watching.

For more information about both lighthouses, visit the Yaquina Lights Web site at www.yaquinalights.org.

Chapter 9

SEASON BY SEASON

Mother Nature's clock is as accurate as a Swiss watch, yet local families need not rely on her precise timing to anticipate seasonal changes. Instead, they can coordinate their annual rhythms to the region's cycle of traditional festivals and performances and favorite celebrations. The Ringling Bros. & Barnum & Bailey circus is in town? It must be fall. A towering evergreen commands its place of honor in Pioneer Courthouse Square? It must be winter. Packy the elephant digs into his birthday cake? It must be spring. The Willamette River teems with dragon boats? It must be summer.

This month-by-month listing of metro-area family events is designed to ensure your calendar is never blank.

WINTER

JANUARY

New Year's Day Ride
Waterfront Park
503-281-9800
www.bikegallery.com

Get the New Year off to a rolling start with this family-oriented, 8- to 10-mile bike ride that starts in Waterfront Park and ends in Laurelhurst Park, where refreshments are served.

Portland Boat Show
Expo Center
503-246-8291

Boating enthusiasts delight in this show that features 360,000 square feet of everything that's fun on, in or under the water.

Rose City Classic All-Breed Dog Show
Expo Center
503-661-9669

Purebred dogs and their owners compete in conformation, obedience and agility events. A junior showmanship competition is open to youngsters and their purebred pets.

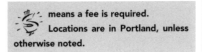

means a fee is required.
Locations are in Portland, unless otherwise noted.

FEBRUARY

Great American Train Show
Expo Center
503-736-5200
www.gats.com

Train enthusiasts will find plenty to be excited about here, with a variety of trains set up for hands-on play. Workshops address such issues as how to get started collecting model trains. (Month may vary.)

Pacific Northwest Sportsmen's Show
Expo Center
503-246-8291

The largest and oldest show of its kind in the region, the Sportsmen's Show spotlights hundreds of new recreational products and services. Free seminars and demonstrations cover everything from fly-fishing to hunting. Kids can fish for trout in the on-site pond.

Period Clothing Fashion Show
Fort Vancouver
800-832-3599, ext. 10
360-696-7655, ext. 10
www.nps.gov/fova

This event highlights the types of clothing worn in the historic reserve over the last 175 years.

Portland International Film Festival
503-221-1156
www.nwfilm.org

During a two-week period, some 100 films from more than 30 countries around the world are screened at a variety of locations.

Teddy Bear Tea
Governor Hotel
503-650-0978

Feast on treats, get artsy with craft projects and enjoy face painting, storytelling and sing-alongs at this fundraiser for the Marylhurst Early Childhood Center. And don't forget to bring your teddy along for a checkup!

Unique Animal Expo and Pet Fair
Washington County Fair Complex
Hillsboro
503-738-6996

This fund-raiser for the Multiple Sclerosis Society lets you check out hundreds of birds, reptiles and mammals of all kinds.

SPRING
MARCH

Annual Winter Games of Oregon
Mount Hood SkiBowl, Timberline
503-520-1319

Skiers and snowboarders of all ages are eligible to compete in Olympic-style events at these two ski resorts. (There is an entry fee for participants,

but no fee for spectators.)

Lewis & Clark International Fair
Lewis & Clark College
503-768-7305
www.lclark.edu/dept/iso/islc_intlfair.html

The foreign students at Lewis & Clark showcase their cultures and customs with multiethnic food booths along with music and dance performances.

St. Patrick's Irish Festival
Kells Irish Restaurant & Pub
503-227-4057
www.kellsirish.com

The region's largest St. Patrick's event, this authentic festival features live Irish music and activities for kids. Some proceeds benefit Providence Children's Center.

Shamrock Run
Waterfront Park
503-226-5080

A benefit for the Doernbecher Children's Hospital Foundation, this fitness event consists of the Leprechaun Lap (a 1K run, walk or jog), the Shamrock Stride (a 4-mile walk) and an 8K race.

Shrine Circus
Expo Center
503-682-4420
www.shrine-circus.com

This is a good-time, old-fashioned, three-ring circus with acrobats, big cats and clowns. (Month may vary.)

Spring brings out kids who enjoy nature oriented celebrations.

Woodburn Tulip Festival
Woodburn
503-982-8221 (Woodburn Chamber of Commerce)
800-711-2006 (Wooden Shoe Bulb Company)

Tour the tulip fields at their peak, in late March and early April. Entertainment and activities are offered at various locations.

EASTER EVENTS

Alpenrose Dairy Easter Egg Hunt
Alpenrose Dairy
503-244-1133
www.alpenrose.com

Youngsters are invited to search for eggs, gifts and prizes.

Rabbit Romp
Oregon Zoo
503-226-1561
www.oregonzoo.org

This event features egg hunts, games, crafts and a petting zoo. The Oregon Humane Society sponsors an exhibit of adoptable pets.

APRIL

Children's Tree Trail
World Forestry Center
503-228-1367
www.worldforestry.org

One of the nation's biggest Arbor Day celebrations, Children's Tree Trail features a guided walk through Hoyt Arboretum and special hands-on activities on the trail and in the World Forestry Center.

Earth Day Celebration
Tryon Creek State Park
503-636-4398
www.tryonfriends.org

Nature oriented, kid-friendly activities coincide with the presentation of the winners of the park's annual tall-tales writing contest.

March of Dimes WalkAmerica
Rose Quarter
503-222-9434

Enter a 3K, 10K or 20K walk and help raise money for the March of Dimes Campaign for Healthier Children.

Packy's Birthday Party
Oregon Zoo
503-226-1561
www.oregonzoo.org

Watch Portland's popular elephant feast on his special whole-wheat cake with peanut butter frosting. Kids' games and people food are also provided.

Packy and Sunshine of the Oregon Zoo.

Trillium Festival
Tryon Creek State Park
503-636-4398
www.tryonfriends.org

Hands-on crafts and activities center on horticulture and gardening. Purchase native plants, trees and shrubs to support Tryon Creek State Park educational programs.

WonderWalk
Rose Quarter
503-222-9434

Sponsored by the March of Dimes, this pledge walk includes activity stations for kids.

MAY

1860s Baseball
Fort Vancouver (Washington)
800-832-3599, ext. 10; 360-696-7655, ext. 10
www.nps.gov/fova

Take a step back in time as Fort Vancouver hosts 1860s-style baseball games between soldiers and townsfolk. (These games take place throughout the summer, so ask for a schedule.)

Cinco de Mayo
Waterfront Park
503-222-9807
www.cincodemayo.org

This Hispanic celebration features ethnic foods, entertainment, dancing, and arts and crafts booths.

Herb Festival
Pomeroy Living History Farm, Yacolt (Washington)
360-686-3537
home.pacifier.com/~pomeroy/index.html

Visit the farm to see thousands of herb plants and take in the live entertainment.

SUMMER

JUNE

Oregon Safe Kids Day
Oregon Zoo
503-226-1561
www.oregonzoo.org
Exhibits and hands-on activities emphasizing safety issues are the highlight here. (Free with zoo admission.)

Queen Victoria's Birthday
Fort Vancouver (Washington)
800-832-3599, ext. 10
360-696-7655, ext. 10
www.nps.gov/fova

Come celebrate the birthday of her Royal Highness at "British" Fort Vancouver.

St. Johns Parade
St. Johns neighborhood
503-283-1175
This down-home, neighborhood parade is a 40-year tradition and includes marching bands, floats, clowns and horses.

Soldiers' Bivouac
Fort Vancouver (Washington)
800-832-3599, ext. 10
360-696-7655, ext. 10
www.nps.gov/fova
Delve into military history at the Vancouver Barracks on the parade ground.

Berry Festival
Portland Farmers Market, South Park Blocks
503-241-0032
www.portlandfarmersmarket.org
Celebrate Oregon's berry bounty with free strawberry shortcake at the Portland Farmers Market.

Cruisin' Sherwood
Old Town, Sherwood
503-625-5207
www.ci.sherwood.or.us
A display of more than 300 souped-up show cars, from old to new, Cruisin' Sherwood also features crafts, food and games for children.

Festival of Flowers
Pioneer Courthouse Square
503-223-1613
www.pioneersquare.citysearch.com/1.html
This celebration of flowers showcases a show-stopping, artist-designed floral display.

Lake Oswego Festival of Arts
George Rogers Park and Lakewood Center for the Arts, Lake Oswego
503-636-1060
An art show and sale with more than 1,000 works by regional artists, this festival also spotlights craft activities and

performances for children. Kids' Day is traditionally the first day of the festival, with lots of hands-on activities.

Midsummer Night City Bike Tour
Various locations, Portland
503-281-9800
www.bikegallery.com

This Bike Gallery-sponsored, family-friendly ride gets you out and about in the middle of the night in Portland. Choose from various route and distance options.

Rose Festival
503-227-2681
www.rosefestival.org

Consistently ranked among the world's top 10 festivals, the Rose Festival dates to 1907, when Portland's first floral parade was accompanied by two days of activities celebrating the rose. Today, more than 80 events span three weeks and dozens of area venues. Below is a chronological sampling of some of the festival's family events.

■ Waterfront Village
Waterfront Park

Carnival rides, games, entertainment and food booths take over Waterfront Park for 10 days. The first night typically includes a fireworks display.

■ Starlight Parade
Downtown Portland

The first of three festival parades, this nighttime event features clowns, marching bands and eccentric floats.

■ Li'l Britches Rodeo
Alpenrose Dairy

Children ages 3 through 12 compete in silly rodeo-style events (there is no riding, however): calf-flagging, pig scramble, cowhide race, three-legged race and ring-a-ribbon.

■ Alpenrose Milk Carton Boat Races
Westmoreland Park

Participants vie to keep afloat in their creations.

■ Rose Festival Fleet
Waterfront Park

More than 20 ships arrive, dock and are open for tours.

■ Junior Parade
Hollywood district

With more than 10,000 child participants, this is the largest parade of its kind in the world.

■ Grand Floral Parade
Downtown Portland

The highlight of the Rose Festival, this event is the country's second-largest all-floral parade. Dozens of floats, meticulously decorated with live, natural materials, are joined by equestrian teams, marching bands and celebrity guests.

■ Showcase of Floats
Rose Quarter

Here's your opportunity to view the parade floats up close.

■ Arts Festival
Portland State University
South Park Blocks

A three-day celebration with works by more than 100 national, regional and local artists, along with food, music and live entertainment.

■ Dragon Boat Races
Waterfront Park

Teams of paddlers race in traditional, colorful shells.

■ Air Show
Hillsboro Airport

Bring earplugs to this airborne spectacle with flying and sky-diving exhibitions and jet races.

■ Budweiser/G.I. Joe's 200
Portland International Raceway

World-class race-car drivers compete for prize money and points in this National Championship Auto Racing Team contest.

Settling In: Making Oregon Home
End of the Oregon Trail Interpretive Center, Oregon City
503-657-9336

Learn how the pioneers made their new life in Oregon and enjoy hands-on pioneer demonstrations and activities.

Tigard Festival of Balloons
Cook Park, Tigard
503-590-1828

Colorful hot-air balloons ascend at dawn, then "park" on the lawn at night, festooned by lights. Carnival rides plus food booths are also on-site.

JULY

Brigade Encampment
Fort Vancouver (Washington)
800-832-3599, ext. 10;
360-696-7655, ext. 10
www.nps.gov/fova

Kick off summer at the Tigard Festival of the Balloons.

Witness a reenactment of the annual return of fur-trapping brigades.

Da Vinci Days
Oregon State University, Corvallis
541-757-6363
www.davinci-days.org

Celebrate art, science and technology at this unique festival. Enjoy live music and the antics of street performers, take in the sidewalk chalk-art competition and play in the children's village.

Molalla Buckeroo
Molalla Buckeroo Grounds, Molalla
503-829-8388
www.molalla.net/community/buckeroo.htm

Sure, there are bucking broncos, but

kids also like the train rides, parades and the carnival that comes to town.

Multnomah County Fair
Oaks Amusement Park
503-289-6623

Displays of livestock are interspersed with carnival rides and craft and food booths.

Oaks Park Fireworks
Oaks Amusement Park
503-233-5777
www.oakspark.com

Celebrate the day with all-American fireworks, rides and a picnic. Alcohol and personal fireworks are not allowed.

Portland Scottish Highland Games
Mount Hood Community College
Gresham
503-293-8501
www.phga.org

Dancing, athletic events, children's games, clan tents, and border collie and Highland cattle demonstrations highlight this event.

St. Paul Rodeo
St. Paul Rodeo Arena
503-633-2011
www.stpaulrodeo.com

For more than 65 years, this smaller-scale rodeo has been an ideal event for families. Carnival rides and games, a parade and fireworks displays are other featured activities.

Salem Art Fair and Festival
Bush's Pasture Park, Salem
503-581-2228
www.salemart.org

With a history that spans more than 50 years, this festival has lots to offer: an area where kids can create their own works of art, a children's stage that features puppet shows and live entertainers, as well as good food, and lots of arts and crafts for sale.

Sherwood Robin Hood Festival
Stella Olsen Park, Sherwood
503-625-4233
community.oregonlive.com/cc/hobbehod

This multiday event features a "knighting" ceremony of community leaders, a parade, games, crafts and nonstop entertainment. There's also an annual archery tournament.

Taste of Beaverton
Griffith Park, Beaverton
503-644-0123
www.beaverton.org/taste/

This family festival features lots of entertainment and fine food from a variety of popular area restaurants.

Turkey Rama
McMinnville
503-472-6196
www.mcminnville.org/turkeyrama

This event got its name way back when McMinnville was home to many turkey farms. Now the town features sidewalk art shows, a carnival, children's fair and the "Biggest Turkey" talent contest.

Vancouver Fireworks
Fort Vancouver Parade Grounds
(Washington)
360-693-5481

Considered the largest fireworks display west of the Mississippi, this extravaganza is preceded by an all-day festival.

Washington County Fair and Rodeo
Washington County Fair Complex,
Hillsboro
503-648-1416
www.faircomplex.com

Visit with livestock, watch a rodeo or 4x4 truck pull, then stay for live entertainment.

Waterfront Blues Festival
Waterfront Park
503-282-0555
www.waterfrontbluesfest.com

 (donation)

Enjoy four days of live outdoor performances by local and international blues artists, plus a Fourth of July fireworks display. Proceeds benefit the Oregon Food Bank.

AUGUST

Antique Airplane Fly-in
Evergreen Field, Vancouver
(Washington)
360-892-5028
www.nwaac.org

More than 300 aircraft that predate 1940 arrive from around the country for this weekend event. Model kits, toy airplanes and other related merchandise are on sale.

Bridge Pedal
503-281-9198

In 2001, this noncompetitive 35-mile bike ride had 18,000 participants. The ride takes in all 10 Willamette bridges. Families may opt to try the shorter, 12-mile route from the Fremont Bridge to the Marquam Bridge. In 2002, a kids-only ride is planned for the day before the Bridge Pedal.

The Bridge Pedal attracts thousands of participants.

Celebration of Cultures Festival
Downtown Gresham
503-618-2521

Hosted by the Gresham Sister City Association to honor its three sister cities, this open-air festival features multiethnic food, entertainment and special activities.

Clackamas County Fair
Clackamas County Fairgrounds, Canby
503-266-1136

www.co.clackamas.or.us/fair

Livestock displays and rodeos are joined by a carnival and food and craft booths.

Clark County Fair
Clark County Fairgrounds, Ridgefield (Washington)
360-397-6180
www.clarkcofair.com

This fair features 4-H exhibits and a carnival, plus a special kids' park complete with pony rides, a petting zoo and live entertainment.

Family Camperoo
Oregon Zoo
503-226-1561
www.oregonzoo.org

Set up camp with your family on the concert lawn and take part in fun events and activities. Children must be at least 6 years old.

Festa Italiana
Pioneer Courthouse Square
503-223-1613
www.festa-italiana.org/
An outdoor street festival complete with live music and dance entertainment, this event nonetheless focuses on Italian food. Kids like the pasta, pizza and gelato.

Fiesta Mexicana
Legion Park, Woodburn
503-591-3365
This celebration spotlights the traditional folk dances, music, foods, and arts and crafts of Mexico.

Founder's Day (August 25)
Fort Vancouver (Washington)
800-832-3599, ext. 10;
360-696-7655, ext. 10
www.nps.gov/fova
Celebrate the birth of the National Park Service. At Fort Vancouver, the focus is on the Oregon Trail and the impact of the fort on its history.

Homowo Festival for African Arts
Portland State University
503-288-3025
www.homowo.org
An outdoor festival, this cultural event features traditional African music, dance and storytelling performances.

India Festival
Pioneer Courthouse Square
503-223-1613
Dancing, music, crafts and food typical of India take over the heart of downtown.

KidsFair
Rose Garden, Rose Quarter
503-797-5577
Hosted by Fred Meyer, this event features interactive activities and demonstrations, plus stage entertainment for children throughout the day.

OBT Exposed!
Behind the Arlene Schnitzer Concert Hall, SW Broadway & Main
503-227-0977
www.obt.org
Oregon Ballet Theatre rehearses publicly under tents outdoors for two weeks in preparation for the new season.

Obonfest
Oregon Buddhist Temple
503-234-9456
This Japanese-American Buddhist

festival features ethnic foods, dancing
and crafts.

Oregon State Fair
Oregon State Fairgrounds, Salem
503-947-FAIR (3247)
www.fair.state.or.us

With its big-name entertainers, cultural arts, 4-H exhibits, livestock displays,
carnival and special lineup of kids' activities, this is the mother of all fairs.

Summer Loaf
Portland Farmers Market
South Park Blocks
503-241-0032
www.portlandfarmersmarket.org
Enjoy artisan bread as well as a multitude of other locally grown and created foods.

Tigard Blast
Main St, Tigard
503-670-0260
This is a family-oriented street fair
with arts and crafts, kids' activities, petting zoo, food booths, an entertainment
stage and a miniature train display.

The Bite
Waterfront Park
503-248-0600
www.soor.org

 (donation)

"Grazing" takes on new meaning at
this annual feast, where noshers nibble
their way through à la carte samples
from dozens of area restaurants. Family activities abound and continuous
entertainment is featured on multiple
stages. Proceeds benefit Oregon Special Olympics.

Tualatin Crawfish Festival
Tualatin Community Park
503-692-0780
www.tualatincrawfish.com
A Tualatin tradition for some 50
years, this annual celebration features
live music, craft and food booths, and a
crawfish-eating (shells and all!) contest.

AUTUMN

SEPTEMBER

Art in the Pearl
Northwest Park Blocks
503-231-2810
www.artinthepearl.com
This outdoor arts festival features
more than 100 artists showing their
works along with music, dance and other
performing artists on stage. Kids can take
part in many hands-on art activities.

Candlelight Tour
Fort Vancouver (Washington)
800-832-3599, ext. 10; 360-696-7655,
ext. 10
www.nps.gov/fova
Take a candlelight tour of Fort Vancouver as it was in 1845. Some 70 volunteers dressed in period costumes
re-create the era.

Mount Angel Oktoberfest
Mount Angel
503-845-9440
www.oktoberfest.org

Bavarian delicacies, music, dance, sporting events and traditional arts and crafts entice the entire family, while the free Kindergarten, with its rides and entertainment, is a big hit with the kids.

Oktoberfest
Oaks Amusement Park
503-233-5777
www.oakspark.com

This event is a family-oriented celebration of German culture.

One Stop Kids' Health Fair
Legacy Mount Hood Medical Center, Gresham
503-674-1122
The hands-on activities here help promote safety and good health.

Oregon Air Fair
Linn County Expo Center, Albany
800-874-0102
View military and Coast Guard aircraft, plus helicopters, seaplanes and hot-air balloons, at this aviation event. Hands-on activities run the gamut from creating paper airplanes to operating flight simulators.

Portland Juggling Festival
Reed College
503-249-1135

This is the largest regional juggling festival in America. Attend a Saturday-night juggling extravaganza or sign up to have a ball at any of 30 different workshops.

Ringling Bros. and Barnum & Bailey Circus
Rose Garden
503-321-3211

www.ringling.com

The nation's premier three-ring circus brings on the lions, tigers and bears—plus clowns, acrobats and a whole lot more.

TomatoFest
Portland Farmers Market, South Park Blocks
503-241-0032
www.portlandfarmersmarket.org
Taste more than 50 varieties of tomatoes and pickled vegetables during the height of the season's bounty and enjoy a petting zoo, live music, apple cider pressing and scarecrow making.

Wintering-in Harvest Festival
Bybee House, Sauvie Island
503-222-1741

Watch demonstrations of candle making and rope making. Then sample freshly pressed apple cider and tour the historic house.

OCTOBER

Costume Rummage Sale
Northwest Children's Theater and School
503-222-2190
www.nwcts.org
Drop in at the theater's costume shop for this fund-raising costume sale. Proceeds benefit the NWCT.

Great Pumpkin Event
Portland Farmers Market
South Park Blocks
503-241-0032
www.portlandfarmersmarket.org

Kids dress up for the Great Pumpkin event at Portland Farmers Market.

Kids can taste pumpkin pancakes, strut their stuff in a children's costume parade and compete in a pumpkin-carving contest.

Hood River Valley Harvest Fest
Hood River Expo Center
800-366-3530
business.gorge.net/fruitloop/

The bounty of the fertile Hood River Valley—its produce and crafts—is showcased at this annual event.

Howloween at the Zoo
Oregon Zoo
503-226-1561

Combine trick-or-treating with learning about wildlife at this zoo event.

Portland Greek Festival
Holy Trinity Greek Orthodox Church
503-234-0468
www.goholytrinity.org
Come to fill up on souvlaki, baklava and other Greek specialties, and to enjoy Greek music and dancing.

Portland Marathon
Downtown Portland
503-226-1111
www.portlandmarathon.org

Kids are invited to join in the Mara-fun Kids' 2 Mile Run. Other events include a 5-mile run, the 10K Mayor's Walk and wheelchair competition.

Pumpkin Festival
Pomeroy Living History Farm, Yacolt (Washington)
360-686-3537
home.pacifier.com/~pomeroy/index.html

Feed chickens and goats, make scarecrows, wind through the hay maze, then take a hay ride to the pumpkin patch for a prize squash.

Pumpkin Run
Flower Farmer, Canby
503-266-3581
www.flowerfarmer.com

Climb the straw mountain, make your way through the hay maze and take a spooky train ride.

Salmon Festival
Oxbow Regional Park
503-797-1850
www.metro-region.org/parks/salmon.html

Celebrate the annual return of the migrating salmon with guided salmon-viewing walks, hands-on nature activities, cultural performances, music and food.

Spooktacular
Jenkins Estate, Aloha
www.thprd.org/Facilities/Jenkins/jenkins_estate.htm
503-642-3855

This not-so-scary Halloween event, with its carnival, crafts and contests, is recommended for children 10 and under.

Safety Safari
Oregon Museum of Science and Industry (OMSI)
503-222-7161
www.nwosteo.org

Learn safety skills, explore emergency vehicles, watch simulated rescues and enjoy activities and demonstrations from nearly 40 safety organizations. (Kids 13 and under are free; adults pay OMSI admission.)

NOVEMBER

American Girls Fashion Show
Governor Hotel
503-416-6328

Bring your favorite doll to a dress-up tea party. Proceeds benefit the Oregon Symphony Youth Concerts.

Christmas at Pittock Mansion
Pittock Mansion
503-823-3623

Pittock Mansion is all dolled up for the holidays in accordance with a different theme each year, some especially appropriate for children.

Christmas Tree Lighting
Pioneer Courthouse Square
503-223-1613
Join a chorus of carolers at the official lighting of Portland's Christmas tree.

Clackamette Gem and Rock Show
Oregon City High School
503-631-3128
This two-day gem and mineral show features specimens, finished jewelry, demonstrations, a fluorescent exhibit and a kids' corner with a dig site, special activities and crafts.

Columbia Gorge Model Railroad Show
2505 N Vancouver
503-288-7246

Examine one of the nation's largest model railroad layouts and hobnob with other hobbyists. As many as 30 different trains run each day during the railroad club's monthlong open house.

Festival of Lights
The Grotto
503-254-7371

The largest choral festival in the Pacific Northwest, Festival of Lights showcases 130 school, church and civic choral groups. Performances are held in the Grotto's 600-seat chapel, which is known for its cathedral-quality acoustics. Outdoors, a walk-through lighting display depicts the story of the birth of Christ, and there are puppet shows and a petting zoo for young children.

Festival of Lights Hanukkah Gift Fair
Mittleman Jewish Community Center
503-244-0111
You'll find lots to choose from here:

books, fine art, jewelry, toys, children's clothing and special Hanukkah supplies. (Month varies.)

Hanukkah Celebration
Mittleman Jewish Community Center
503-244-0111

This one-day fair features klezmer music, dancing, food and crafts. Join in the singing, and stay for the candle-lighting ceremony. (Month varies.)

Hanukkah Menorah Lighting
Pioneer Courthouse Square
503-223-1613

In an annual tradition, a large menorah is erected in Pioneer Courthouse Square and Hanukkah candles are lit at public gatherings. (Month varies.)

Meier & Frank Holiday Parade
Downtown Portland
503-203-9166

Welcome the season with a post-Thanksgiving parade of floats, bands, celebrities and—the guest of honor—Santa Claus.

O.O. Howard Birthday
Fort Vancouver (Washington)
800-832-3599, ext. 10;
360-696-7655, ext. 10
www.nps.gov/fova

Celebrate the birthday of one of the post commanders of the Vancouver Barracks.

Portland Turkey Trot
Oregon Zoo
503-646-RUNR (7867)
www.orrc.net

Get yourself ready for Thanksgiving

dinner by running in the Turkey Trot on Thanksgiving morning. Sponsored by the Oregon Road Runners Club, the event includes a 4-mile walk and a 5-mile fun run through Washington Park and the Oregon Zoo.

Singing Christmas Tree
Keller Auditorium
503-557-TREE (8733)

Fifty children and 300 adult volunteer performers are joined by a live orchestra in this popular, annual holiday program.

Ski Fever & Snowboard Show
Expo Center
503-249-7733
www.portlandskifever.com

Held the first weekend of November, this event features representatives from local ski resorts, dozens of vendors selling new equipment and lots of used equipment for sale as well.

Wild Arts Festival Show and Sale
DoubleTree Hotel, Lloyd Center
503-292-6855

Sponsored by the Audubon Society of Portland, this showcase celebrates nature in art, crafts and books. Activities for children include face painting, hands-on crafts and visits with authors of children's books.

WINTER

DECEMBER

Alpenrose Storybook Lane
Alpenrose Dairy
503-244-1133

Visit the flocked, indoor fantasy forest and its baby farm animals. Meet Santa Claus, and stay to watch cartoons in the old opera house.

Christmas at Fort Vancouver
Fort Vancouver (Washington)
800-832-3599, ext. 10; 360-696-7655, ext. 10
www.nps.gov/fova

Enjoy traditional Scottish and Irish holiday music in a historic setting.

Christmas Ships
Willamette River, Columbia River
503-275-8355
www.christmasships.org

Festively lit vessels ply the waters of the Columbia and Willamette rivers on select nights in season.

Festival of Trees
Oregon Convention Center
503-215-6070

This multiday event features 8-foot trees thematically decorated by sponsoring companies, groups and individuals, plus gingerbread creations.

Holiday entertainment is provided by area choirs and dance groups, and children can visit Santa.

Holiday Cheer & Authors' Party
Portland Art Museum
503-306-5200

Sponsored by the Oregon Historical Society, this is one of the oldest and largest book signings in the nation. Many of the region's finest authors and illustrators are spotlighted.

Holiday Woodcarving Show
World Forestry Center
503-228-1367

The Western Woodcarvers' Association displays its unique wooden creations, leads demonstrations and offers useful tips.

Kids' Holiday Concert
Arlene Schnitzer Concert Hall
503-228-4294

Join the Oregon Symphony in its annual celebration of the holiday season with music from around the world. Bring a bell to help Santa Claus find his way to town.

The Nutcracker
Keller Auditorium
503-227-0977

The Oregon Ballet Theatre's elegant production of The Nutcracker runs for three weeks with 22 performances.

Peacock Lane
SE Stark St & Peacock Ln

Plan to meet with a mob of gawkers on this street, where every house is done up in lights.

Queen Anne Victorian Mansion
1441 N McClellan
503-283-3224

More than 1 million white lights are ablaze on the grounds of this 6,300-square-foot house.

Santa Land
Downtown Meier & Frank
503-223-0512

The 10th floor of the downtown Meier & Frank department store is transformed into a winter wonderland. Kids under 51 inches tall can ride the monorail for a bird's-eye view of Santa.

ScanFair
Smith Hall, Portland State University
503-244-3697

Sponsored by the Scandinavian Heritage Foundation, this traditional holiday festival features folk dancing, singing, craft activities for children, art demonstrations, ethnic food and hand-crafted items.

Tuba Christmas
Pioneer Courthouse Square
503-223-1613
www.pioneersquare.citysearch.com

This quirky, fun-filled event features about 200 tuba players playing favorite holiday songs.

Winter Solstice
Tryon Creek State Park
503-636-4398
www.tryonfriends.org

Celebrate the changing of the seasons at Tryon Creek State Park with natural themed crafts and educational activities.

Winter Wonderland
Portland International Raceway
503-232-3000

The racetrack is converted into a drive-by lighting display with animated characters and broadcast holiday music.

ZooLights
Oregon Zoo
503-226-1561
www.oregonzoo.org

This month long display of thousands of lights and animated animal silhouettes delights visitors of all ages. Come for a train ride, entertainment and refreshments.

Chapter 10

BASICS

Unless you have a sleepy infant or an adventurous teenager, you probably don't expect a relaxing four-course meal when you head to a restaurant with the family. In truth, the places that focus on families have found that the recipe for success features a heaping dollop of noisy commotion. Family-oriented restaurants are often high-energy, kid-appealing places, but the noise level and activity (which help mask poor table manners!) preclude serious conversation and good digestion. In other words, you don't go out to eat with the kids for the food or the ambience. You go out to have fun.

Each of the restaurants described below offers added value to families in particular—special playrooms, reasonable prices, friendly, attentive service and kid-friendly foods, as well as varied selections for parents. Some up the ante with take-home treats, free meals and/or fully equipped changing facilities. But beyond the crayons, finger foods and high chairs, these restaurants have proven they know kids. For parents it's most reassuring to realize your children can't create any chaos these folks haven't seen before—and mopped up with a smile.

Restaurants

Byways Café
1212 NW Glisan, Portland 97209
503-221-0011
Breakfast & lunch Tues-Sun
Prices: $6-$10

No matter what your age, going out to breakfast at a cafe is a special occasion. Byways is a small restaurant in Portland's Pearl District that is a treat for young and old. Walk into Byways and you are on the road in America's heartland: Adorning every square foot of the restaurant are vintage souvenirs from the highways of all 50 states: mugs, pennants, salt shakers, plates and even suitcases. You and your children can play a version of the license-plate game by trying to find a relic from every state. Each table even has its own View-Master with "3-D" pictures of national parks and national treasures.

The food at Byways is wholesome, generous and hearty. Their milkshakes are made the old-fashioned way: blending real ice cream and a little bit of milk. The salads are big enough to share. The fare at both breakfast and lunch is classic with a few modern twists. When you are done eating, you can walk off your hearty meal enjoying one of Byways' finest attributes: its neighborhood, "the Pearl." If you are dining late enough in the morning, you will want to roam this jewel's galleries and shops. Children can enjoy quick trips in and out of galleries while they get a sense of Portland's lively contemporary art scene.

Chevys Fresh Mex Restaurant
Five area locations, including 8400 SW Nimbus Ave, Beaverton 97008
503-626-7667
Lunch & dinner daily
Prices: $7-$15/adult meal, $3.99/child meal

In a city where there are numerous successful restaurant chains that cater to families by offering satisfying meals at affordable prices (Red Robin, Stanford's, Chili's, Tony Roma's and Olive Garden come to mind), Chevys is the big enchilada. The Mexican food here is good (the restaurant prides itself on using strictly fresh ingredients), and the festive south-of-the-border, anything-goes atmosphere particularly suits parents and their unpredictable table mates. Yet, while other eateries also offer helium balloons and kids' place-mat menus with games and take-home crayons, Chevys has something more: a tortilla machine. (See also Active Play: Indoor Fun, Behind the Scenes.)

Adults are just as fascinated as kids to watch it work, and have even been known to sneak a pinch or two from Junior's wad of dough to play with while awaiting dinner. If your little ones are too young for chips, request a basket of warm tortillas instead. But beware: You'll be hard-pressed to refrain from spoiling your own appetite. Tortillas turn up yet again as the crispy cones of the free ice-cream treats for the kids.

The Beaverton Chevys—the region's largest, with a seating capacity of 320—may be the best bet for families. Because it serves as a training facility for managers, its service is especially consistent and efficient. Perhaps even more important, it accepts reservations.

Chuck E. Cheese
Two locations, including 9120 SE Powell Blvd, Portland 97266
503-774-7000
Lunch & dinner daily
Prices: $5-$9

Chuck E. Cheese is for hard-core parents only. In the world of family dining, it is an extreme sport. With masses of kids freely roaming, bells going off from arcade games and a giant mouse giving hugs, it is clear that Chuck's is not designed with adults in mind. With pizza, arcade games, prizes to select, play structures and kiddie rides, it's all about kids—and they love it.

Before you head for Chuck's, look for their coupons, which usually appear in the Sunday Oregonian. You can usually find a coupon good for several dozen free tokens with the purchase of a whole pizza pie. The tokens will keep your little ones busy and happy until the pizza arrives. It will also help them win lots of tickets that can be traded in for much-coveted little plastic trinkets.

Only the hardiest parents dare go to Chuck's, and you will find yourself in remarkably agreeable and patient company. Another plus is the great diversity of the clientele, with many Hispanic, Southeast Asian and African-American families playing skee-ball and the ever-popular spider stomp.

In case you are interested in eating something other than pizza and drinking something other than soda, Chuck hasn't completely forgotten the parents: There are sandwiches, a good salad bar and even beer and wine. Go ahead, dare to do Chuck E. Cheese! Your kids will love you for it.

Cucina! Cucina! Italian Cafe
130 Center Court, Portland 97227
503-238-9800
10205 SW Washington Square Rd., Tigard 97223
503-968-2000
Lunch & dinner daily
Prices: $7-$16/adult meal, $3.95/child meal

This Seattle-based chain of Italian eateries attracts families with more than

its menu. Sure, kids (and many adults) favor pizza and pasta, but when you're allowed to scribble on the menu and tablecloth, and invited to play with pizza dough, you're bound to look forward to a return visit.

Even at its slowest, Cucina! Cucina! seems to buzz with activity. Perhaps it's the colorful decor, the bicycles suspended from the ceiling (can you find the tricycle?) or the television sets tuned to sports games (Portland only). There's nothing staid about Cucina! Cucina! The only problem with the Cucina! Cucina! formula is that it works so well. It's not unusual to have to wait for a table. If you can plan ahead, take advantage of the Telephone for a Table program. Call as you leave for the restaurant, and the hostess will add your name to the waiting list in advance.

Located adjacent to the Rose Garden, the Portland outlet is a zoo on event nights, but is relatively calm at other times. (Reservations are accepted for all groups on nonevent nights.)

It's best to call ahead to inquire about the Rose Garden schedule; even if you don't mind a crowded restaurant, you might feel differently when confronting a crowded parking lot. Ask for a validation stamp when paying your restaurant tab, which entitles you to two and a half hours of free parking in arena garages. On nights when the Trail Blazers play at home, the fee structure changes dramatically: You could be charged up to $13 or more with validation to park in arena garages.

The Ivy House
1605 SE Bybee Blvd, Portland 97202
503-231-9528
Lunch & dinner daily; brunch Sat-Sun
Prices: $5-$18/adult meal, $1/child meal

RESTAURANTS

Open five years now, the Ivy House is the inspired creation of Brian and Lisa Quinn, two chefs who met at the California Culinary Institute and have two children of their own. What the Quinns have created is what they longed for as parents who enjoy fine dining: a charming restaurant that serves ambitious gourmet meals to discerning adults and simple conventional favorites to kids.

Located in a quaint older house festooned with vines, the two-story restaurant has a main-floor dining room with a working fireplace and sunporch. Families have the upstairs to themselves. Four tables are set with white tablecloths and linen napkins, and a plastic tot-size table commands one wall. The adjacent alcove is given over to top-quality toys such as a train set, dollhouse, play kitchen and storybooks. If you're the only family upstairs, or if you can reach agreement with neighboring diners, a television set with a videocassette recorder is also available (it's hidden behind curtains when not in use).

Just outside the rest room, a countertop outfitted as a changing table is stocked with disposable diapers and wipes, and a comfortable settee serves as a private nursing station. A smaller downstairs playroom accommodates overflow families.

The children's menu is short but sweet: hot dog, grilled cheese, peanut butter and jelly, and noodles with butter. Older kids can order double portions or consult with the chef regarding other options, such as a grilled chicken breast with pasta. Brunch choices include French toast, waffles and scrambled eggs. Far more interesting are the seasonal adult selections, and even parents whose children are well behaved may find themselves planning to return without the brood to give full attention to the food.

Legin Restaurant
8001 SE Division St, Portland 97206
503-777-2828
Hours: Sun-Thur, 10 am-midnight; Fri.-Sat, 10 am-2 am
Prices: $5.50-$31

Hailed as one of the best Chinese restaurants in the city, Legin is especially known for its dim sum, available in a sort of rolling buffet that's served every day from 10 am to 3 pm. During these hours it's best to forgo the regular menu, which features more than 240 items, including everything from Shark's Fin with Triple Delight Soup to sautéed squid, roast duck to broccoli with tangy sauce.

If you're feeling a bit adventurous, arrive early for dim sum to avoid a wait (particularly on Sunday, when the parking lot is packed by noon). Take time to let the kids admire the colorful koi in the giant tank just inside the entrance, then be sure to check out the crabs and other crustaceans in the bubbling tanks off to the left of the hostess's station.

After being led to a seat in one of a labyrinth of rooms, you'll find a seemingly endless parade of carts weaving their way among the tables. Friendly servers dispense such savory fare as egg rolls, steamed bok choy, sweet yeast rolls filled with barbecued pork, pork-filled potstickers and sticky fried rice. And then, of course, there are the dishes that are harder to name, but just as delicious.

It's fun for adults and kids alike to discover just what's next in this sort of progressive meal, and even if your child isn't fond of one particular selection, you can reassure him or her that the next cart harbors a multitude of other options.

As you choose an item from a cart, the server marks your ticket with a code to indicate the cost. And though it may be a little disconcerting not knowing exactly what each of the symbols means, it's easy enough to enjoy a meal—complete with a shared warm, sweet, soupy tofu dessert at the end—and pay less than $30 for a family of four.

Mother's Bistro & Bar
409 SW Second Ave, Portland 97204
503-464-1122
www.mothersbistro.citysearch.com
Breakfast Sat-Sun; lunch Tues-Sun; dinner Tues-Sat
Prices: $7-$25

Mother's Bistro & Bar is an elegant anomaly in family dining. No chaos or animal mascots here. The restaurant has fine old-fashioned decor: chandeliers, framed artwork, black-and-white photos of mothers, huge glass windows and curtains. The bar is safely tucked away in another room with a separate entrance. An aberration, Mother's is a fancy restaurant that loves families and reveres moms. Each month, Mother's features a particular Mother of the Month (M.O.M.) and her favorite recipes. The honored mother usually isn't a famous person, but she often represents a particular ethnic or regional background, expressed in her cooking. The restaurant features several of her recipes, along with her "story."

Children are pampered at Mother's, as well, with their own menu, particularly generous offerings of pens and crayons, and patience for spills. Mother's is a great opportunity to practice manners. Perhaps a trip to Mother's could be a reward for good manners at home or an excuse to read a good kids' book on manners. (Manners by Aliki and Oops–the Manners Guide for Girls by Nancy Holyoke of the American Girl Library are particularly good.)

Being a good mother, Mother's has a fondness for mac and cheese, and it features a mac and cheese of the day, as well as the tried-and-true cheesie kind that kids always devour. Also delicious are the fabulous matzo-ball soup and yummy potato dumplings. In true motherly spirit, Mother's has an upholstered bench outside the bathroom in lieu of a changing table. And if you have any leftovers, Mother's will wrap them up for you to take home in a labeled, dated and signed doggie bag. Guaranteed, you will go home full and nurtured!

Old Spaghetti Factory
Four area locations, including 0715 SW Bancroft St, Portland 97201
503-222-5375
Lunch & dinner daily
Prices: $5-$8/adult meal; $3.50/child meal

"Factory" is not a word usually associated with fine dining, which goes far in explaining this restaurant's success with families. The Old Spaghetti Factory has hit on a winning formula: simple, good food at reasonable prices; fanciful antique decor; and friendly, efficient service.

The flagship of a 30-restaurant chain, Portland's outlet on Bancroft, overlooking the Willamette River, seats 450 at capacity, and patrons regularly wait up to 45 minutes for a table at dinnertime. Weekend evenings are especially busy. To avoid the crowds, families are encouraged to arrive before 6 pm, visit for lunch or call ahead to assess the estimated wait. If you do get stuck in a long line, send your children upstairs, where, in view of the lobby, they can watch G-rated videos and play video games.

Children can choose from three pasta entrees at dinner. Kids under age 7 eat from colorful dinosaur plates and are treated to take-home plastic cups. If

RESTAURANTS

they're not won over by the view of the river or the authentic Council Crest trolley car (good luck getting a table inside!), they'll likely be entranced by the miniature loaf of bread that arrives on its own wooden board to be sliced by hand.

Old Wives' Tales

1300 E Burnside, Portland 97214
503-238-0470
Breakfast, lunch & dinner daily
Prices: $5-$17/adult meal (less for breakfast); $1-$3/child meal

The first inkling that Old Wives' Tales emphasizes nutritious, alternative foods comes when you notice the candy jar at the cash register by the front door. It's full of sugar-free lollipops. Of course, most kids don't notice the difference, as long as they can choose for themselves. The number of choices is what makes this restaurant work for families. That and the legendary playroom, of course.

A brightly painted circus-train climbing structure equipped with navigational controls, peek-a-boo windows, stairs and a tunnel occupies a carpeted corner room. At first glance the playroom appears best suited to preschoolers, but when the restaurant's busy it's a free-for-all, and parents are encouraged to supervise the chaos lest a toddler end up at the bottom of the heap. Families are virtually guaranteed a table near the playroom; the far half of the main dining room, as well as a more private room at the rear, are reserved for others.

When the kids are ready to break for some food, they may have difficulty making up their minds—and so will you. The menus for each meal fill two pages, with the options for children ranging from sandwiches and natural turkey franks to burritos and noodles in Parmesan cream sauce. The best selection for picky eaters is the salad bar, which features daily ethnic specialty preparations plus fresh rolls, wheat crackers and rice cakes.

Lunchtime, when many local business people come to dine, and brunch, a meal favored by families, are hectic at Old Wives' Tales. Come virtually any evening to avoid a noisy crowd.

Sisters of the Road Cafe

133 NW Sixth Ave, Portland
503-222-5694
Lunch Mon-Fri
Price: $1.25/meal

Portland has a quiet treasure in Sisters of the Road Café. For 20 years "Sisters" has practiced its philosophy of nonviolence and "gentle personalism" by welcoming anyone who would enjoy a solid $1.25 meal. Sisters is like a bustling small-town coffee shop except that almost everyone here, including most of the cooks, is homeless or poor. You and your children will immediately feel the friendly atmosphere and enjoy the kid-friendly amenities: high chairs and booster seats, simple foods (such as peanut butter and jelly or cornbread, 25 cents each) and a small playroom.

The daily Sisters menu offers two entrees: rice and beans or the special of the day. Eating at Sisters is a great way to expand your family's horizons and talk about poverty and homelessness. Many of the customers will defy your stereotypes of homelessness, but one thing is for sure: Sisters is one of the friendliest places you will ever eat in.

Tipping is almost unheard of at Sisters. Instead, you and your children could make a donation to the restaurant. Sisters is also always looking for new teddy bears to give to kids, gifts for children who may not have any other place to celebrate their birthdays and food donations (call ahead to check what is needed). You can even buy Sisters food coupons that can be given to people in need for a free meal. No matter what you give to Sisters, you and your children will go home with a full belly and heart, and lots to think about.

Sushi Takahashi

(aka "the train place")
24 NW Broadway, Portland 97209
503-224-3417
Lunch & dinner Mon–Sat
Prices: $6-$10; special discounts Wed night and Sat

How often do your kids beg to go out for sushi? With Sushi Takahashi it becomes a regular affair. Your children are likely to shout, "Let's go to the train place!" Sushi Takahashi sports a toy train that delivers surprisingly affordable sushi on its flatbed cars to customers sitting at the circular counter (parties of more than four not guaranteed space together at the counter). A few tables are located away from the train, but kids prefer to sit at the counter, watch the sushi chefs at work and grab their dinner from the train as it goes by.

"Sushi?" you may ask incredulously, but, yes, there are lots of things for even the most culinarily conservative toddlers to enjoy. From the train they can take fruit salad, a plain-tasting sweet roll with pork or beans inside, or very plain cucumber and rice rolls. And from a waiter they can order rice, ramen, miso soup, deep-fried shrimp or vegetables.

One of the hardest things about taking kids out to eat is waiting for the food to arrive. At "the train place," kids get immediate gratification as they grab their favorites off the train. The train also offers other surprises, such as the ability to write notes to fellow dinners and send them around on the train. And if you have a real train aficionado in your younger set, why not stop by the train station after your meal for a complete outing? It is only a few blocks away.

Shopping

If you think we're lucky to be parents in a region that overflows with specialty stores catering to kids' needs, whims and dreams, think how lucky our children are! Here are some of the best places to find quality kids' clothing, toys, books and furniture.

CLOTHING

Baby Gap
Washington Square, Tigard 97223
503-684-4545

Bambini's Children's Boutique
16353 Bryant Rd, Lake Oswego 97034
503-635-7661

Gap Kids
- Clackamas Town Center
  Portland 97266
  503-654-3661
- Pioneer Place, Portland 97204
  503-228-8115
- Washington Square, Tigard 97223
  503-620-3965

Gymboree Store
- Clackamas Town Center
  Portland 97266
  503-654-0927
- Lloyd Center, Portland 97232
  503-281-6892
- Pioneer Place, Portland 97204
  971-544-1760
- Washington Square, Tigard 97223
  503-620-2898

Hanna Andersson
327 NW 10th Ave, Portland 97209
503-321-5275

Hanna Andersson Outlet Store
7 Monroe Pkwy, Lake Oswego 97035
503-697-1953

Lads & Lassies Frocks & Britches
11651 SW Beaverton-Hillsdale Hwy
Beaverton 97005
503-626-6578

Lil' Britches
325 N Main Ave, Gresham 97030
503-492-9378

Mako
732 NW 23rd Ave, Portland 97210
503-274-9081

Old Navy Clothing Co.
- 3115 SW Cedar Hills Blvd
  Beaverton 97005
  503-626-4661
- Clackamas Promenade
  Clackamas 97015
  503-659-3009
- 747 NW 12th St, Gresham 97030
  503-492-7943
- 18065 NW Evergreen Pkwy
  Hillsboro 97
  503-533-4421
- 1752 Jantzen Beach Center
  Portland 97217
  503-289-8975
  www.oldnavy.com

Ragazzi
720 NW 23rd Ave, Portland 97210
503-227-7095

Water Babies
3272 SE Hawthorne Blvd
Portland 97214
503-232-6039

RESALE/CONSIGNMENT CLOTHING

Angel Kisses
2700 SE 26th, Portland 97202
503-963-8548

Baby to Baby
8120 SW Beaverton-Hillsdale Hwy
Portland
503-296-6055

Child of Mine
40 NW Second St, Gresham 97030
503-667-2245

Children's Delights & More
733 SW 185th Ave, Aloha 97006
503-356-8550

Frocks-N-Britches
13815 SW Pacific Hwy, Tigard 97223
503-624-7782

Just 4 Kids
1925 NE 42nd Ave, Portland 97213
503-249-7556

Little Darlings Children's Boutique
10527 SE 42nd Ave, Milwaukie 97222
503-654-1034

Mulberry Bush
19279 SW Martinazzi Ave, Tualatin 97062
503-691-1119

Once Upon a Child
18033 NW Evergreen Pkwy
Beaverton 97006
503-439-8911

Second to None
6308 SW Capitol Hwy, Portland 97201
503-244-0071

Tyke Towne USA
16144 SE 82nd Dr, Clackamas 97015
503-557-3557

We Love Kids
11200 SE Fuller Rd, Milwaukie 97222
503-775-9946

Zanzibar
1315 NE Fremont, Portland 97212
503-284-1276

MATERNITY

Angel Kisses
2700 SE 26th, Portland 97202
503-963-8548

Baby & Me
1295-B NW Cornell Rd, Beaverton
503-646-2021

Generations
4029 SE Hawthorne Blvd
Portland 97214
503-233-8130

Mimi Maternity
Pioneer Place, Portland 97204
503-241-1536

Motherhood Maternity
- Clackamas Town Center
  Portland 97266
  503-652-2450
- Lloyd Center, Portland 97232
  503-249-0373
- Washington Square, Tigard 97223
  503-639-0400
  www.maternitymall.com

Mulberry Bush
19279 SW Martinazzi Ave
Tualatin 97062
503-691-1119

185

Other Mothers Childrens & Maternity Exchange
17112 SE Powell Blvd, Ste 3
Portland 97236
503-491-4787

We Love Kids
11200 SE Fuller Rd, Milwaukie 97222
503-775-9946

TOYS

Bridges A Toy & Book Store
218 A Ave, Lake Oswego 97035
503-699-1322

Child's Play
907 NW 23rd Ave, Portland 97210
503-224-5586

Christmas at the Zoo
118 NW 23rd Ave, Portland 97210
503-223-4048

Finnegan's Toys & Gifts
922 SW Yamhill St, Portland 97205
503-221-0306

Kay-Bee Toy & Hobby Shop
- Clackamas Town Center
  Portland 97266
  503-652-1472
- Lloyd Center, Portland 97232
  503-284-2997

KB Toys
9779 SW Washington Square Rd
Tigard 97223
503-684-9174

Kids at Heart
3435 SE Hawthorne Blvd
Portland 97214
503-231-2954

Learning Palace
- 3861 SW 117th Ave, Beaverton 97005
  503-644-9301
- Gresham Town Fair, Gresham 97030
  503-661-0865
- Mall 205, Portland 97216
  503-251-1833
- Vancouver Plaza, Vancouver
  (Washington) 98662
  360-896-1574

MudPuddles Toys & Books
16190 SW Langer Dr, Sherwood 97140
503-625-7699

OMSI Science Store
1945 SE Water, Portland 97214
503-797-4626

Small World Surprises
3225 SW Cedar Hills Blvd
Beaverton 97005
503-646-3202

Spoiled Rotten
1626 SE Bybee Blvd, Portland 97202
503-234-7250

The Disney Store
- Clackamas Town Center
  Portland 97266
  503-786-4020
- Lloyd Center, Portland 97232
  503-249-8311
- Washington Square, Tigard 97223
  503-684-8121

Thinker Toys
7882 SW Capitol Hwy, Portland 97219
503-245-3936

Timeless Toys
16006 SW Boones Ferry Rd
Lake Oswego 97035
503-675-8548

Toy Bear Ltd.
130 N Main Ave, Gresham 97030
503-661-5310

Toys R Us
- 12535 SE 82nd Ave, Clackamas 97015
  503-659-5163
- 1800 Jantzen Beach Center
  Portland 97217
  503-289-4691
- Lloyd Center, Portland 97232
  503-335-5955
- 10065 SW Cascade Blvd
  Tigard 97223
  503-620-9779

Treehouse Toys
4907 SW 76th, Portland 97225
503-292-4447

Warner Bros. Studio Store
Washington Square, Tigard 97223
503-620-0405

BOOKS

A Children's Place
1631 NE Broadway, Portland 97232
503-284-8294
www.achildrensplacebooks.com

Annie Bloom's
7834 SW Capitol Hwy, Portland 97219
503-246-0053
www.annieblooms.com

B. Dalton
- Lloyd Center, Portland 97232
  503-288-6343
- Mall 205, Portland 97216
  503-255-5650
- Washington Square, Tigard 97223
  503-620-3007

Barnes & Noble Booksellers
- 18300 NW Evergreen Pkwy
  Beaverton 97006
  645-3046
- 9078 SE Sunnyside Rd
  Clackamas 97015
  794-9262
- 1720 Jantzen Beach Center
  Portland 97217
  503-283-2800
- Lloyd Center, Portland 97232
  503-335-0201
  10206 SW Washington Square Rd.
- Tigard 97223
  503-598-9455

Borders Books & Music
- 2605 SW Cedar Hills Blvd
  Beaverton 97005
  503-644-6164
- 687 NW 12th St, Gresham 97204
  503-674-3917
- 708 SW Third Ave, Portland 97204
  503-220-5911
- 16920 SW 72nd Ave, Tigard 97223
  503-968-7576

Broadway Books
1714 NE Broadway, Portland 97232
503-284-1726

Looking Glass Bookstore
318 SW Taylor St, Portland 97204
503-227-4760

Oregon Book Co.
1900 SE McLoughlin Blvd, Ste. 52
Oregon City 97045
503-657-0706

Powell's Books
- 8725 SW Cascade Ave
  Beaverton 97008
  503-643-3131
- 1005 W Burnside, Portland 97209
  503-228-4651

- 3747 SE Hawthorne Blvd
  Portland 97214
  503-238-1668
- Portland International Airport
  Portland 97218
  503-249-1950
  www.powells.com

Portland State Bookstore
1880 SW Sixth Ave, Portland 97201
503-226-2631
www.psubookstore.com

Water Tower Books
The Water Tower at Johns Landing
5331 SW Macadam Ave, Portland 97201
503-228-0290

FURNITURE

A. Jay's Baby Shoppe
12435 NE Glisan St, Portland 97230
503-254-0991

America for Kids/America The Beautiful Dreamer
- Beaverton Mall (Cedar Hills Blvd)
  Beaverton
  503-469-1470
- Hillsboro (1001 SE Tualatin Valley Hwy)
  503-648-9161
- Cornell Home Center, Beaverton
  503-645-8200
- Clackamas Town Center
  Portland 97266
  503-786-4661
- Lloyd Center, Portland
  503-493-2202
  www.atbd.com

Babies R Us
- 9650 SE 82nd Ave, Portland 97266
  503-777-3006
- 7805 SW Dartmouth, Tigard 97223
  503-670-7539

Baby Depot at Burlington Coat Factory
10506 SE 82nd Ave, Portland 97226
503-774-8955
www.babydepot.com

Goodnight Room
1517 NE Broadway, Portland 97232
503-281-5516

Segal's for Children
14356 SW Allen Blvd, Beaverton 97005
503-626-1010

Stork's Nest
227 N Main Ave, Gresham 97030
503-666-6289

Tidee-Didee Infant Department
6011 SE 92nd Ave, Portland 97266
503-775-4729

USA Baby Child Space
12244 SW Scholls Ferry Rd
Tigard 97223
503-521-9900
www.usababy.com

PARTY SUPPLIES

Current Factory Outlet
2770 Cedar Hills Blvd, Beaverton 97005
503-646-2822
11364 SE 82nd Ave, Portland 97266
503-653-4023

Lippman Co.
2727 SE Martin Luther King Blvd,
Portland 97202
503-239-7007

Paper Caper
16829 SW 65th Dr
Lake Oswego 97035
503-620-9460

Party City

- 8664 SE Sunnyside Rd
  Clackamas 97015
  503-653-3500
- 11930 NE Glisan St, Portland 97220
  503-255-5907
- 9160A SW Hall Blvd, Tigard 97223
  503-684-5400

Party Depot

8620 SW Hall Blvd, Beaverton 97008
503-646-3145
4500 NE 122nd, Portland 97230
503-252-6032

Party Mart

16200 SW Pacific Hwy, Tigard 97224
503-639-9414

Party Place

- 10101 SE Stark St, Portland 97216
  503-252-3466
- 8904 SW Canyon Rd, Portland 97225
  503-292-8875
  www.portlandrental.com

Snead's Party Time

14105 SW Tualatin Valley Hwy
Beaverton 97005
503-641-6778

SHOES

Haggis McBaggis

6802 SE Milwaukie, Portland 97202
503-234-0849

Stride Rite Bootery

Washington Square, Tigard 97223
503-639-3399

Shopping Malls

Beaverton Mall

3205 SW Cedar Hills Blvd, Beaverton
503-643-6563
http://beavertonmall.citysearch.com/

Single-level Beaverton Mall has 65 stores, a small food court and rest rooms equipped with changing facilities. Anchor stores include Emporium, G.I. Joe's, Ross Dress for Less, Best Buy, Old Navy, WinCo Foods, Tower Records. Children's stores include Game Trader, Learning Ladder, Magic Fest and Small World Surprise.

Clackamas Town Center

12000 SE 82nd Ave, Portland 97266
503-653-6913
www.clackamastowncenter.com

This busy mall features 185 stores, a five-theater cinema complex, a food court with 20 eateries and an ice-skating center. A soft-sculpture play area geared for children 6 and under is located on the lower level near Sears. Double and infant rental strollers are available. Anchor stores include J.C. Penney, Meier & Frank, Nordstrom and Sears. Children's stores include the Disney Store, Gap Kids, Gymboree, Limited Too and Children's Place.

Jantzen Beach Supercenter

1405 Jantzen Beach Center
Portland 97217
503-286-9103

This was the site of an amusement park until 1970. There's an original, hand-carved wooden carousel ($1 per ride) in the enclosed mall, plus 25 to 30 specialty stores. About 18 superstores are on the grounds, including Barnes & Noble Booksellers, Copeland's Sports, Home Depot, Linens 'N Things, Old Navy Clothing Co., REI, Ross Dress for

Less, Sleep Country USA, Staples and Toys R Us.

Lloyd Center

2201 Lloyd Center, Portland 97232
503-282-2511
www.lloydcentermall.com

This three-story mall holds more than 200 specialty stores, a food court with more than 20 eateries, an eight-theater cinema complex and an ice-skating rink. Children under 12 enrolled in Planet Kid receive a free newsletter, gifts and coupons. Anchor stores include Marshalls, Meier & Frank, Nordstrom and Sears. Children's stores include the Disney Store, Gymboree, Kay Bee Toys and Toys R Us.

Mall 205

9900 SE Washington, Portland 97216
503-255-5805
www.mall205.com

Single-level Mall 205 has some 30 specialty stores. Stores include Home Depot, Target, PayLess Shoe Source and Learning Palace.

Pioneer Place

700 SW Fifth Ave, Portland
503-228-5800
www.pioneerplace.com

This newly expanded, four-story, glass-enclosed mall has more than 70 specialty stores as well as a Saks Fifth Avenue department store. The food court with 17 eateries features a cascading fountain/wishing well. Rest rooms are equipped with changing facilities. Children's stores include Gap Kids, Gymboree and the Children's Place.

Washington Square

9585 SW Washington Square Rd,
Tigard 97281-3635
503-639-8860

www.shopwashingtonsquare.com

Washington Square is a popular mall with 140 specialty stores and five anchor stores. The food court has 10 eateries, and 15 other food services are scattered throughout. Single and double rental strollers are available. Anchor stores include J.C. Penney, Meier & Frank, Mervyn's, Nordstom and Sears. Children's stores include the Disney Store, Gap Kids, Gymboree, Stride Rite, Warner Bros. Studio Store and the Discovery Channel Store.

Westfield Shoppingtown Vancouver

8700 NE Vancouver Mall Drive
Vancouver (Washington) 98662
360-892-6255
www.vancouver.shoppingtown.com

The food court hosts the region's largest mall kids' club every fourth Tuesday of the month, 10:30 am to 11:15 am. Free entertainment is provided by theater troupes, magicians, puppeteers, clowns, jugglers and storytellers. The mall houses more than 140 specialty stores, plus a public library. Anchor stores include J.C. Penney, Meier & Frank, Mervyn's, Nordstrom, Old Navy and Sears. Especially for kids: Game Crazy and the Tilt, a video arcade.

Resources

Portland is home to two free monthly parent-oriented publications, both of which carry calendars of events and articles of interest. Both may be found at public libraries, in some kid-friendly restaurants and in many area doctors' offices:

Portland Family Magazine

P.O. Box 16667, Portland 97292
503-255-3286

Portland Parent

P.O. Box 80040, Portland 97280

503-638-1049

Community Service Numbers
- **Emergency:** 911
- **Poison Control Center:** 503-494-8968

- **Boys and Girls Aid Society of Oregon:** 503-222-9661
- **Child Abuse Hotline:** 503-238-7555
- **Clackamas County Office for Children and Families:** 503-655-8288
- **Harry's Mother Runaway Youth Agency:** 503-233-8111
- **Metro Child Care Resource and Referral:** 503-253-5000

Mental health numbers
- **Clackamas County Mental Health:** 503-655-8401
- **Multnomah County Mental Health:** 503-215-7082
- **Washington County Mental Health:** 503-291-9111
- **Multnomah County Community and Family Services:** 503-988-3691
- **Multnomah County Commission on Children and Families:** 503-988-3897
- **Oregon SafeNet for Women, Children and Teens:** 800-723-3638 or 503-988-5858
- **Portland Women's Crisis Line:** 503-235-5333 (hot line); 503-232-9751 (office)
- **Teen Health InfoLine:** 800-998-9825
- **Washington County Boys and Girls Aid 24-Hour Crisis Line:** 503-641-7820
- **Washington County Child Abuse and Neglect:** 503-648-8951
- **Washington County Children's Mental Health:** 503-846-4541
- **Washington County Commission on Children and Families:** 503-846-4539

Parenting Groups
Attachment Parenting Groups
- **Attachment Parenting International:** 503-245-9868; www.attachmentparenting.com
- **Northwest Attachment Parenting:** 503-234-6004; www.nw-ap.org

Breastfeeding
- **La Leche League:** 503-282-9377; www.lalecheleague.org/Web/Oregon.html
- **Nursing Mothers Council, Portland:** 503-293-0661

Mothers of Multiples Groups
- **Columbia Mothers of Twins Club,** Vancouver (Washington): 360-573-3318
- **Northwest Association of Mothers of Twins Clubs:** info@nwamotc.org; www.nwamotc.org
- **Triplets and More of Oregon,** Portland: 503-524-0909

Other Support Groups/Programs
- **Healthy Start of Clackamas County:** 503-513-0436
- **MOMS Club:** www.momsclub.org. To find a chapter near you, call 503-648-6125, e-mail momsclub@aol.com or write Inquiries, MOMS Club, 25371 Rye Canyon Rd., Valencia, CA 91355
- **Moms' Group of Vancouver:** 360-571-9858
- **Mom's Home,** Tigard: 503-524-1936
- **Mothers & More, Portland** (east side): 630-941-3553; www.mothersandmore.org
- **ParentCare:** Portland (northeast), 503-493-8959
- **Parents Again** (for grandparents raising grandchildren), Vancouver (Washington): 360-694-6577

RESOURCES

- **Portland Asperger's Network** (for parents of children with Asperger's Syndrome or high-functioning autism): 503-284-4507; www.aspergersnet.org
- **SIDS Resources of Oregon:** 503-287-8265
- **Vancouver MOMS** (Moms Offers Moms Support), Vancouver (Washington): 360-883-3160.

- **Waverly Children's Home** (offers parenting groups, support groups and social-skills groups for children diagnosed with high-functioning autism or Asperger's Disorder): 503-234-7532
- **Young Parent Opportunity Program** (for Clackamas County teens ages 15 to 21 who want to continue their education, increase their parenting skills and prepare for employment): 503-657-6958, ext. 2592

QUICK INDEX

Birthday Parties

Classes/Workshops

Field Trips

QUICK INDEX

Free Fun

Restaurants

Wheelchair Accessible

QUICK INDEX

INDEX

INDEX

INDEX

INDEX

INDEX

INDEX

W

Y

Z